David Abulafia is Emeritus Professor of Mediterranean History at the University of Cambridge, and a Fellow of Gonville and Caius College, Cambridge. His previous books include *Frederick II* (1988), *The Discovery of Mankind* (2008), *The Great Sea: A Human History of the Mediterranean* (2010) and *The Boundless Sea: A Human History of the Oceans* (2019). He is a Fellow of the British Academy and a Member of the Academia Europaea. He is also a visiting professor at the College of Europe in Warsaw and a visiting Beacon professor at the newly founded University of Gibraltar. In 2020 he was awarded the Wolfson History Prize for *The Boundless Sea.*

THE MEDITERRANEAN IN HISTORY

Edited by
David Abulafia

Texts by
David Abulafia
Oliver Rackham
Marlene Suano
Mario Torelli
Geoffrey Rickman
John Pryor
Michel Balard
Molly Greene
Jeremy Black

With 28 illustrations

On the cover: Details from a map of the Mediterranean, Henry
Martellus, 15th century. British Library, London.

First published in the United Kingdom in 2003 by
Thames & Hudson Ltd, 181A High Holborn, London WC1V 7QX

This compact paperback edition 2021

The Mediterranean in History © 2003, 2021
Thames & Hudson Ltd, London.

Designed by Mark Bracey

British Library Cataloguing-in-Publication Data
A catalogue record for this book is available from
the British Library

ISBN 978-0-500-29621-9

Printed and bound in the UK by CPI (UK) Ltd

CONTENTS

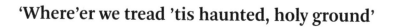

'Where'er we tread 'tis haunted, holy ground'

Byron – Childe Harold, II 88

PREFACE

The history of the Mediterranean is more than the sum of its parts. There are those who write the history of lands which border the Mediterranean; they number a great many historians throughout the world, in Europe, the Americas, around the Mediterranean itself, and increasingly in Japan as well. But this book aims to be much more than a compilation of Spanish, North African, southern French, Italian, Greek, Turkish, Levantine and Egyptian history across the centuries. It brings together the history of the lands that faced each other across the Mediterranean Sea, and places some emphasis on the role of the islands that have acted as bridges across the sea. For it was around the shores of the Mediterranean that many of the great civilizations of antiquity developed: Egyptians, Minoans, Mycenaeans, Greeks, Etruscans, Romans, to mention the most obvious, while from its Levantine shores spread out not merely the merchants of Phoenicia, from whose writing system the alphabet in which these words are written is descended, but the belief in one God which originated with the ancient Israelites and forms the core of Judaism, Christianity and Islam. And this serves as a reminder that the Mediterranean has also been the main seat of the clash of religions, as, from the seventh century onwards, Christianity and Islam began a battle for dominance that lasted into the nineteenth century, when Christian powers annexed or brought under their influence the Muslim shores of the Mediterranean. Some would argue that the conflict of religions is far from dead in the twenty-first century, though, as I suggest in the final chapter, the 'globalized

Mediterranean' of our own times has begun to develop a very different character to the more closed sea of the previous millennia.

The authors of each chapter have been allowed to speak for themselves, in the sense that some have wanted to lay more emphasis on, say, the eastern Mediterranean (as one might in the age of the great empires of antiquity or in the Ottoman era), while others have shifted the focus further to the west (as in the Roman period and during the period of barbarian invasions that followed). Some are more concerned with political or economic or cultural developments. For some periods the evidence has to be pieced together from minute and scattered fragments, as during the 'Dark Ages' between Mycenaean and Archaic Greek civilization. But what the authors have in common is a concern to relate developments on one side of the sea to those on another, and to show how the Mediterranean is far more than an empty space between the landmasses of Europe, Africa and western Asia. In the interstices between chapters I have inserted my own assessments of some of the other aspects of Mediterranean history that did not fit neatly into their own chapters. A constant theme in these linking passages has been the emergence and diffusion of the three 'Abrahamic' religions of Judaism, Christianity and Islam, which, despite the tensions between them and the divisions within them, have given shape to the civilizations that have developed in and around the Mediterranean. It may seem presumptuous of someone whose main speciality is the Mediterranean in the late Middle Ages and Renaissance to express views about Minoans, Etruscans and Carthaginians; however, having been brought up on the rich diet of the books in Glyn Daniel's *Ancient Peoples and Places* series, and having observed with fascination the new theoretical approaches of more recent archaeology, I have found it a particular pleasure to revisit these old haunts, all the more so when my publisher is the same one who served Professor Daniel so well, Thames & Hudson.

This project could not have come to fruition without the constant support and encouragement of a large team: the authors of the individual chapters, whose texts I have been allowed to mould in ways that do not, I hope, mangle their ideas. The Master and Fellows of Gonville and Caius College, Cambridge have facilitated my research trips around the Mediterranean since I joined their society in 1974. Finally, I owe a very special debt to those of my colleagues in the History Faculty at Cambridge University who made it possible by their efforts for a Professorship of Mediterranean History to come into being.

Since the first edition of this book appeared in 2003, the stream of books and articles on Mediterranean history has not ceased to flow. At the same time, the variety of approaches becomes ever richer. My own approach, which I describe as the 'human history' of the sea, focusing very much on the sea, ports and islands of the Mediterranean and on movement back and forth across this space, is just one perspective; I have developed it further in my lengthy history of the Mediterranean, *The Great Sea*, published in 2011. Most recently Greg Woolf has adopted the perspective of Mediterranean cities in his book *The Life and Death of Ancient Cities*, taking us back on land in what he describes as a 'natural history' of the Mediterranean. Within this book, some authors have laid an emphasis on naval history, looking at the great conflicts that took place on the surface and around the edges of the Mediterranean; cultural interactions between three continents across this space are an important theme of most chapters; this cultural interaction was stimulated by the movement of goods back and forth across the Mediterranean; a very important aspect of that cultural interaction was the spread of religious ideas, whether the arrival of stories about the Greek gods in Etruscan Italy, or the rise of Christianity and Islam in later centuries. This book is intended to convey not just the richness of Mediterranean history but the variety of ways in which it can be treated.

David Abulafia

Gonville and Caius College, Cambridge

What is the Mediterranean?

DAVID ABULAFIA

The question does not admit of a straightforward answer. At first glance the boundaries of the Mediterranean appear well defined by the coastline that runs from the rock of Gibraltar along Spain and southern France, around Italy and Greece to Turkey, Lebanon, Israel and then the entire coast of North Africa as far as Ceuta, the Spanish town on the tip of Morocco, opposite Gibraltar. But the Mediterranean cannot simply be defined by its edges. Within this space there are dozens of islands which have enormous significance for the history of the Mediterranean: the largest is Sicily, closely followed by Sardinia, but any historian of the Mediterranean would also wish to lay heavy stress upon the importance of Crete and Cyprus, as well as much smaller islands such as Santorini (Thera), the home of a flourishing prehistoric culture, or Elba, source of iron to the Etruscans. Small islands abound between the Greek and Turkish mainlands and along the coast of Croatia. But the Mediterranean is also divided into a western and eastern section by the Sicilian Straits between Sicily itself and Tunisia, an area of water that contains the remarkable Maltese islands, home to a Christian society which has preserved for over a millennium the language of its medieval Arab conquerors.

The first question is whether to identify the Mediterranean in terms of its water, its islands, its coasts or indeed the civilizations and states that have emerged along its coasts. For the highly influential French historian Fernand Braudel, lauded in his day as 'the greatest living historian', what was important was the way the physical geography of the Mediterranean moulded the civilizations that grew up on its shores, and (as will be seen) a long way inland. His was a view that laid considerable emphasis on the physical constraints that had determined human behaviour. Thus in his classic work *The Mediterranean and the Mediterranean World in the Age of Philip II* he paid detailed attention to land forms, particularly the contrast between mountain and plain, in order to argue that there were also fundamental differences between the societies that grew up in mountain and plain. This theme emerged out of his intense study of geography and his experiences as a young academic in French Algeria. His emphasis on the *longue durée*, the features of Mediterranean society that changed only slowly over time, sat rather uneasily alongside his attempt to explain the policies of the Spanish king Philip II in the late sixteenth-century Mediterranean, and it is fair to say that his work is still consulted for its insights into the relationship between geography and history, but rather less for its information about King Philip II. His school of historians was long scornful of the sort of history that was built around the study of political events; to be accused of writing *histoire événementielle* was for a time regarded as a damning criticism, particularly among French historians. But for Braudel this confinement of Philip II to the end of the second volume of his great work was right, since even the triumph of the Spaniards over Ottoman sea power was a reflection of deeper realities rooted in the geography of the Mediterranean lands. It was a history 'in which all change is slow, a history of constant repetition, ever-recurring cycles', and therefore poor Philip II recedes from view in most of Braudel's work, while the Mediterranean at times enlarges to include not merely Madeira but Cracow.

The need to take individuals into account in understanding the history of the Mediterranean, even what would now be called its economic history, was well understood by one of its first historians: Thucydides. His *History of the Peloponnesian War* is significant here because it stresses the ways in which sea empires or 'thalassocracies' are created, and shows an exceptional understanding of the nature of political rivalries, all the more startling since he had only a relatively modest group of predecessors in the art of writing history. He portrays at the start of his work a prehistoric Hellas which had no great interest in the sea, and tries to explain the transformations that occurred when the great Cretan King Minos assembled the first great navy in the Mediterranean. But it was an age of pirates, in which raiding and seizing what one required was regarded as a perfectly honourable way to secure a livelihood; and Minos, followed by the rulers of Mycenae, is credited by Thucydides with the achievement of chasing away the pirates, establishing governors on the Aegean islands, and fostering the prosperity of the region; this, then, provides us with an image of the maritime stability that Thucydides saw as ideal.

Then, after the discord of the Trojan War, it took time for Corinth to emerge as the leading naval power in Greece, capable of seeing off threats from Phoenicians, Carians and others, but blessed too by its position astride the isthmus of Corinth, which gave it access to the seas both to the east and to the west, and enabled it to grow rich on trade. Indeed, its influence spread across the central Mediterranean with the foundation of Corcyra (Corfu), and then by the Corcyrans of Epidamnos (Dyrrachium, Durazzo (Dürres), in modern Albania); at this point, the literary evidence and the archaeological, discussed by Mario Torelli with great authority later in this book, neatly converge. Thucydides explains with precision how a dispute over a relatively remote city such as Epidamnos eventually brought Athenian fleets into the waters of the Ionian Sea. What is important here is his sense of what would now be called geopolitics (a word that only came into use in the second half of the twentieth century). In fact, Thucydides trounces Braudel by showing an understanding of the human element in the making of Mediterranean history.

Braudel was concerned with the Mediterranean as a sea but also with extensive lands alongside that sea. This book takes a rather different approach. A history of the Mediterranean could be written, rather easily written, in the light of present knowledge, which recounted the ups and downs of the many civilizations that have flourished by the shores of the Great Sea: Egyptians, Minoans, Mycenaeans, Greeks, Etruscans, Romans, Byzantines, Arabs ... and so on, making a sort of encyclopaedia of human history in the area where three continents, Europe, Asia and Africa, meet. Medieval mapmakers certainly understood the Mediterranean as the meeting point of three landmasses, only one of which was dominated by Christians. That this region had an absolutely fundamental importance in the history of the entire planet cannot be denied: whether it is the cultural history of the world, with its roots in the classical civilizations of Athens, Rome, Renaissance Italy; whether it is the religious history of the world, so significantly shaped by Judaism and its two daughter religions, Christianity and Islam; whether it is the history of empire, in which the Iberian peninsula has played such a dominant role; whether it is the economic history of this planet, in which Genoese, Venetians and Catalans helped mould the commercial institutions with which we still operate; and so on.

In this book, an attempt has been made not to write the history of each of the societies that developed within the Mediterranean space, but to understand how contemporaneous societies interacted with one another across the sea. Lands far distant from one another enjoyed trading and cultural, even political, ties as a result of ease of movement across the open sea. A good case of this is offered by Muslim Spain. There we find a flourishing civilization which depended on cultural models derived from Syria, Egypt and Iraq, which entertained strong commercial relations with the East, and which also acted as a bridge between cultures, facilitating the transmission of Greek and Arabic texts, by way of translators, to western Europe; most of these translators were themselves either Jews or Arabized Christians native to Spain (Mozarabs). Thus the history of the Mediterranean Sea is not just the history of fleets and traders, though that is a crucially important aspect; the movement of ideas and religions needs to be documented as well. It is not just with politics, but with the way that objects and ideas moved across this space that this book is concerned: with the ships, their cargoes, their passengers and what went on in the heads of the passengers – allowing also for movement by land along the shores of the sea, which could have major consequences, as in the age of Turkish conquest. In such a history, the islands are all-important. It may be a cliché to describe islands such as Sicily as 'stepping stones' between the different cultures of the Mediterranean world, but it is nonetheless true. It remains true now, when that island is a focus for new waves of immigration from North Africa into Europe, just as it was such a focus in the ninth and tenth centuries of this era, and in the classical world, when Sicily was colonized by Greeks and Phoenicians among others.

The emphasis in most chapters is on trade and politics, and on the relationship between the two. Given the breadth of the topics that need to be discussed in a volume with such an ambitious agenda, it has seemed important to provide linking passages between the historical chapters, which attempt to contextualize what the chapters themselves focus on, and which attempt to provide continuity across the centuries. One area where continuity and caesura can often be observed is the religious history of the Mediterranean region, and it is therefore in these bridging passages that comments can be found about the rise of the three monotheistic religions that did much to mould the civilizations of the Mediterranean, Judaism, Christianity and Islam, religions with a vast number of common beliefs and ideals, though nonetheless often in bitter conflict with one another.

The parts and the whole

'List of the freight which is in the ship of the first prophet of Amun under the authority of the scribe of the treasury Hori ...' Here is a document from over three thousand years ago which seems to have uncanny similarities to the information about cargoes and commerce in the letters left by Jewish merchants of Old Cairo a mere thousand years ago. Year in, year out, the rising and falling of the Nile gave life to Pharaonic Egypt as it did to Roman, Byzantine and Islamic. This very long continuity has only recently been broken with the building of the Aswan Dam. It is tempting to see in the Phoenicians the remote precursors of the Genoese and Venetian masters of Mediterranean trade; like the Italians, they also linked the Mediterranean to the outside seas, essaying voyages to Cornwall for tin, just as the Italians travelled to Hampshire for wool nearly two thousand years later.

Yet the assumption that the Phoenicians are in some sense the precursors of later Mediterranean merchants begs questions about continuities from the remote past to more recent times; in particular, the assumption treats the Mediterranean as a unity, with a distinctive history of its own. It is not necessarily the history we would expect: not a compôte of the history of (say) tough Spartans brutalizing their sons, Roman conquests crushing the peoples of Italy, Visigoths conquering in turn the Romans and horrifying them by rubbing rancid butter into their hair... Nor in modern times is it solely the history of the War of Greek Independence, of the Young Turks, Fascism in Italy, the creation of the State of Israel, the radicalization of the Arab world, all developments which have had a decisive influence on political relationships within and beyond the Mediterranean. These events took place within the physical space of the Mediterranean, but do not by themselves help us understand how man and the sea interacted across that space.

Thus the sort of history being written here will, where appropriate, place its emphasis on great maritime empires or 'thalassocracies', such as the Athenian empire in antiquity, the Venetian empire in the Middle Ages, the British empire in the Mediterranean in the age of Admiral Nelson. But sometimes the principal actors will be slightly less familiar ones: Carthaginian and Etruscan merchants, the sailors of medieval Amalfi or Majorca, Sephardic Jews expelled from Spain in 1492, and indeed modern migrants from Africa and Asia to Europe, the people who have carried both goods and ideas across the Great Sea. Nor should one exclude the large numbers of north Europeans who have developed an intense fascination with the Mediterranean since the days of the Grand Tour. The character of the north European (and north American) presence in the Mediterranean changed dramatically in the second half of the twentieth century, as mass tourism enabled quite enormous numbers of northerners to spend their vacations in Majorca, the Greek islands and virtually every other corner of the European shores of the Mediterranean. It will be seen from the final chapter of this book that it was in this period that the Mediterranean became 'globalized', a process which began with the opening of the Suez Canal in the late nineteenth century, and which has been taken much further with the economic integration taking place within the European Union.

The term 'Great Sea' to describe the Mediterranean was sanctioned by the rabbis of the ancient world when they set out the blessing to be recited by Jews when they set sight on the Mediterranean, in praise of God 'who has created the Great Sea'. In the eyes of ancient and medieval observers, this was indeed the sea that stood at the centre of the world; as Geoffrey Rickman observes, in his valuable study of the Roman Mediterranean in this volume, the term *Mare Mediterraneum* seems to have come into use only between the late third century and the sixth century, and the Romans themselves spoke of the 'Great Sea', the 'Inner Sea' or simply *Mare Nostrum*, 'Our Sea'. The Ocean Sea surrounded the three continents of Asia, Africa and Europe, and even if navigators found evidence of other lands offshore, these were merely drops in a vast Ocean, sometimes rich in spices and other exotica, but external to a world that revolved around that Great Sea. A question that then arises is the identity of the seas that feed into the Mediterranean: the Adriatic may be fairly seen as a branch of the Mediterranean, and the Aegean is clearly

an island-studded corner of the Mediterranean; these were seas
through which Mediterranean merchants passed in order to reach
more distant markets – ancient Greek traders carrying their pottery
to Spina on the northeast coast of Italy; Venetians and Ragusans
bound for the spice markets of the Levant.

By contrast, the Black Sea has in many respects a separate identity,
tying the world of the steppes to eastern Europe, and linked to the
Mediterranean by a narrow passage that only opened in recent geological history. Its link to the Mediterranean has lain first, perhaps,
in Troy, with its position dominating the entrance to the Dardanelles,
and latterly in the city known successively as Byzantion, Constantinople and Istanbul. Certainly there were times, such as the fourteenth
century, when Black Sea grain fed several cities of the Mediterranean,
notably Genoa, and thus the Black Sea at certain points achieved
a degree of commercial integration into the Mediterranean world
(a theme brought out very clearly by Michel Balard in these pages).

Looking mainly at the sixteenth century, Fernand Braudel portrayed a series of links that brought towns as remote as Cracow in
southern Poland into the commercial nexus of the Mediterranean, by
way of Genoese merchants trading through the Black Sea ports across
the open spaces of eastern Europe. Thus his was a vast Mediterranean.
It stretched too beyond the Pillars of Hercules, guarded by Ceuta
and Gibraltar, to the 'Mediterranean Atlantic' which was opened up
in the later Middle Ages by merchants and conquistadors active in
Madeira, the Canaries, the Azores. From the time of the European
discovery of the Americas this interaction between Mediterranean
and Atlantic was certainly of the greatest significance: the emergence
of an 'Atlantic economy' by 1600 had major economic consequences
for the Mediterranean lands which had previously supplied northern
markets, and this continued to be an important issue well into the
period studied in this volume by Jeremy Black: the eighteenth and
early nineteenth centuries saw Great Britain, France and others
squabbling over their prizes within the Mediterranean Sea.

This vast Braudelian Mediterranean is reflected in modern historical writing in several ways. In the first place, there has been a rise in interest in the history of the region over the entire period from antiquity to contemporary times. We can identify several different schools of Mediterranean historian by looking not at books about the history of the Mediterranean, but at the surprising number of journals of Mediterranean history which have been published by the generation of historians who were brought up on the works of Braudel; it is here that the different schools tend to congregate, masters and pupils, professors and protégés.

The obvious place to begin is the *Mediterranean Historical Review*, which was first published in 1986 by a team of historians based in Tel Aviv, under the leadership of Shlomo Ben-Ami, who later became an active figure in Israeli politics, but began as an expert in modern Spanish history. Its approach is to study the history of the countries around the Mediterranean, but there is often space for articles about trade and other maritime links across the sea, and the journal has a particular interest in the role of the Jews as vectors of economic, religious and cultural change in the region, which is hardly surprising given its Israeli editors. Still, this journal could be said to embody the view that Mediterranean history is in essence the history of the lands surrounding the Mediterranean not just collectively, by way of examining their interactions, but individually, looking at the internal affairs of Italy, Spain, Greece or Egypt. The Mediterranean is thus seen as a broadly defined region, one that has many distinctive features.

Moving beyond even this generous approach to Mediterranean history, there is the philosophy of the 'Society for Mediterranean Studies', based in the United States since the 1990s. Here the emphasis, notably in its annual publication *Mediterranean Studies*, is on Mediterranean culture as the foundation of a world culture. Thus the society takes great interest in the links between the Mediterranean and Portugal, a land which was the product of the Christian struggle against Islam in Iberia, where the language is derived from classical Latin with some Arabic vocabulary. An excellent case can certainly be made for including Portugal among the ranks of Mediterranean countries, on cultural, religious and other grounds, as a sort of honorary Mediterranean country. In fact this society held two of its earliest conferences not in the Mediterranean but in Portugal, followed by one in Salvador de Bahía in Brazil, an offshoot of an offshoot of Mediterranean culture. For South America too can be seen as a cultural extension of Mediterranean civilization. Here, then, 'Mediterranean' effectively means 'Latin' (as in 'Latin America'). Mediterranean history thus becomes world history, seen through the lens of Iberian overseas expansion, but the Great Sea itself recedes from view. This is a perfectly legitimate approach, but it is not the one that will be adopted here, where the focus will remain that 'Inner Sea' and its edges.

Another 'world history' approach is to see the Mediterranean Sea as one of several Mediterraneans, or Middle Seas, areas of the world where land masses are separated by intervening water across which commodities, ideas and people regularly cross; sometimes therefore the contact will be between vastly differing societies, which were not in physical contact by land. The most successful attempt to export Braudel's approach to the Mediterranean elsewhere has been in the exciting books and articles of Kurti Chaudhuri on the Indian Ocean on the eve of the age of European expansion and during the period when Portuguese, Dutch and others irrupted into a sea whose commerce was previously dominated by Muslim and Hindu merchants, with the occasional appearance of Chinese warships too in the early fifteenth century. Like the 'classic' Mediterranean, it was an area where continents met (East Africa facing the many societies of South Asia), and different religions, including Buddhism and Islam, spread across vast distances.

A similar case could be made for presenting the Caribbean together with the Gulf of Mexico as a sort of Mediterranean in the era before Columbus, in which trade goods and migrant peoples moved between islands and the predominant feature was not isolation, but ease of contact. Another rich example is the 'Mediterranean' formed by the South China Sea, flanked by Malaysia, Indonesia, Vietnam, the Philippines, Taiwan and China; just as Italy half closes the Mediterranean Sea, so the waters between Korea and Japan form a narrow point through which trade and ideas were easily transmitted in the Middle Ages, with the Japanese port at Hakata-Fukoaka tapping into Korean and Chinese trade and even acting as host to resident Chinese merchants. These trade routes brought books and religious ideas as well, and provided the basis on which Buddhism laid down firm roots in Japan. Given the many similarities between this 'Japanese Mediterranean' and the classic Mediterranean, it is possible to learn much from a comparative approach to the maritime history of the two seas.

But there are other examples which have a more direct bearing on the history of the Mediterranean Sea, because these other 'Mediterraneans' had important commercial and cultural links with the classic Mediterranean. A distinguished historian of the medieval Mediterranean, Roberto Lopez, wrote (somewhat confusingly) of the Baltic and North Sea as the 'northern Mediterranean' where similar commercial developments took place to those visible in the classic Mediterranean; Viking and Frisian merchants played the role of the early Amalfitans and Venetians in the Mediterranean (within the period of John Pryor's chapter in this book), while the great trading confederation known as the German Hansa shows some parallels with the operations of the Genoese, Catalan and Venetian merchants of the late medieval Mediterranean, though it was rather more united than the Italian merchants ever became. This Mediterranean of the North interacted with the Mediterranean of the South by way of the trade routes that led from Bruges to the Mediterranean Sea, overland or (after the 1270s) by sea past Gibraltar. Not just trade goods such as furs and amber went south, and spices came north:

so did ideas and techniques of the most varied sort, such as the methods and iconography of Flemish painters or the new ideas of antiquity favoured by Renaissance scholars; possibly too the type of heavy ship known as the cog was copied by Mediterranean navigators from northern ships that entered the Mediterranean. And, as has been seen, the Black Sea is both an extension out of the classic Mediterranean and a small Mediterranean in its own right, linking the contrasting shores of Europe and central Asia.

These 'Mediterraneans' do not need to contain water: the Sahara Desert is another Mediterranean that interacted closely with the classic Mediterranean, criss-crossed by caravans consisting of ships of the desert, dromedary camels, taking gold from Black Africa to the shores of the Maghrib, trudging from oasis to oasis just as ships might hop from island to island. Thus Mediterraneans become the theatre for cross-cultural trade and for the exchange of ideas and populations, a subject examined comparatively by the American world historian Philip Curtin. Again, this multiplication of the Mediterranean, though intellectually stimulating, is not the theme of this book.

Another approach to the Mediterranean can be found in the contributions to a journal called *al-Masāq: Islam and the Medieval Mediterranean*, founded by an indefatigable scholar originally from Malta, Dionisius Agius, who also set up a Centre of Mediterranean Studies at the University of Leeds in the north of England. This journal is a genuinely innovative one, which seeks to cross the Christian–Islamic divide in the medieval Mediterranean, often examining commercial and religious contacts from the perspective of the Muslim presence in the Mediterranean. With *al-Masāq* we seem to be coming nearer to a history of the Mediterranean which is about interactions, rather than about an infinite number of localities: about the meeting of cultures in Norman Sicily or Muslim Spain, about Venetian merchants in Islamic lands, and so on. But the idea of an infinite number of localities also has its appeal: two British historians, Peregrine Horden and Nicholas Purcell, have suggested that the localities themselves are very much part of the history of Mediterranean interactions. It is to their view, presented in a massive volume called *The Corrupting Sea*, that we should now turn.

Changing visions of a Mediterranean world

Ambitious though Braudel's vision was, that of Peregrine Horden and Nicholas Purcell has been conceived on an even vaster scale. The chronological range of their book takes us from ancient Hellas to early medieval times, with occasional peeks earlier and later. In three words, their thesis is that of diversity within unity. Horden and Purcell stress the relationship between the very diverse localities of the Mediterranean and the 'connectivities' that bind one locality to another. Paradoxically, the fundamental geographical feature of the Mediterranean is thus the enormous complexity of the region. Complexity means richness, diversity in a very positive sense, facilitating exchanges over short and long distances. How tightly packed the different environments are can be seen from the example of western Sicily; there, one can ascend in late summer from the steamy heat of the salt-pans of Trapani into the cold, thick clouds that shroud the ancient mountain city of Erice, with its own distinctive microclimate.

Moreover, this is a sea of jagged coasts, of islands scattered across the sea (so that sailors are rarely, in good weather, out of sight of land), many of them tiny ones which must exchange goods across the sea if the population has any hope of surviving. It is a sea with marshy coastlands, such as the Valencian *horta*, famous for its rice, or the insalubrious sea coast of Albania, with its salt supplies; yet along the coastline plains and mountains are dramatically juxtaposed, feeding off one another, especially in the regular transhumance of sheep from lowlands to highlands as one presses into the interior. Indeed, Horden and Purcell have taken issue with Braudel's famous characterization of mountain communities as immobile and isolated, insisting that the mountains are more, not less, 'connected': the imperatives of exchange tie the mountains to the rest of the Mediterranean world, and routes through the mountains prove not to be obstacles, but ways of binding mountain micro-ecologies into greater ecological networks. Isolated enclaves are a rarity in areas close to the sea. Mountains like the Apennines were barriers to armies but not to the mule trains that carried considerable quantities of grain and salt from the Romagna to thirteenth-century Florence.

And yet the sea was what provided the most flexible link, even if the changing seasons sometimes (but less than is generally supposed) imposed a close season when maritime contact had to be reserved for emergencies. This regular interchange had a transforming or 'corrupting' effect on the societies which were reached by systems of trade and exchange; 'corrupting' is a word that implies negative change, and in many ways what Horden and Purcell have described is a highly positive set of stimulants. Rather than a 'Corrupting Sea' it would be appropriate to call it an Enriching Sea: 'enriching' in the figurative sense, as one society benefits from cultural contact with its neighbours and with societies further across the water, but 'enriching' also in a literal sense, as merchants make heavy profits from the business engendered by the exchange of essential commodities, such as grain and salt. Theirs, then, is a history of the Mediterranean which places its emphasis not on the grand trade routes bringing spices and dyes from the East (most of them in any case produced very far from the shores of the Mediterranean, as far away as the East Indies), but on systems of exchange which sought to satisfy primary needs: for grain, wine, oil, metals and timber.

The ecological diversity of the eastern Mediterranean led the rulers of Egypt in ancient and medieval times to look, politically as well as commercially, towards the forests of Lebanon and Cilicia in order to obtain wood for their fleets and a hundred other uses. The need for base metals attracted Greek merchants to the territory of the Etruscans, which still contains gigantic slag heaps left by the iron producers who processed the iron of Elba in the region round Populonia (close to the modern Piombino). Indeed, for Horden and Purcell it was precisely the imperative of local exchange within such a varied ecological setting that bound the ancient and medieval Mediterranean together.

Interchange across the sea and between its margins and the hinterland may indeed have created population centres, even helped generate sea empires; but Horden and Purcell are also arguing that there existed a fundamental consistency across time. Ecological catastrophes, they opine, were never so drastic that they fundamentally altered the economic structures of the region, and in this their views chime with those of Oliver Rackham, whose essay on the ecology of the Mediterranean opens the series of chapters in this volume. Horden and Purcell note that the destruction of Pompeii did not have long-term economic consequences outside a small region, where the massive lava outflow revitalized the soil; however, it is possible that other volcanic eruptions, notably that which covered Santorini (Thera) in ash, were far more destructive, and the end of Minoan civilization has even been attributed to that eruption, a point raised by Marlene Suano and Mario Torelli in this book.

Still, Horden and Purcell are not satisfied with the classic view that alluvial flows modified the landscape throughout time, destroying as well as creating resources on which communities had based their existence. This view was powerfully expounded by the historical geographer Claudio Vita-Finzi, in a study called *The Mediterranean Valleys*, even if it was only able to examine a few hand-picked examples in such areas as western Anatolia and North Africa; Vita-Finzi's approach was eagerly grasped by historians of Byzantium and other societies, in search of explanations of economic crisis and decline. The Horden-Purcell view is quite different: 'alluviation is a great constant of Mediterranean life'. In a word, there are swings and roundabouts. There is no dark history of mankind corrupting a terrestrial paradise by environmental incompetence. That is a familiar

myth, widespread in the Mediterranean societies themselves; but
the myth is not an accurate portrayal of physical reality.

More recently, Oliver Rackham expressed not dissimilar doubts
about the damage human beings have inflicted on the Mediterranean
environment, in his chapter in this book, and in his larger study,
written with A. T. Grove, *The Nature of Mediterranean Europe*. His
own approach is heavily informed by a deep knowledge of ecological issues, and close study of examples in Sardinia and elsewhere.
The Mediterranean of Horden and Purcell therefore sees societies
move forward at different speeds, some stimulated into life by
access to new sources of raw materials, others deprived of access
(perhaps by political factors, such as invasions and warfare between
states, no less than because of geological change). Thus, alongside
intensification of human activities, there are cases of 'abatement',
letting go; and rather than a general Mediterranean trend, these are
localized trends, so that micro-regions are out of rhythm with one
another, and, more importantly still, 'long-term change is almost
never unilinear'. Indeed, it makes sense to argue that it is precisely
the disjunctures that take place which stimulate innovation and
experimentation: thus the Turkish advances of the late Middle Ages,
which made access to the eastern Mediterranean more difficult for
Italian merchants, also indirectly stimulated the growth of sugar
plantations in Sicily and Spain, since the Italians were looking for
alternative supplies of this much-valued article away from the main
battle zones (and the longer-term effects of the Turkish presence in
the Mediterranean are beautifully described by Molly Greene in her
chapter in this book).

Human beings thus responded to local disasters such as ecological transformations or political upheavals by developing new
strategies, and even the apparently desperate strategy of emigration from afflicted regions should be seen as another example of
the 'connectivities' binding together the Mediterranean area. For
Horden and Purcell, the constant movement of population, whether

as slaves or economic migrants (or indeed as conquerors) is another of those factors that binds together the Mediterranean region. We could go further, and argue that even the cataclysm of conquest often masks real continuities. The rise of Islam led to the adoption of many practices from the previous rulers of the lands the early Arabs overwhelmed, that is, from the Byzantine Greeks and the Persians; thus this invasion did not in fact break a great many important continuities, notably in government. The Arabs could never have governed Egypt after it fell to their armies in 640 without the help of Copts, Greeks, Jews and Samaritans who showed them how the land had been governed in the past. On the other hand, the Arab conquests stimulated the movement not just of Arabs but of Berbers, eastern Christians and Jews westwards to North Africa, Sicily and Spain, along with plants which, if not always unknown, were at least never before so intensively cultivated; the watermelon that one sees propped on a plank along the roadside in modern Greece, advertising that more of the same is available around the corner, traces its heritage back to the Muslim conquests. By looking briefly at the legacy of Islamic conquest by way of the foods that the Muslims brought to the Mediterranean world, we can understand more clearly how the Mediterranean functioned as the meeting point of three continents and of three religions.

The legacy of the Islamic conquests appears not just in the mosque at Córdoba but in the lemons we squeeze, the sugar we stir and the marzipan we savour. A vast array of products on sale in any modern Mediterranean food market arrived originally from the Islamic world, reaching Sicily and Spain before penetrating deeper into Europe: sour (or Seville) oranges, limes, artichokes, bananas, aubergines, watermelon, spinach, rice. Their origins often lay far to the East, in Persia or the Indies, but they were soon cultivated throughout the Muslim lands. Some were favoured by the early caliphs in Baghdad, setting new standards of elegant cuisine whose influence spread as far as Spain. The aubergine even had its praises sung in early Arabic poetry. A Spanish Muslim wrote that 'the prince must ensure that the greatest encouragement is given to the cultivation of the soil', and agronomy was an art in medieval Spain, pursued with a similar passion to that of modern kibbutz workers desperate to extract the maximum benefit from apparently dry and hostile soils.

The spread of these crops transformed the countryside, necessitating massive irrigation projects to moisten the dry soils of the Middle East, North Africa and southern Spain. Superbly built underground ducts (*qanats*) carried water across hills and prevented evaporation; the construction of these tightly fitted tunnels owed something, too, to local precedents, reaching back through the ancient Romans to the early tunnel builders of ancient Etruria. But the Asian model counted for much: South Arabia had long been the centre of surprisingly lush cultivation, and settlers from as far away as Yemen taught the Spaniards how to create an equally lush countryside around Córdoba, filled with orange groves, which in the tenth century had an ornamental as much as a nutritional role. Palace gardens adorned with fruit trees, flowers and fountains were seen as an image of Paradise. In tenth-century Córdoba the Jewish poet Dunash ibn Labrat sang of how 'pomegranates, dates, tamarisks, grapes and pleasant anemones fill the garden rows', and the garden became a standard theme of Arabic and Hebrew poetry in Muslim-ruled Spain. By the late thirteenth century, paddy fields around Valencia produced another Asiatic food, rice, exported as far as Plantagenet England, along with Majorcan figs, yet another product brought westwards by the Arabs.

It was not just upmarket food which was introduced into Europe by the Muslims. There was the famous hard wheat, milled into semolina out of which couscous and pasta were made. From the Arabic name for noodles, *fidawsh*, came the Spanish name which is still in use, *fideos*. The names of many other crops are of Arabic origin: the artichoke, in Spanish *alcarchofa*, was the Arabic *kharshuf*, and was probably first cultivated in North Africa, before its adoption in Spain. But it was sugar that had most impact; its origins lie in the Far East, though it rapidly spread across the Islamic world. By 1400 Levantine sugar was eagerly traded by Italian merchants who carried it to England, Flanders and Germany. As has been seen already, with the Turkish advance into Europe, these merchants became keener to buy their sugar further west, and sugar plantations were developed in Sicily, Muslim Granada and even in Braudel's 'Mediterranean Atlantic', in Madeira. By the sixteenth century the New World became the great source of sugar; but it was to Islam that Westerners owed their taste for sugar, and it was out of the Mediterranean that it reached the New World. Mixed with mountain snow and juices, sugar was the basis for sherbet or sorbet, which the crusaders encountered in the East. Interestingly, around 1400 the Muslim lands of the eastern Mediterranean reciprocated by demanding western European honey, particularly the honey of Narbonne. Thus (in accord with Horden and Purcell's concepts) shortages in one area were compensated by trade with another.

The Muslim world was also a great source of spices sent to Europe throughout the Middle Ages. In fact, not many of the famous spices were cultivated in Mediterranean lands; pepper and ginger were carried along the shores of the Indian Ocean from the Spice Islands, but their sale to Christian merchants in Alexandria made the fortune of medieval Egypt. In that sense they too are part of the history of the Mediterranean. The West was itself the source of one spice which was eagerly traded by the merchants of San Gimignano and Volterra, two Tuscan towns that were, in the thirteenth century, the international centres for the production of saffron; and later other centres emerged, in the Abruzzi and north of the Alps, to meet both Oriental and European demand for what was one of the most precious spices of all.

But it was in the Mediterranean that demand for all these items was most ferocious, and this demand helped mould the economic activity of several of the leaders in international trade during the medieval and early modern eras: the Genoese, who diversified from grain and cloth in order to buy pepper and ginger in the Levant; the Venetians, who left behind them their origins as humble salesmen of fish and salt, to become the leading spice merchants of the fifteenth century. Until Vasco da Gama circumnavigated Africa in 1497 these products were only obtainable in Muslim lands bordering the Mediterranean, and were used not just to flavour food but in medicines and as dyestuffs. Of course, they were goods which rapidly passed beyond the coasts of the Mediterranean, to be put up for sale in Champagne, Flanders, Germany, even England and the rest of the 'Mediterranean of the North'; but this too is testimony to the way the Mediterranean functioned as the main bridge between the economic systems of East and West.

With the image of the Mediterranean presented by Peregrine Horden and Nicholas Purcell, we are still not so far from Braudel: the *longue durée* has lengthened considerably, yet the people who inhabit this landscape are masses and waves. Micro-regional history must surely also emphasize the often considerable effects of micro-regional politics and individual endeavour. The catalyst may be a rude Macedonian king from the backwoods, a conquering Arab general who ignores his superiors, or a Genoese merchant with an eye on the alum monopoly. This human Mediterranean was the focus of the research of the great scholar of the Jews of Islam, Shlomo Goitein, who died in 1985. His five-volume work, *A Mediterranean Society*, was based on the documents of the Cairo Genizah, literally a rubbish dump of medieval papers (mainly from about 950 to about 1200) found a century ago in an ancient synagogue in Old Cairo, and mostly preserved in Cambridge University Library. Though Horden and Purcell cite Goitein as one of a select group who have transformed our understanding of Mediterranean history, they recognize that it is in the detail rather than in any overall conception of Mediterranean history that his importance lies.

Goitein brilliantly evoked a world of Jewish merchants trading from India to Sicily; and the letters he analysed concerned not just sales of silk and spices, but family relationships – all the hopes and fears of generations of Jews of all social classes. How typical they were of 'Mediterranean society' is a question no one has been able to answer, and they certainly avoided some types of business which were more favoured by Muslim or Coptic merchants, such as the trade in wheat. But they were an integral part of Mediterranean society, not ghettoized, and they can be studied in far more detail than contemporary Muslims; thus they were not so much a 'Mediterranean society' as part of wider Mediterranean society. Still, by dedicating volumes to the individual, the community and the family as well as to economic links, Goitein's work serves as an important reminder that it is essential to restore individual human beings to their place in Mediterranean history.

The fundamental characteristic of this and other Mediterraneans (like the Japanese example briefly examined earlier in this Introduction) was the relative proximity of opposing shores, but also the clear separation between shores, enabling different cultures to interact with one another across what may at times seem almost impermeable cultural barriers, such as the Christian-Muslim divide in the Mediterranean Sea. Distances were also narrowed by the presence of islands which, in the Mediterranean, tended in fact to serve as bridges between the cultures and economies of the Mediterranean: islands such as Minoan Crete in the Bronze Age or Catalan Majorca in the late Middle Ages. Some islands, it is true, became isolated societies relatively untouched by the outside world, and this isolation can be seen in the way that Sardinia was only slowly integrated into the cultural and political world of medieval Europe, as a result of Italian colonization; or the way Malta preserved the otherwise vanished Arabic idiom of early medieval Sicily. But even these societies, though conservative in some ways, were affected by trade and adapted their production to meet the needs of foreign demand: for Maltese cotton, for Sardinian grain, leather and pecorino cheese.

Of course, all seas both join and divide landmasses. But what is important about the Mediterranean lands is the scale of the challenge posed by the sea, and the relative ease of movement that is possible within its compass compared to the open ocean. This ease of movement produces further dividends: the history of the Mediterranean Sea is a history of coexistence, commercial, cultural, religious, political, as well as a history of confrontation between neighbours aware of their often powerful ethnic, economic and, again, religious differences. Ecological questions certainly cannot be ignored; but to the historian their great importance lies first of all in the living conditions that they imposed on human settlers, and second in the ways the settlers subsequently modified the environment. In writing the history of the Mediterranean it is essential to write a human history of the Mediterranean Sea expressed through the commercial, cultural and religious interaction that took place across its surface.

ONE

The physical setting

OLIVER RACKHAM

One way to define the Mediterranean region is in terms of climate. Summers are hot and dry; winters warm and wet, without much frost. At low altitudes winter and spring are the growing season, summer the dead season. This odd and harsh climate is confined to about 1 per cent of the world's land area, some of it in other continents. Yet this definition can have many variants. As one goes north winters get colder and summers less arid. Southward and eastward it merges more gradually into desert. The towering mountains of Mediterranean coasts create intense local rain-excesses and rain-shadows. Indeed, the Mediterranean includes the driest place in Europe (Almería in southeastern Spain) and the wettest place in Europe (Crkvice in Montenegro). Mediterranean mountains have a rigorous climate with two dead seasons: the cold, snowy winter is separated by only a few weeks in spring from the dry summer.

Combined with the varied and mountainous topography, diverse geology and the diversity of human cultures, Mediterranean lands are dramatically varied. Generalizations about the Mediterranean should be treated with suspicion.

For instance, the islands are not mere extensions of the mainland. Crete, a splinter of land some 250 by 50 km (155 by 31 miles), is a miniature continent with its Alps, its deserts and jungles, arctic wastes and tropical gorges, and many bizarre animals and plants found nowhere else. Although the native animals are nearly all long extinct, their effects can be seen in the plant life, which still survives.

Islands, too, have their own peculiar human cultures. Crete, with its dangerous coasts and pirate-haunted seas, has been inward-looking for much of its history. The Iron Age civilization of Sardinia put thousands of massive towers called *nuraghi* on the hilltops: and yet there is not one elsewhere, even on Corsica. The human landscapes of these two islands remain utterly different to this day.

Mediterranean lands are now in a transitional state not typical of their history. Throughout almost all the European Mediterranean there has been a shift of population from the mountains to cities and settlements on the coast, previously inhospitable and dangerous. This is not only a matter of coastal and urban tourism. Mechanization has limited agriculture to relatively flat land, where tractors and bulldozers can be used, and where there is scope for irrigation with plastic pipes and for market-garden crops grown in greenhouses. Steep terrain, formerly terraced, is abandoned and turns into forest or pasture; much of the remoter pasture-land, in turn, is abandoned. Rivers are dammed (which causes their deltas to retreat) and ground-water is pumped out to the point at which the supply is threatened by the intrusion of salt and other noxious substances.

As a base-line for comparison with the past, it is helpful to use, not the present state, but the situation before this recent phase of mechanization, urbanization and land abandonment ('Greece Yesterday', as Anthony Snodgrass puts it). However, it must not be supposed that what preceded it was a 'traditional' landscape whose land-uses were unchanged since antiquity. Declining rural populations today must be seen against a time of abnormally high population in the late nineteenth and early twentieth centuries, coinciding with an earlier phase of globalization and technological change based on steam-engines, mules, windmills and sailing ships.

Moreover, much of the African and Asian Mediterranean is still in this earlier phase, with populations still increasing and cultivation still being pushed to its limits.

Climate and climate history

The Mediterranean climate is very undependable. Rainfall in any one season can easily be either more than twice or less than half the average. Some mountains, such as Mont-Aigoual in the south of France, are peculiarly prone to deluges, when half a year's average rainfall or more falls in two days.

The climate is dusty. Dust is picked up from the Sahara and transported in the upper atmosphere. In Crete it is deposited almost annually in 'red rains' in sufficient quantities to be an appreciable input to the soil.

However, the present climate appears to have existed for only a few thousand years. The evidence comes partly from the pollen record (see later) but also from parallel changes in Alpine glaciers and in Africa. In the first half of the Holocene, to judge by the vegetation, it was less seasonal and less arid. Between 4800 and 2400 BC there was a change, known as the aridization, to the present drier and more strongly seasonal climate.

Deluges were concentrated around particular periods in history, such as the peaks of the Little Ice Age in the early fourteenth, late sixteenth, late seventeenth and early nineteenth centuries AD. These periods of unstable weather are well known from records as well as the deposits which they leave. Evidence is emerging for earlier periods of instability and deluges, for example around 1600 BC and AD 700. The last 180 years, in which there are abundant instrumental weather measurements, now appear (like the Roman period) to have been a time of unusually stable weather.

Watercourses typically run only during the rainy season; in drier areas they may run for only a few days, or not every year. Perennial rivers either derive their water from outside the region (like the Rhône) or are fed by springs. In recent years the growth of irrigation and dams has dried up many rivers and springs. There is some evidence that in the Little Ice Age more rivers were perennial.

Mountains, earthquakes and deserts

The Mediterranean is a very lively region geologically, the zone where the European and African crustal plates collide, crumple and splinter. The Alpine mountain-building belt runs from Morocco through the Pyrenees and Alps to Turkey and beyond; ripples of it form the mountains of Spain, Italy and Greece, the volcanoes of Sicily, and the island arcs of the Aegean. The Mediterranean Sea itself is the relic of a much wider sea in Tertiary times, some 70 million years ago.

Tectonic uplift (and local depression) results in the earthquakes to which much of the region is subject. It is the ultimate driving force of the various kinds of erosion (except wind erosion) of Mediterranean landscapes.

Mediterranean geology is very varied; much of it is limestone, different kinds of which generate startlingly different landscapes. Wide tracts of country, especially at low altitudes, are covered with material brought down by erosion at earlier stages of the mountain-building. Palaeozoic igneous and metamorphic rocks are limited to areas spared in the Tertiary disturbance, such as the interior of Spain, Sardinia, Libya and Egypt.

Soils in Mediterranean lands are formed partly from the weathering of underlying rocks (or of overlying rocks that have disappeared), and partly from material brought from elsewhere by water or wind, for example fall-out of volcanic ash or dust from the Sahara. Glacial deposits are insignificant.

Soil-forming materials have been moved around by erosional processes, ancient and recent, and have accumulated in places where they make cultivation possible.

Vegetation is particularly dependent on moisture, a combination of rainfall, the water-holding capacities of soil and bedrock, and the ability of roots to penetrate the soil or bedrock. The latter is specially important, as is shown by the recent practice of bulldozing soft limestones and growing vines and other crops in the broken-up bedrock.

The Mediterranean has several small, curious and beautiful deserts. Some are in areas of very low rainfall, as in southeastern Spain and southeast Crete. Some are where the rock fails to retain moisture, as in the alpine desert of west Crete. Others are determined by poor root penetration. Massive hard limestones, where there are no ledges or rock-pockets to retain soil and no fissures for trees to root into, are sometimes brilliantly white or pink deserts; so are the hard, compact forms of conglomerate. Even soft limestones, such as the marls of middle Crete, can be very poorly vegetated if roots cannot penetrate.

Some limestones form *karst*, when fissures and sinkholes are gradually enlarged as rainwater percolates through and dissolves the limestone. Karst tends to be well-vegetated, and cultivable soils are lodged in pockets and sinkholes. Caves in the karst form important prehistoric sites.

Badlands are tracts of gullies, filling the landscape and intersecting to leave sharp jagged ridges. They result from water erosion in certain types of sediment, especially clays, laid down in earlier phases of mountain-building and then tilted by further uplift to angles where they are no longer stable. They can also be set off by a river cutting back its headwaters and breaching a sediment-filled basin. These extraordinary and beautiful landscapes have had their peculiar interactions with the human inhabitants in prehistoric, ancient and modern times.

Coastal changes

The Mediterranean Sea has been connected to the Atlantic for at least five million years. It is topped up by a net inflow of ocean water which balances the excess of evaporation over input from rivers. The link to the Black Sea results from a breakthrough in the early Holocene.

The outline of the Mediterranean depends on the general level of water in the oceans, which was about 100 m (328 ft) lower during the last glaciation and rose to its present level about 7,400 real years ago. From that time onwards, erosion on land has produced sediment which has filled in bays and built up deltas at the mouths of rivers. The coastline is still not completely adjusted to the sudden rise in sea-level. Many changes have occurred in historic times, such as the silting up of ancient harbours on the Turkish coast and the appearance above sea-level of the Ebro delta. These local changes depend on the erodibility of deposits upstream, the supply of sediment, and the presence or absence of badlands.

Coastlines are also affected directly by local tectonic uplift or subsidence. The western half of Crete was suddenly uplifted by some 9 m (29 ft) in the sixth century AD; the east of the island has subsided. Big river deltas, such as the Nile, Rhône and Po tend to subside under their own weight; there is often a nice balance between the subsidence of a delta, the input of sediment, and the local tectonics. A famous example is Thermopylae, the site of ancient battles in Greece, where the ancient topography has dramatically changed because of the interaction of several of these factors.

In the twentieth century most Mediterranean coasts have retreated. This is ascribed to the fashion for damming rivers: the sediment that used to top up deltas and reinforce soft coasts now fills dams instead. Deltas have come in the recent past and may disappear in the near future.

Vegetation

Mediterranean lands have a very rich flora. Although they experienced the peripheral effects of Pleistocene glaciations, they were never so covered with ice as to wipe out all plant life. The small, high, isolated mountains and mountainous islands have encouraged the evolution of new species, hence the many endemic plants which are confined to a particular region, island, mountain or cliff. About one-eighth of the flora of Crete is peculiar to Crete or to some part of it.

Here, too, generalizations are unrealistic. Vegetation is not all the same, still less is it a mere part of the environment. Anyone studying

Mediterranean vegetation has to begin by knowing the behaviour of a dozen common tree species and a score of undershrubs, and how each reacts to different human activities.

The plant life of the Mediterranean is ill-adapted to a climate which has existed for little more than 5,000 years. Only a few plants, such as *Euphorbia dendroides*, have the knack of shedding their leaves in summer. Typical Mediterranean trees are thought of as evergreen, their leaves lasting a little over a year (or just less than a year, as in the cork oak). Many, however, lose their leaves in winter, and do their growing during the dry summer, presumably a relic of their ancestry in a climate which was differently seasonal.

As in other climates, different plants react in different ways to browsing (by wild animals or domestic livestock) and woodcutting. Pines die when felled; most oaks sprout. Goats love ash and will eat oak, but leave the strong-tasting cypress and sage until they have run out of more palatable plants. Some plants protect themselves by spines, strong flavours, poisons and distasteful fluff. These adaptations, requiring as they do tens of thousands of years of evolution, are presumably a response to deer, elephants and so on, rather than to domestic animals.

Many Mediterranean trees and shrubs are the same species according to circumstances. Prickly-oak (*Quercus coccifera*), for instance, can be anything from a big oak tree to a shrub a few centimetres high, according to how much woodcutting, browsing or burning it gets. If circumstances change it can grow up from a shrub into a tree.

Fire is important in Mediterranean ecosystems. It is an adaptation, not a misfortune: trees and other plants that will burn do so because they make fire-promoting chemicals. Most combustible trees are adapted in various ways to withstanding or recovering from fire. Aleppo pine is very flammable and is killed by a fierce fire, but the seeds in the cones may be stimulated to germinate. Cork oak, which is only moderately flammable itself but grows among fire-promoting undershrubs, withstands fire by its heat-resistant bark.

Forests, in the sense of trees growing close together, in Mediterranean countries are mainly in the mountains. Other types of wild vegetation include:

Maquis, macchia: trees reduced to the form of shrubs. Typically these are evergreens such as prickly-oak, but deciduous trees are often also involved.

Phrygana (sometimes called *garrigue*, but this word is also applied to the dwarfer forms of maquis): vegetation composed of undershrubs, woody plants – usually short-lived – which are not potential trees. Examples are the species of *Cistus* and Labiatae which give Mediterranean landscapes their colours and scents.

Steppe: vegetation of herbaceous (non-woody) plants, including grasses, bulbous and tuberous species, and many dandelion-like species.

Savanna, *'pseudo-savanna'*: trees scattered in phrygana or steppe, as in the Portuguese *montado* or Spanish *dehesa*.

Most of the pasturage, especially for sheep and goats, depends on maquis and steppe. Honey comes mainly from phrygana.

These types of vegetation sometimes form separate tracts, but often there is a mosaic of maquis, phrygana and steppe, organized according to moisture and root penetration. In the Mediterranean, as elsewhere, in a partly treed landscape the trees tend to grow on patches of rock and the other plants on patches of soil. Trees also congregate round the edges of screes. Shrubs, like trees, tend to occupy rock outcrops or buried archaeology where their roots penetrate fissures; undershrubs are shallow-rooted and less constrained; steppe favours areas with more soil.

Savanna and maquis are partly natural and partly artificial, and it is not easy to tell the difference. In wetter climates trees grow in forests, where a full-sized tree gets enough moisture from the ground directly beneath it. Where there is not enough moisture trees can either be reduced to the stature of shrubs (maquis) or can grow widely spaced, spreading their roots to catch the rain that falls between the trees as well as on them (savanna). In still less favourable places even shrubs are absent.

Historians from northern Europe or influenced by north and central European habits of thought, tend to view Mediterranean lands as 'degraded' landscapes. The original vegetation (so the argument runs) was continuous forest – some say 'magnificent forests'. The present 'typical' Mediterranean wild vegetation of maquis, phrygana, steppe and savanna are traditionally interpreted as derivatives of forest through different degrees of degradation by woodcutting, browsing and burning. Much of this change is supposed to be very recent. Scholars claim that degradation is progressive and more or less irreversible: changes wrought by successive human cultures, from the Neolithic to the age of railways, have added up over the centuries to the 'ruined landscape' that there is today.

This theory is largely untenable. Degradation is difficult to establish as a historical event: it has rarely been shown, as a matter of record, that a certain area now phrygana was once maquis, or that a tract of maquis was forest earlier in history. There are, of course, plenty of historical records of people cutting down trees, but without knowing about regrowth it is impossible to say whether this constituted deforestation. The Roman Empire, with its dense populations and fuel-using activities and industries, presumably consumed timber and wood as never before, but it is not known whether there was more or less tree-land in the Mediterranean at its end than at its beginning.

In reality, Mediterranean vegetation is resilient. If grazing, burning or woodcutting cease, maquis and savanna turn towards forest: shrubs grow into trees and new trees fill the gaps in savanna, up to a new limit set by climate. Undershrubs are often shaded out, and steppe remains as steppe. Abandoned cultivation turns into phrygana or forest: often the new trees are already there as bushes in terrace walls. These changes happen at least as rapidly as in temperate climates. They bring further consequences. Trees and undershrubs of abandoned land, especially pines and *Cistus* species, are mostly very fire-promoting. Much of the recent increase in fires is due to the landscape becoming more combustible (although some is probably due to increased diligence in reporting fires). Landscapes no longer dominated by browsing or cultivation tend to become fire-dominated. Modern forestry encourages this change, because foresters hate goats and love pines and eucalyptuses.

Animals

The native mammals of Mediterranean mainlands are not very different from those of adjacent Eurasia and Africa. They have gradually and unevenly declined, probably because of human activities. Elephants disappeared from Europe and Asia in the Palaeolithic; lions survived in Greece into the Classical period and in Algeria until modern times; bears still persist in a few remote places. Not all native mammals disappeared. Wild pig, surprisingly for a water-loving animal, is abundant even in very dry parts of Spain and also in Italy, but not Greece. The jackal still exists in Greece, and is abundant on Mount Athos, the republic of monks. The most significant introduction is the black rat, with its fatal consequences for humanity via plague, which came from India in the Roman period.

All the main domestic animals appear to have been domesticated outside the Mediterranean, and from the Neolithic onwards have displaced most of the large native herbivores. The last arrival was the domestic cat. Cattle were once as widespread as sheep and goats, but declined in the twentieth century in most of the drier areas.

The islands are different. Most of them had a peculiar set of native mammals, which arrived irregularly and by chance and having once reached an island diverged by evolution from the mainland population. For some reason large carnivores did not reach islands, so that the fauna was very unbalanced. Crete, for example, had an elephant the size of a calf, a non-aquatic hippopotamus the size of a pig, several species of deer that could not run (for there was nothing to run away from), a bewildering variety of rodents, but no carnivore fiercer than a badger (or maybe a giant flightless owl); only one mouse and one shrew still exist. People settled on the islands late, and sometimes coexisted with the native mammals for centuries before exterminating them, as on Cyprus and Sardinia. It is very likely that the first people to reach the islands would have found them in a state that would now be called overgrazing, with numbers of herbivores limited by food supply, not predation.

Cultivation history: introduced plants

Of the staple crops, olives and some legumes are native to parts of the Mediterranean. Wheat and barley originated in the Near East, in an environment sufficiently like the Mediterranean to be transferred there in the Neolithic without obvious difficulty. The vine – least well adapted of the five to the climate – is central European, but Jennifer Moody points out that it was probably domesticated from outliers, relics from before the aridization, which survived (and still survive) in the mountains of west Crete.

The Mediterranean has taken crops from almost all over the world except the 'mediterraneoid' regions of California, Chile, South Africa and Australia with similar climates. In antiquity peaches, carob and fig-mulberry (*Ficus sycomorus*) came from the Near East; white mulberry from the Far East; date-palm from Africa. In the Middle Ages apples came from central Europe (and ultimately from Central Asia); citrus fruits, rice, sugar-cane, black mulberry and cotton from Southeast Asia and China. Since the late Middle Ages parts of Italy and Spain have been almost as rice-dependent as Japan. In the last 150 years Canary Island pine has come out of Africa; kiwi-fruit out of tropical Southeast Asia. Eucalyptus came from non-mediterraneoid parts of Australia.

American contact strongly affected land-use, and to a lesser extent landscape. Maize came with the discovery of America, and tobacco a little later; prickly-pear and agave were established by the eighteenth century. Tomato, potato, French bean, sunflower and American species of cotton were not widely accepted until the nineteenth century. Later introductions include *Pinus radiata* and avocado pear. Greek cuisine is now based on American plants.

Exotic crops (except wheat and barley) are almost all ill-adapted to the Mediterranean environment, which partly explains the cultural practice of making a living by labour-intensive cropping of small areas of very productive land, leaving the rest as pasture. Most of them require irrigation, and are part of the reason for the ingenious irrigation traditions of all the drier regions. Even the vine needs labour in digging, weeding and pruning to keep it alive.

As well as deliberately imported foreign crops, the Mediterranean has acquired many accidentally introduced plants. Examples are *Oxalis pes-caproe*, the South African plant that carpets olive groves and thrives on ploughing and weedkilling, and Johnson grass, *Sorghum halepense*, one of the 'universal tropical weeds' of irrigated orchards. False Acacia (*Robinia pseudacacia*) from America and Tree of Heaven (*Ailanthus altissima*) from China are trees that spread by suckering and get out of hand in an environment very different from the one that they are adapted to. The Mediterranean, however, is not as overrun with foreign weeds as the other mediterraneoids.

Crop diseases, too, have come from other continents, especially nineteenth-century America (potato blight, chestnut blight, *Phylloxera* and downy and powdery mildews of vines).

Fields and terraces

The Mediterranean is as varied in its field systems as in other cultural aspects. Most fields are irregular and of unknown date; occasionally detailed study reveals several superimposed patterns of land division (as on the Frangokástello Plain, Crete).

Centuriation is the Roman practice of dividing land, regardless of topography, into exact squares of 709 m (2,326 ft), oriented exactly north–south (or occasionally at 45°). It still covers huge areas of the Po plain and the rugged mountains of Croatia. There are earlier and later examples of similarly doctrinaire land planning (Classical Greek in Basilicata; Venetian on the Lassíthi Plain, Crete).

Another type of organized landscape is strip-cultivation, which spread over Europe in the Middle Ages. Land was divided into strips typically 200 by 10 m (656 by 328 ft), but often bigger, which were allocated among different owners, and went with communal farming practices. This was rigorously adopted in Sardinia and is still abundant there. In various forms it penetrated as far as Greece and even Crete.

In the nineteenth and twentieth centuries land 'reform' again gave planners the opportunity to put doctrinaire theories (usually derived from the Enlightenment philosophy of eighteenth-century northern Europe) into effect. Common lands were thought to be bad and were privatized. Marshes were drained in the hope that this would prevent malaria (despite Dutch experience to the contrary). Forests were taken over by the state and managed as if they were French or German forests, depending on which state. Many existing field-systems were reorganized along centuriation lines. The traditional ecology was marginalized – especially if, as with savanna, it did not fit into pre-conceived categories – and its inhabitants not listened to. The extent of these changes depended on the degree to which Enlightenment penetrated particular countries. More survives of pre-Enlightenment practices in Spain, Crete and Corsica than in Sardinia or Italy.

Cultivation terraces are the most characteristic feature of many Mediterranean landscapes, and the least known. There are many styles and types, for example the floodwater terraces of southeastern Spain, cunningly constructed downstream of badlands to catch the water, and the fertile silt it brings, whenever there is a minor deluge. They are common in Provence, Liguria, Majorca, Croatia and Crete; uncommon in most of Spain (with the notable exception of the Alpujarra) and in Sardinia (with the exception of Barbagia).

Terraces are notoriously difficult to date. They are under-represented in historic pictures and documents. Archaeological dating is problematic, but a few datable examples show that at least some terraces existed in Bronze Age Crete and Classical Greece. Written and pictorial evidence begins as late as *c.* 1500 AD and steadily increases thereafter.

Nobody now living knows for certain why most kinds of terrace were made. The reason given in textbooks, erosion control, is part of the story, but hardly explains the lack of correlation between terracing and erodibility: terraces are common in erosion-resistant Crete and absent from very erodible Basilicata. Another common function is to break up bedrock and allow roots to penetrate. Terraces are an example of people investing labour – nobody knows how much labour, or over how long a period – in increasing the carrying capacity of land. In many countries they reached their greatest development in the late nineteenth century.

Settlements

As in the rest of the world, Mediterranean civilizations have waxed and waned for reasons that are not obvious in environmental terms. Not all the changes are known from documents. The dense population and high culture of Crete in the late Roman period, like those of Minoan Crete, are almost unknown from written sources but are very evident from archaeological survey. The magnificent architecture of Roman Spain has left almost no contemporary written record.

Attempts to show that Mediterranean cultures flourished or declined for environmental or ecological reasons have produced meagre results. Whatever caused the collapse of Bronze Age Crete, or the decline and fall of the Roman Empire, it was not sudden drought or running out of trees, and was probably not plague. How much influence malaria had is an open question.

Settlement can take many forms: towns in an otherwise empty landscape (Sardinia), villages (Greece), hamlets (west Crete) or scattered farms (parts of Italy). This is to do with cultural and social factors rather than environment, and can change with time in no obvious pattern. Sardinia in the Iron Age was a land of hamlets, as Corsica still is. In the Middle Ages some peoples moved from their scattered homes into villages, often with castles (the Italian *incastellamento*). Mediterranean peoples in general insist on living near water sources and refuse to spend time carrying water. If there are no springs or wells they store rainwater in cisterns.

The Mediterranean, with its stormy seas, jagged promontories and scarcity of dependable harbours, was dangerous for ancient shipping, as Xerxes and St Paul found to their cost. In classical times most seafaring shut down for half the year. Only in late medieval times did developments in ship design and rigging reduce the risks.

Piracy was a hazard on land as well as sea. Pirates flourished in much of antiquity, until the Romans made a point of executing them and the seas were safe for nearly a thousand years. In the Middle Ages and for long after, half the Mediterranean was in Christian and half in Muslim hands. Piracy became institutionalized in the form of corsairs, whose duty was to plunder the other religion's shipping and raid their coasts. In Spain, Sardinia and Crete, people dared not live on the coast except in fortified towns, and even these were not always immune. Only in the nineteenth century did they venture back to cultivate coastal plains and resume coastal shipping.

Vegetation history

The history of vegetation in the Mediterranean is different from that of northern Europe. The impact of human activity is not so clear; it overlaps with climate change and is not easily separable.

The Mediterranean climate is unfavourable to preserving fossil pollen. The pollen record is not abundant, and is mainly from high altitudes or the fringes of the Mediterranean, such as north Greece. Many important Mediterranean plants, especially undershrubs, produce little pollen. The bias caused by pollen deposits being in the wettest parts of the landscape is particularly severe in a semi-arid region. There are no established criteria for differentiating forest from coppice-woods, maquis or savanna: a prickly-oak produces pollen whether it is a forest tree, a free-standing tree or a shrub less than a metre high.

Very few endemic species are shade-bearing: the great majority are species of phrygana, which grow on cliffs, deserts and mountains above the limit of trees. Mediterranean forests tend to have poor floras with few endemics; on an evolutionary time-scale the predominant vegetation has thus been non-forest.

The period corresponding to the last glaciation was evidently dry as well as cold. The predominant vegetation was steppe, sometimes with scattered trees. Trees evidently retreated to favourable spots. It was not cold enough to exterminate frost-sensitive endemics, especially in Crete, which being endemics could have retreated only to the land exposed by the then lower sea-level.

After the last glaciation trees returned to form what was (so far as the pollen evidence reveals) a more tree'd landscape than in historic times. At least in the eastern Mediterranean, deciduous trees (especially oaks) were abundant and often predominant. However, forest was not universal. Savanna was widespread, but phrygana seems to have been more restricted than now. Central European trees such as lime, hazel and birch extended much further south than they do now, some of them even to Crete.

Palaeolithic and Mesolithic human inhabitants are traditionally supposed to have had little effect on the landscape, being few in numbers and not tilling the soil. They may, however, have had a disproportionate influence by altering the frequency of fire, and by exterminating large mammals such as elephants.

The change to something like the present landscape began in the Neolithic and went on into the Bronze Age (typically *c.* 6000 to *c.* 1000 years BC). It was partly the result of the slow spread of cultivation and keeping of domestic animals. Deciduous oak, for example, was probably the characteristic tree of the more fertile soils and was destroyed because it competed with cultivation; it is now returning as cultivation retreats. However, this is not the whole story. Central European trees slowly and irregularly disappeared from the pollen record. Their surviving outliers tend to be in specially cold sites such as high-altitude north-facing cliffs, which indicates that their decline was not due to human activity. Had lime, for instance, been specially sensitive to burning or woodcutting (which it is not), it should survive on cliffs in general, not on special kinds of cliff.

This indicates that, as well as increasing human activity, there was also a change towards a drier and more strongly seasonal climate between 4800 and 2400 BC. This aridization is best recorded from Greece, where it corresponds to a movement of the vegetation zones northward by 500 km (310 miles). It also occurred in Spain, and there is supporting evidence from North Africa. Italy, however, was less affected, and trees such as alder still reach the southern tip.

Erosion in the Mediterranean has had a bad press. It is traditionally thought of as an evil consequence of human activity, especially deforestation and cultivation. Originally (we are told) the landscape was forested and was stable. Soils are fragile and were held in place by forests. People cut down the forests, which then disappeared or turned into maquis or savanna; the soils were washed away into the sea or depleted of nutrients. On this theory, at its most pessimistic, agriculture is ultimately unsustainable. But it fails to explain how soils survived the 'deforestation' of the last glaciation. It overlooks the fact that much erosion is not soil erosion – for example, in badlands the gullies dig into bedrock, not soil.

There are many types of erosion: sheet erosion (where soil creeps uniformly down a smooth slope, rill erosion (where small gullies form temporarily), gully erosion (where gullies eat into bedrock), slumps and landslips, downcutting and side-cutting of rivers, wind erosion, karst erosion (where rainwater dissolves limestone) and frost action splitting stones off cliffs (mainly during the Pleistocene).

Some, like wind erosion, are strongly influenced by vegetation or the lack of it; others, like gully erosion, weakly so.

In such a violently uplifted part of the world erosion is an inevitable force of nature. (Without it there would be landscapes of spiky mountains and towering inland cliffs, as indeed there are in Crete.) Sediment accumulated from past erosion has created most of the cultivable land, for example in river deltas (all of which have formed in the last 7,400 years since the sea-level rose).

Erosion is roughly correlated with particular types of geology and geomorphology, but not with the intensity of human activity. Badlands, for instance, form in particular types of sediment, themselves the product of erosion in earlier phases of the uplift of the mountains, and often near unstable faults, as around the Gulf of Corinth. They are not related to particular kinds of vegetation, and often occur in forest. They are not especially prevalent in the neighbourhood of Athens or Rome, and are not the end-product of very intensive land-use.

Some types of human activity do promote some kinds of erosion, though not to the extent implied by those writers who allude to prehistoric activity (usually unspecified) 'stripping the soil' from hillsides. Such claims often depend on a vague coincidence of date between an erosional event and a phase in a human culture, themselves often poorly dated. The significant activity appears to be ploughing, not deforestation. Trees have no unique power of preventing soil-erosion; at least as significant are the crusts of mosses, lichens, *Selaginella* and other small plants, at most a few millimetres high, which form on exposed, undisturbed sediment surfaces.

In the last half-century people have invented powerful technologies for promoting erosion. Tractor ploughs, bulldozers and road-making have attacked landscapes on a far larger scale than was possible before. Erosion does indeed result (especially from poor standards of road-building), but on a limited scale: archaeologists are not struggling to record the last remaining earlier deposits before they are overwhelmed by new ones. The twentieth century is likely to go down in erosional history as a relatively quiet period. It is hard to believe that prehistoric ards and harrows destabilized whole landscapes where tractors and bulldozers have failed.

Water erosion tends to be episodic: the heaviest single fall of rain in a hundred years shifts more sediment than a century's worth of ordinary rains. A big deluge overwhelms the mechanisms that stabilize the landscape. Deluges, and the alluvial deposits that result, can be dated, not only in historical records, but archaeologically by the artefacts that they bury: for example if a medieval church is buried by a flood deposit and a new doorway, in a later style, is built to give access from the new land level. These deposits tend to be of local extent but to cluster around certain historical periods. They are particularly associated with peaks of the Little Ice Age.

Understanding the Mediterranean means appreciating that it
is far more than a series of connected stretches of salty water.
The Australian historian John Pryor has observed that the
Mediterranean possesses several distinctive features that result
from its character as an enclosed sea: in modern times the
Mediterranean loses water through evaporation more rapidly
than its river systems replace the water, which is not surprising
when it is remembered how puny some of the rivers feeding into
the sea are: the little rivers of Sicily and Sardinia, the historic
but not substantial rivers Tiber and Arno (the latter of which
becomes a trickle upriver from Florence in high Summer).

It is true that the Mediterranean draws down water from
the massive river system of the Nile, and the Po and Rhône also
make some contribution. Among European rivers, the Danube
and the Russian river systems make an indirect contribution,
because the Black Sea draws in water from several great arteries
stretching deep into the land mass. The result is that the Black
Sea has an excess of unevaporated water, and this creates a fast
current that rushes past Istanbul into the northeastern Aegean.
But even this only compensates for less than one twentieth of
the water loss in the Mediterranean, and the principal source
of water to compensate for losses by evaporation is the Atlantic
Ocean. There is thus a steady in-flow of cold Atlantic water,
but even this is to some extent counter-balanced by an outflow
of Mediterranean water which (because of the evaporation) is
saltier and therefore heavier.

The fact that the Mediterranean is open at two of its
ends is thus crucial to its survival as a sea. Indeed, in remote
geological time it was a closed area, and evaporation reached
the point where the Mediterranean basin was a deep and empty
desert. The opening of a third end, at Suez, has perhaps had
more limited effects since the sea route passes through canals
and locks, but it too has perceptible effects, for example in
the arrival in the eastern Mediterranean of Indian Ocean fish
species. The Mediterranean has, of course, a reasonably rich

stock of fish of its own, though the salty water keeps numbers down; man has always hunted its tunny and swordfish, while crustaceans and molluscs have also formed part of the diet of most Mediterranean peoples.

The inflow has been sufficient to deter navigators from making a regular passage out of the Strait of Gibraltar, though it has not deterred Vikings, crusaders and others from entering the Inner Sea. It will be seen in this book how late the traffic out of the Strait was in developing. The major currents follow the coasts of Africa eastwards from Gibraltar, swing past modern Israel and Lebanon and around Cyprus, and then round the Aegean, Adriatic and Tyrrhenian Seas and along the French and Spanish coasts back to the Pillars of Hercules. These currents have had a significant impact on the ease with which ships have been able to move around the Mediterranean, at least in the days of oar and sail. It has even proved possible to use the currents to sail against the wind, tacking back and forth but gradually moving in the face of the Mediterranean winds. These winds themselves could be profitably exploited to carry shipping in the Spring time down from the ports between Barcelona and Pisa towards Sardinia, Sicily and the Levant; the weather systems in the region tend to move from west to east, though the major influence in the western Mediterranean during winter is the north Atlantic weather system, while in the summer it is the Atlantic sub-tropical high, stationed over the Azores.

Wet and windy weather in the winter is characterized by the mistral bringing cold air into the valleys of Provence, but it has many close cousins such as the *bora* or *tramontana* of Italy and former Yugoslavia. John Pryor has pointed out that the 'Gulf of the Lions' off Provence is so named because the roar of the mistral resembles that of a lion. No one should underestimate the unpleasantness of a winter storm in the Mediterranean, despite the modern image of a sun-drenched sea which the final chapter of this book seeks to dissect. In any case, occasionally low pressure weather systems develop over the Sahara and are dragged north as the unsettling wind known as the *scirocco* (Italy), *xaloc* (Catalonia) or *hamsin* (Israel, Egypt); vast amounts of red Saharan dust may be dumped on the lands surrounding the Mediterranean. The coasts of North Africa were all the more dangerous for sailors because the prevailing northerly winds threatened to throw their ships on the sandbanks and reefs of the southern Mediterranean shores, while (as Pryor observes) the steeper inclination of most of the north Mediterranean shores made them much more attractive to navigators, as did their coves and beaches; one might add, however, that the coves were also a longstanding temptation to pirates in search of a nook and cranny.

The overall impression, however, is that passage from west to east, the famous Levant trade, was easier for ships setting out in the spring and following the northern shores of the Mediterranean, past Sicily and Crete and around Cyprus; to reach Egypt from Genoa or Marseille it was not apparently standard practice to cut across from Crete to the mouth of the Nile until the coming of the steamship. The seasonal character of ancient and medieval shipping can, certainly, be exaggerated: there is evidence from thirteenth- and fourteenth-century Majorca which indicates that ships criss-crossed the western Mediterranean all through the year, barely missing a single day even in January and February. But evidently the big sailings over longer distances did make more use of favourable winds.

Of course, we cannot be completely sure that the winds and currents have remained more or less the same. There are enough references in classical and medieval sources to such winds as the *Boreas* from the northwest to make it clear that the *bora* has indeed a very long history. And yet land use has affected the flow of rivers; slight cooling and warming (such as the cooling in late medieval Europe identified by some) would affect water retention and therefore foliage and tree cover; human intervention, in the form of cutting wood for ships, even if regeneration was often fairly rapid, led to local variations which could still disturb weather patterns. Dams, notably the Great Aswan Dam in Upper Egypt, have changed the pattern of flow of water into the Mediterranean, with effects on currents and also on humidity generated by the new lakes carved out behind the dams. In particular, it is man who has in recent history altered the seasonal cycle of the Nile, decisively changing the economic life of Egypt and putting to an end the annual floods which the ancient Egyptians attributed to their gods. It is to the dawn of history in the Mediterranean that this book now turns.

TWO

The first trading empires: prehistory to *c.* 1000 BC

MARLENE SUANO

The ancient Mediterranean world, geographically and historically speaking, stretches from the Pillars of Hercules (the Strait of Gibraltar) across the Middle East to the Fertile Crescent (the valleys of the Tigris and Euphrates). The cultural strains, commercial routes and political movements of the ancient world drained into the Mediterranean just as do the rivers that flow into the Inner Sea. The great number of cultures, states and chronological periods, as well as the sheer difference of the documents available, has forced its historiography to be built on very specialized knowledge in the traditionally distinct fields of Assyriology, Egyptology, Hittitology, Greek and Roman history, and European prehistory, all of which need to be considered side by side if sense is to be made of developments within the early Mediterranean. The aim of this chapter, therefore, is not to present a general and superficial view of all the separate Mediterranean peoples one by one but, quite to the contrary, the links between them. For, when trying to understand the history of the Mediterranean, one encounters what might figuratively be described as curious knots, which the fragmented historiography we practise is not able to unravel. By addressing these particular problems, we may be able to make sense of the history of our area.

Stuart Piggott, the British archaeologist, wryly noted in 1965 that it has been technological considerations that have been, for the previous 100 years, the prime determinant of the study of the remote past, given the traditional emphasis on the idea of the Stone and Metal Ages. The result has been a chronological framework which has proved almost impossible to escape. But another approach was adopted by J. G. D. Clark, who in 1952 showed that it would be fruitful to analyse human development in other terms, looking at questions of subsistence and economic life. Such a perspective was present, although quite dimly, in nineteenth-century French archaeology, in the attempt to classify men not only in terms of their artefacts but also according to the large mammals they depended on for their subsistence (a *Mammoth Age*, a *Reindeer Age*). However, the technological approach was then too strong to be modified and continued to be adopted, not least because of its sheer usefulness.

Clark inherited and was able to put to good use a long European tradition of considering the environment of early man and offered a new model for considering man's prehistory. Thanks to him, the different ecological settings within Europe and the stages through which the economy developed, such as the transition from a hunter-gatherer society to farming communities, were clearly established as the basis on which material culture rested (taking as evidence houses and settlements as well as handicrafts) and also as the basis of trade networks (including travel and transport). Different zones had different economic profiles, so that one area might be devoted to hunting and gathering while another one saw a farming economy develop. It is also important to bring to bear on Clark's insights those of Fernand Braudel; although his comments about the prehistoric Mediterranean need modification in the light of current knowledge, his overall approach must be borne in mind: his goal was to show that Mediterranean experiences and successes could only be understood if taken on as a whole and, even more, that they ought to be brought into relation with one other, as the present chapter will try to do.

The earliest times

In trying to understand the relationship between man and the sea in the Mediterranean area, not only the vegetation must be considered, but coastal and maritime economic activities must be taken into account and seen against environmental knowledge that helps to account for the presence of hunted seals, during the Upper Palaeolithic period, in the Dordogne caves, at some 200 km (124 miles) from the sea coast, and many other otherwise inexplicable archaeological data. Rivers and coastlines must be examined together in order to grasp something of early men's movements and conquest of physical space. Rivers were, indeed, natural ways of transport, a point clearly stated by the Roman writer Strabo. From the Mediterranean system access can be gained to the European network of big rivers such as the Danube and the Rhine, and it is quite interesting to note how deeply inside Europe Egyptian and Cretan pieces have been found. However, although the river valleys were not always the main vehicles of internal trade, as Clark believed, the Danube played an extremely important role in connecting East and West before the Mediterranean became the main link between these regions. This period runs for about 25,000 years, from 35,000/30,000 to around 10,000/8,000 years before the present.

Such a long and complex period in the history of man cannot be briefly summarized, and it would be wrong to assume a lack of cultural change throughout this lengthy period. Even so, archaeological sites in Israel reveal a Stone Age culture quite similar to that known in the western Mediterranean, from the limestone caves of Spain, France and northern Italy. The Galilee Skull and the skeletons found on Mount Carmel are quite similar to those of European Neanderthal men and women whose bones have been found as far west as the rock of Gibraltar (indeed, the first discovery of what are now known as Neanderthal bones occurred in Gibraltar, but 'Gibraltar Woman' was not at first recognized for what she was). Neanderthal man was to a large degree an Ice Age phenomenon, a type of hominin who adapted well to the harsh climate of Upper Palaeolithic Europe, but showed less inventiveness than the modern humans who, peacefully or otherwise, came to replace the Neanderthals, and were the authors of the magnificent cave paintings of Lascaux in southern France, Altamira in northern Spain and many other sites. That population spread into Italy, Spain and Greece is abundantly clear, but what languages developed among these peoples and how the different ethnic groups came to diverge from one another is still a mystery. It is possible, as the geneticist Luigi Cavalli-Sforza has argued, that the Basque language is a remnant of the tongue spoken in large areas of Europe as far back as the Upper Palaeolithic period.

The Levant, however, demands special attention, though at this time it was not yet subject to the powerful influences from Egypt and Mesopotamia that were later to mould its civilization at the dawn of recorded history. The Levant is seen today as the place where plants were first cultivated, by the late eleventh to early tenth century BC. It was here, along with Anatolia, that concentrated settlements, effectively the first cities, emerged for the first time. Thus Jericho has an impressive sequence of Neolithic buildings, polished walls and floors, a portico with wooden pillars and no pottery, although the last seven levels (out of seventeen) revealed copper implements. Both flint and copper implements from Jericho were suitable for agricultural practice, a point which sheds doubt on the old assumption that agriculture and pottery production were intimately intertwined. For in fact the 'Neolithic Revolution', which is generally seen as the process of the domestication of plants and animals, took several thousand years to develop, starting in the Palaeolithic and culminating, as far as the present data allow us to surmise, in the creation of farming villages in South Asia around 10,000 to 7000 BC. Research on this topic continues to produce striking results: the data we need are clearly present from the Zagros to the centre of Anatolia, through the Fertile Crescent and the Levant and are still being identified, especially in the Levant and Anatolia, where the vital site of Çatalhöyük has been excavated by a British-American-Turkish team.

During the Neolithic, our references to the use of the Mediter-ranean Sea are scanty. Men certainly explored the sea in order to compensate for poor harvests and game during drought on land, exploiting among other assets the presence of nutritious tuna fish which, though difficult to catch, could be found in plenty in the Black Sea region as well as in the Mediterranean proper. Although none of their sea crafts are known to us, some scholars suggest that they might have been something like the *papirella* (the reed rafts still present in the island of Corfu, one of which crossed in 1988 from Laurion to Melos, with five people on board) or rafts sustained by inflated leather bags. Reed rafts were known on the Nile up to the twentieth century; and dugout canoes, a worldwide, timeless, solu-tion, certainly lie at the starting point of the extremely long history of seafaring craftsmanship. It is interesting to note that the term 'binding together' is the most common term in Egyptian shipbuild-ing vocabulary; thus our attention is drawn to the environment, to timber and metal resources as well as the implements and binding technology, especially metal rivets, rods and nails since, as the eminent Marxist archaeologist Vere Gordon Childe observed, the axe and the chisel gave birth to the true ship. Land and sea resources were, therefore, almost literally bound together by mankind as the necessary basis for its mobility and for the conquest of Mediter-ranean space.

The Bronze Age

This is one of the most staggering periods in the history of man, and the eastern Mediterranean was its epicentre. However, when talking about 'Bronze Age', we must make it clear that there is not a single chronological definition for it. The Central European Bronze Age has been dated from the fourteenth to the eighth century BC; and this has been lately refined with the use of radiometric and dendrochronological (tree-ring) methods. Mediterranean Europe has had its chronology established from the combination of central European dates with those from the Aegean world, which is further linked to dates established for Egyptian and Mesopotamian sites: this chronology, called 'historical-archaeological', situates the Bronze Age between the years 3000 and 1200 BC. Not everyone is happy with the existing date sequences, and radiocarbon, dendrochronology, archaeomagnetism and thermoluminescence are gradually rewriting the Mediterranean chronology; but for the moment these are the correlations with which archaeologists have to work. Calibrated radio-carbon evidence from Anatolia can be cross-linked to the southern Aegean Bronze Age cultures, and although further research is still needed, the current view is that both chronologies – the 'classical' and the 'dendro-dated' – roughly concur.

Not only the Levant, but also the lands from Anatolia to Persia, had an important role in the development of farming, trade and in the creation of an unprecedented concentration of wealth. Some fea-tures of the combination of wealth and power are found in Anatolia at the same time as they appear in early Bronze Age Mesopotamia and Egypt, during the third millennium. For, at a time when the western Mediterranean and continental Europe were going through several different phases of Neolithic cultural development, the eastern Mediterranean was giving shape to the features that would create the most impressive and best balanced structure of political power in the history of ancient man. This new political structure can be observed from four points of reference, and could be schematically displayed in the form of a rough cross that would have as its four arms Hittite Anatolia, Pharaonic Egypt, the Minoan Aegean and the Mesopotamian civilizations. Taken together, they are generally referred to as the 'Bronze Age Empires'.

These large regional units operated on the basis of a central authority (the Great King, the Pharaoh) which delegated regional powers to lesser kings or princes. Such a structure meant that the greater territory was divided among small realms with local dynasties subject to a higher level of imperial authority, that of the Palace, which took responsibility for common aspects of political and economic life. Although differences between these units existed, and were by no means irrelevant, the similarities allowed for quite a harmonized system. To the east, Sumerian civilization was experiencing a period of great wealth, and its metal industry produced bronze (tools, weapons, ornaments and other vessels, with a tin content of 5 to 10 per cent). Later Mesopotamian polities, ruled by the Akkadian, Babylonian and Assyrian empires, depended on long-distance trade for both the importation of raw materials (especially metals) and the export of manufactured goods (textiles, bronze implements, artisan goods of various kinds, which would reach Egypt, Syria, Anatolia, the Aegean and even central Europe).

This also served as a link to Egypt, which was notably dependent on Mesopotamian trade and had close political ties to the Syrian lordships which stood between the lands directly ruled by the Pharaohs and the Mesopotamian empires. To the north, the Hittites, the overlords of Anatolia, from north Syria to the borders of the Black Sea, had a very significant part in the history of the Bronze Age, and particularly in its final crisis, a role that is only recently coming to light. And to the west, there stood the Aegean, guarded by Troy, the last bastion in Anatolia, standing on the very edge of the Aegean world. Its history, so important to the development of Western culture, was tightly bound to that of the rest of the eastern Mediterranean. Archaeology has turned Troy from a legend to the reality of a city on nine levels, a fortress town overlooking the entry of the Dardanelles (and therefore the entry to the Black Sea and the Danube, one of the key routes into the heart of Europe).

In the middle of these regional units of centralized power, which we know shared relations with one another broadly as equals, stood the Levant, with important principalities such as Ugarit on the coast of Syria, and Cyprus, which experienced a series of attempts by both

Egypt and the Hittites to establish overlordship in the island, not to mention the strong presence of Aegean economic power in and around Cyprus and the Levant. These lesser units of power, in their turn, also related to one other on the same roughly equal level, producing a very formal set of conventions for the 'proper' relationship between a Great King and a 'brother' Great King, between a Small King and a 'father' Great King, between a Small King and a 'brother' Small King. A well-known example of ties between lesser kings from a slightly later period is the relationship between Solomon, king of the Israelites, and Hiram, king of Tyre, as recorded in the biblical Book of Kings.

Hittite civilization has been the last major addition to knowledge of the eastern Mediterranean. Never mentioned in Greek texts, its very existence had disappeared from the history of mankind until the end of the nineteenth century when the discovery of the Amarna Letters revealed a powerful Anatolian kingdom in the second millennium BC. The German excavations at Bogazkoy in 1906 brought to light the archives of Hattusa, the capital city of Hatti. Apart from the tablets written in Akkadian, the diplomatic language of the period, most of the others were in the Indo-European language now known as Hittite. Since then, our information about the Hittites and the Empire of Hatti has grown considerably: 26 temples have been excavated at Hattusa and more than 3,000 royal seal impressions have come to light during excavations. Archaeological work throughout Anatolia has produced masses of data and exposed the balance of imperial powers in the Bronze Age eastern Mediterranean.

Apart from the palace-based economic structure – a major common feature of these societies – we can see how deep their social contact was when considering the recurrent themes of heroic foundation myths. These link Hatti (the 31 sons of the Queen of Carchemish are placed on reed baskets in the river), to Egypt and the Israelites (in the story of Moses and the bulrushes) to Mesopotamia (with similar tales of the childhood of King Sargon II), and these themes are later to be seen in variant forms also in Persia (Cyrus) and even in Rome (Romulus and Remus): the abandoned infant, the motherly gentleness of nature (the waters, kind wild animals), growing up ignorant of their actual origins and their final great destiny of creating a nation for their fellow men. They are neither simple coincidences nor mere copying.

Consciousness of this deep relationship was also present in the myth of Europa, a Phoenician princess kidnapped by Zeus, who appeared as a white bull and carried her to Crete, where she gave birth to Minos, the great Aegean king and supreme ruler of the seas. According to the most widespread version of this myth, her mother and brothers (among whom was Cadmos, who was to be the founder of Boeotian Thebes) went in search of her, but in vain. Neither of them ever returned to the Levant, choosing to stay in the Occident. Recent research suggests that the direction might have been the opposite: Europa may have been a northern Greek name and the heroine would have been invested with Oriental attributes, including a Phoenician origin, due to confusion with her father's name, Phoenix, at a much later date. These contradictions notwithstanding, the myth of Europa provides valuable clues concerning the deep imprint left by an awareness that Crete was an important cradle of culture, with a particular role in joining together East and West.

The Bronze Age economic system

The period that concerns us most here is that of the formation of the first mercantile empires, notably the Mycenaean and the Phoenician trading networks, since they were the first to master the Mediterranean and thus had a critical role in moulding its cultural shape. Of course, it was well before the Bronze Age that seafaring started in the Mediterranean. Obsidian flakes from the island of Melos found on the Greek mainland in the southern Argolid are the earliest known evidence to demonstrate a degree of seafaring ability in the Mediterranean as far back as the Palaeolithic period, around 7000 BC. In any case, ancient seafaring depended very much on the environment. Late spring and summer winds, like the Aegean Etesian winds, allowed secure navigation that made possible the Crete–Egypt crossing in only five days, a point made plain by none other than Odysseus in Book XIV of the *Odyssey*. No doubt coasting was the preferred way of sailing in early times, either because of technical necessities or because of the constant need for a fresh water supply for those on board. Coastal settlements and harbours were, therefore, key pieces in giving shape to the sea routes. The Neolithic and Early Bronze Age remnants of harbours and settlements, combined with other material culture finds and the study of distances and winds indicate a northern route from Attica to Anatolia via Kea, Tinos, Mykonos, Ikaria and Samos; a central route from the Argolid to Anatolia, via the Cyclades; a southern route via Crete, jumping from one island to the next as far as Rhodes and Anatolia.

As for longer distances, it is believed that the most frequent circular route in the ancient Mediterranean was from right to left: from the Aegean to Crete and then Egypt, the Levant, Cyprus, the Anatolian coast, the Cyclades, Crete and back to the Aegean. There were, of course, other regional routes (Aegean/Italy, Crete/Egypt, Egypt/Cyprus, Cyprus/Levant) and alternatives, such Egypt/Crete via the Libyan coast. The remains of stone docks and shore archaeology discoveries indicate the presence of maritime activity throughout the Aegean from the Early Bronze Age and the use of the islands as bridges across the longer distances. Such a practice no doubt allowed the existence of small networks of local or regional trade, as much as it fostered long-distance trade.

Although no physical evidence of Aegean ships has been found so far, there are many graphic representations. The earliest known seem to be the long ships in lead, from Naxos, dated to the third millennium BC, although some suggest that they are not true ships but dugouts. The same design is depicted on the so-called 'frying pans' of terracotta (objects of unknown function) found from mainland

Greece to Anatolia and quite numerous in the Cyclades. There are many other representations of long ships and their technological evolution, as well as that of the double-ended seacraft, identifiable from images on Minoan seals and on pottery. So far, there is no evidence of Minoan warships. The Middle Helladic fragment of a pithos from Aegina, with the only existing representation of armed sailors, and the miniature frescoes from Thera suggest, from the spears carried by the men, that they were not sea warriors but raiders ready for shore battles. The Thera frescoes contain nine different types of ships on the north frieze alone and such a variety has led some scholars to think that the scene refers to a religious procession. Apart from the expected fact that sea-going people attributed cultic significance to their inter-relationship with the sea and its forces, that these ships were fairly reliable seagoing craft is confirmed by a text from Mari referring to a Caphtorite (i.e. Cretan) receiving a load of tin at the port of Ugarit by the end of the eighteenth century BC.

At any rate, the information on Bronze Age seafaring and sea-manship is vast and has been brilliantly put together by Shelley Wachsmann, who studied the technology of construction and navigation techniques as well as the sea routes and sea wars of the period. The variety of solutions presented to shipbuilding problems reveals only too well the individual autonomy of the cultural development of the various Mediterranean peoples in the period. The available data, including later written sources, have been studied from the perspective of a supposed Minoan maritime empire or thalassocracy. Such a concept has been current for some 2,500 years, beginning with the comments of Thucydides about King Minos and his sea empire; but we also read of no fewer than sixteen other thalassocracies (Rhodian, Lydian, Cypriot, Phoenician, etc.) listed in Eusebius' *Chronicon* when he describes, on the basis of much earlier sources, the exercise of military and political control over sections of the Mediterranean during the Late Bronze Age and the Iron Age. However, the concept of thalassocracy has lately been under reconsideration, partly on archaeological grounds, as we shall see below, and partly on the grounds that the idea of a political power guarding the sea for trade and commerce is too closely modelled on Classical Athens. This, rather than any deep awareness by Thucydides of developments in the Aegean region a thousand years before his own time, may thus be the model for what he actually says: 'Minos made himself master of the Greek waters and subjugated the Cyclades, by expelling the Carians and establishing his sons in control of the new settlements founded in their place; and naturally, for the safe conveyance of his revenues, he did all he could to suppress piracy.'

There are, indeed, many 'Minoan' traits on these islands (architecture, pottery, burial customs, religion) and the fortifications in many of them (Melos, Keos, Aegina) have led some scholars to see the Cyclades as a protective ring guarding an unfortified Crete. However, since we have no way of knowing who actually governed these islands, they could equally be Minoan strongholds or, on the contrary as their fortifications could indicate, sites independent of Crete. We must, therefore, move away from the traditional view of Minoan 'colonization' of the waters around Crete, and adopt an approach that emphasizes the social and economic functions of trade.

Long-distance trade

The Minoans had been trading with neighbouring islands since the Neolithic period, and with Lipari and Sicily, Egypt and the Levant since the Early Bronze Age. Harbours and coastal settlements which have been the basis for the widespread notion of 'colonies' have started to be reconsidered in the light of theories about the nature of trading, with the focus no longer on the material results of contact but on the meaning of it, which can be found in the need for prestige goods amongst emergent (and, of course, peripheral) élites. Thus the presence of Minoans is detected as far as Transylvania and on the Danube. Their presence in Italy, from the Early to Middle Bronze Age, is known in the Aeolian Islands (in the so-called Capo

Graziano Culture), Sicily (the Castelluccio Culture) and in Sardinia, but is very meagre in other areas.

The transition from Minoan to Mycenaean culture deserves close attention, since recent archaeological data indicate that both cultures were mutually antagonistic at all times, although around 1450 BC the Mycenaean became dominant. The Caphtor of the Mari tablets and the Bible, the Keftiu or Kefti of the Egyptians, had trade contacts with the Hittites in central Anatolia, Egypt, Mitanni and the Mesopotamian kingdoms. The great palaces of Knossos and Mallia in Crete, and of Pylos on the mainland, leave no doubt about the extensive wealth and power of the Minoan state. It is believed that the Thera eruption of around 1470 BC (though the date is still debated) largely contributed to the dismantling of Minoan power, with people not only from mainland Greece but also from western Anatolia taking over the enfeebled island. How they did it, however, still remains an open question.

The presence of a new form of writing, known as Linear B, from the fifteenth century onwards, prompts some scholars to think that the mainlanders had indeed taken over and the area is, from then on, commonly referred to as Minoan-Mycenaean, and soon after just as Mycenaean; the language of the Linear B tablets of Knossos, as on the mainland, was an early form of Greek, while that of the similar but still only partially deciphered script that preceded it, Linear A, may well have been related to the languages spoken on the coast of Asia Minor, notably Luwian. However, studies indicate occasional similarities between Linear A and ancient Semitic languages, with many words being practically the same. All this, however, remains highly controversial, and the epigraphic evidence includes one inscription, the famous Phaistos disk, which is written in a mysterious script not encountered anywhere else. It would certainly be a mistake to suppose that all Cretans were of the same ethnic origin and language; for example, the Bible records Caphtor as the place of origin of the Philistines, and later there were groups on the island, such as the Eteo-Cretan speakers and, according to Homer's *Odyssey*, the 'Pelasgians', whose culture and possibly origins seem different from those of other Cretans. However, movement in the opposite direction might have been true as well, judging from the astonishing similarities between the Bronze Age palace of Mari, in northern Mesopotamia, and the Bronze Age Cretan palaces.

By taking up the Minoan trade routes and harbours, 'colonies' and clients, the Mycenaeans enlarged even more the territory with which they maintained contact. The nature of their contacts in the eastern and the western Mediterranean was quite different, no doubt owing to the fact that the partners found on each side were fundamentally different. From one side – the eastern lands – we have written remains from highly organized societies presenting similar structural traits, as has been seen already. On the other side, the Italian, Sicilian and Sardinian populations had a completely different social structure and the relations they entered into with the Mycenaeans were bound to be quite different as well. With studies that go beyond simple typologies it is possible to see how the two different social structures used the same kind of material culture established on top of a different economic system, such as the family storage systems present in the Mycenaean settlements in Italy, which was not an Aegean practice.

The Mycenaeans approached Italy making the best use of an environment they knew only too well: the islands and archipelagoes on the Tyrrhenian coast, from the north of Sicily (the Aeolian islands: Lipari, Filicudi, Panarea, Salina) to the Gulf of Naples (Vivara, Ischia). Their presence in Italy is datable to the end of the fifteenth century down to the twelfth century and is concentrated in some sixty sites, a quarter of them on the Gulf of Taranto and the southern Adriatic coast. It is curious to observe that although most scholars see the search for metals as the reason for this contact, the metallurgical zone par excellence in Italy, the central Tyrrhenian area, provides evidence of only three settlements, those of Luni sul Mignone, San

Giovenale and Monte Rovello; and neither Sardinian nor Calabrian metal ores seem to have been exploited before the Italian Late Bronze Age, around the eleventh–tenth centuries BC. Apart from the dating of such evidence, the discussion has been centred on the character of the Mycenaean settlements, and most scholars agree that they were permanent rather than temporary. Two points remain, however, regarding their distance from the metal zone and, therefore, the meaning of their arrival in Italy.

The suggestion that the indigenous élites encouraged such contact in order to obtain prestige goods is quite widespread amongst anthropology-oriented archaeologists such as Bernard Knapp, M. Marazzi and Anna Maria Bietti Sestieri. However, considering the low percentage of prestige goods of Mycenaean provenance and the large amount of locally made wares in the Mycenaean style, a feature normally seen as evidence of permanent residence, I would suggest that the exchange might also have taken the form of apprenticeship in some of the Mycenaean crafts, like metalworking, for instance, in return for the use of harbours, in order to monitor the trade of many articles that passed along those routes (tin and copper, amber, salt, hides, timber, etc.), a situation already detected on the Syrian coast in the Late Bronze Age and also suggested by the Cape Gelidonya Bronze Age shipwreck, which carried metalworking utensils, metal scraps and foundry equipment which was actually working when the ship went down. This possibility should be linked to the exchange of other goods, such as oil, wine and perfumes.

At any rate, the chronology of these almost 300 years needs to be greatly refined in order to contribute to the understanding of the process of occupation of the spaces involved. As it is, we only know that the Mycenaean presence in Sardinia starts later than in the other regions of Italy and that there is an increase of contact from the middle of the thirteenth century down to the eleventh century BC. The idea of a land base, so important for long-distance trade should, again, be examined in the light of the trade routes that such a base might have served; it is also important to take into account the idea that the island stops in the Mediterranean were not just harbours to be used when occasion demanded, but real trading partners involved in this trade network. Amongst those who adopt theoretical approaches to the prehistory of the Mediterranean there have been significant changes in thinking: the old economic models for the study of trade have been superseded by an emphasis on the coexistence of gift-exchange and palace-controlled trade as against commercial trade for profit, the notion of the relationship between the centre or centres and the periphery, as well as ideas of unequal exchange, 'gateway communities' perched on the edge of other cultures and community diasporas, concepts which will prove vital to our final explanation, and which have been applied by such eminent archaeologists as Colin Renfrew, utilizing the approaches of Immanuel Wallerstein in his study of core–periphery relations in early modern times.

The islands

The role of the Mediterranean islands seems to be quite different in the general setting of the Bronze Age. Here we shall concentrate on the islands of the eastern Mediterranean, though it is important to bear in mind that throughout this period Sardinia was the seat of an extraordinary civilization, the Nuraghic culture, which has left evidence in its castles or *nuraghi*, and their surrounding villages, of a warlike and fragmented society, though probably it was a wealthy civilization as well; it has left a record of its metalworking achievements in the large number of bronze figurines that survive from the Nuraghic period, which were being produced from the fifteenth century to the sixth century BC. However, although Sicily and Sardinia are quite obvious stopovers on the western Mediterranean route, Crete functioned as one of the nodal points, a sort of 'gateway' into the Mediterranean linking East and West. Its characteristics as a centre rather than periphery are clearly denoted by the very structure of its palaces, the nature of its material culture in general and its role in the overall functioning of the Bronze Age system network, as its western pole.

The Cyclades and Rhodes were certainly bridges between Crete and Anatolia. One of the interesting characteristics of the Cyclades in this period is their lively economic activity (agriculture, metallurgy, silver mining, trade) that combined both rural and urban settlements. The town of Akrotiri on Thera, an important Aegean port, is often called the Pompeii of the ancient Aegean, thanks to its survival intact under 30 m (98 ft) of debris from a great volcanic eruption around 1470 BC; there is evidence of an impressive urban structure, with multi-storeyed buildings, a feature that the Aegean would only see again, in such a consistent manner, more than a millennium later, in Hellenistic Delos. Cyprus, however, has a quite different nature. Too near the power of Egypt (400 km/248 miles from the Delta) and Hatti (70 km/43 miles from the Anatolian coast) and at only 95 km (59 miles) from the Levant, Cyprus was a channel linking different worlds during the Middle and Late Bronze Ages. It appears as 'Alashiya' in cuneiform and Egyptian hieroglyphic documents. The personal names of the inhabitants of Cyprus that have come down to us demonstrate manifold links with the Levant, although its population was of a multi-ethnic composition: Egyptian, Semites, Hittites, Hurrians, and so on. The role of Cyprus in the Mediterranean regional trade system depended heavily not only on its geographical location, but also on its rich copper ores. Although neutral during the Hittite–Egyptian struggle over the conquest of the Levant during the fourteenth and thirteenth centuries, it never really managed entirely to avoid Hittite overlordship, as well as attempts by the Egyptians and others, such as the rulers of Ugarit, to assert sovereignty over the island.

As for Rhodes and the Dodecanese Islands (the 'Twelve Islands'), they still require fuller archaeological research, but from the northwest of the island we already have impressive data. The Middle Bronze

Age settlement of Trianda presents many Trojan cultural elements and the Late Bronze Age town was spread over 12 hectares (30 acres), more than half the size of contemporary Akrotiri on Thera. Trianda was a very important harbour, not only for the route from Crete to Anatolia, but also for the eastern trade. The 125 Mycenaean-style chamber tombs of nearby Ialysos provide scholars with a rich amount of data attributed to the years 1400–1300 BC. The wealth of material is such that some scholars, seeing it as one of the main Mycenaean centres on the islands, linked it to the *Land of Ahhiyawa*, mentioned consistently in the cuneiform Hittite texts of the fifteenth–thirteenth centuries, a place to which it is now necessary to turn.

The 'Land of Ahhiyawa'

For over seventy years scholars have debated the idea that the 'Land of Ahhiyawa' of the Hittite texts should be identified with Achaia, the land of the Achaeans or, in other words, the early Greeks. In several Hittite texts dealing with eastern Anatolia, there are references to people leaving by sea for Ahhiyawa, a problematic kingdom not bound to Hatti and responsible, as far as the written documents go, for fomenting rebellions in Hatti's western Anatolian vassal territories. The kings of Hatti and Ahhiyawa were both 'High Kings', calling each other 'My brother'; and since the only evidence we have for another Great King off the western Anatolian coast is Mycenae, the identification with the early Greeks at first seemed promising. Linguistic studies point to the possibility that within the word Ahhiyawa there exists the term *Akw-a* (water), with *Ahhiya(k)wa* meaning islands, region of islands. Therefore, the Hittite Ahhiyawa most probably signified both the Aegean and Mycenae. Without diminishing the merit of such a discussion, I believe it worth suggesting that the simple 'fled to the sea' (or by boat) from Millawantha/Miletos is not, on its own, a conclusive argument for locating Ahhiyawa off Anatolia. Whenever these escapes happened, the persecuted were fleeing from Hittite armies which, quite evidently, were occupying the roads just behind the coast.

Although we have references to Hatti's armies being transported by ship – a letter from the King of Ugarit to the King of Alashiya, dated to the late thirteenth century, informs us that the fleet of Ugarit was off the coast of the Lukka, certainly at the disposal of the Hittites, as well as Ugarit's infantry and chariotry – their infantry quite certainly moved mostly overland, and the use of a sea route to escape from these armies would make sense.

The Hittite Wilusa, however, bears on the whole question of Troy and the Trojan War. Countless studies, some serious, others simple guesswork, have tried to find the 'real', historical Trojan War behind Homer's *Iliad*. The American archaeologist Carl Blegen, who divided the mound of Hissarlik in northeastern Anatolia into nine levels, identified Troy VII as the legendary town. Discussion of the subject has increased since then. The simple question is this: if the Achaeans/Ahhiyawans, are present in the Hittite records, where in those records is the Trojan War? Critically considering all available data and studies, Michael Wood's book *In Search of the Trojan War* tried to answer such a question. One of the main documents at our disposal is called the Annals of Tudhaliyas, dated to around 1440–1404 BC. In this document, the Great King of Hatti, who conquered *Arzawa*, in western Anatolia, lists twenty-two states associated with *Assuwa* against Hatti. It is believed that these names are listed from the south upwards, starting with the *Lukka* (Lycia), across the *Land of River Seha*, till the last two names mentioned: *Wilusiya* and *Taruisa*. Although the phonetic association of *Wilusiya* with *Wilios-Ilios* and *Taruisa-Truisa-Troja-Troia* seems possible, a few scholars are still reticent about it.

However, since Homer uses both names, Troy (normally taken as the city) and Ilios (as the country), it seems consistent to think that, during the fourteenth–thirteenth centuries, the remains we now know as Troy, at the site of Hissarlik, were under the grip of the Hittite empire, so much so that Wilusa signed a treaty with Hatti during the time of Muwatallis (1296–1272 BC) and some details of it deserve attention. To begin with, the King of Wilusa mentioned in this treaty is *Alaksandus*, quite rare as an Anatolian name and one which distinctly recalls that of the *Iliad*'s Prince Alexandros of Ilios, better known as Paris. Other evidence may be added to this, such as the gods of Wilusa and Hatti who are invoked as testimonies at the end of this treaty: *Apaliunas* is quite probably an older form of Apollo (the Cypriote Apeilon, the Doric Apellon), the Homeric protector of Troy. As Wood states, Achaiwoi/Akkaiwoi/Ahhiyawa, Alaksandus-Alexandros, Taruisa-Troia, Wilusia-Wilios-Ilios might all be considered by the cautious as mere resemblances, 'but four resemblances is pressing coincidence too far'.

Regarding the chronology of events, Herodotus places the Trojan war in the middle of the thirteenth century, while 1184 BC has become a widely quoted date for the fall of Troy, on the basis of classical sources. Blegen's Troy VIIa, considered by most as the Homeric Troy, is dated to 1250 BC, whereas the references to what may be Troy in the Hittite texts would point to Blegen's Troy VI as the probable fortress-town of the legend. We must be aware that, most probably, there was never a 'Trojan War' of the sort described in Homer's *Iliad*. Many scholars seem to agree that the so-called Homeric society described in his poetry bears elements from three distinct periods: the Mycenaean Bronze Age, the Greek Dark Age and the Early Iron Age. The epic of the Trojan War would have taken centuries to be compiled out of what has been called a 'gradual accumulation of traditions', many of which were probably inspired by a range of historical incidents, none of which is exactly described. Still, considering that western Anatolian archaeology is still in its infancy, there may yet appear new evidence to clinch the identification of Troy in the Hittite sources. At the moment, what is important is the clear evidence that there were serious disputes between the Ahhiyawans/Achaeans and the Hittites over the western Anatolian area. Indeed, the Alaksandus Treaty did not prevent the Hittites from attacking Wilusa soon after signing it, as is painfully apparent from the so-called Manapa-Tarhunta Letter and also from the Tawagalawa Letter, both dated to the mid-thirteenth century BC.

The Tawagalawa Letter is particularly interesting, since it mentions a peace settlement on a previous dispute over Wilusa between Hatti and Ahhiyawa. The Tawagalawa Letter is today used as the main document attesting Ahhiyawan-Mycenaean expansion and pressure in western Asia, since the brother of the Great King of Ahhiyawa, Tawagalawa (or Tawakalawa, whom some equate to Eteowokelewes – Eteokles), was fostering rebellion among the western Anatolian vassals of Hatti, by helping the Hittite renegade Piyramandu. Hattusili III is apparently the Hittite king who wrote this letter to an unnamed king of Ahhiyawa, asking him to send back Piyramandu, since he had fled with Tawagalawa from Millawatha-Miletos, to Ahhiyawa. What is certain is the state of almost permanent belligerency in western Anatolia, from as early as 1450–1430 BC, the date of the so-called Indictment of Madduwatta. This Hittite tablet states that Madduwatta, a lesser king in western Anatolia, has been driven from his country by Attarissiyas, 'the man of Ahhiyawa'. Apart from being the earliest mention of Ahhiyawa, we must take into account this long-term struggle for power when trying to understand the collapse of the Bronze Age system. We might also stop and contemplate the striking similarity between the name Attarissiyas and that of Agamemnon's father, Atreus. This state of affairs did not go unnoticed even in Egypt, where there was reference to 'the islands of the Great Green [Sea] being unrestful'. As a matter of fact, the Egyptian sources open up one of the outstanding enigmas about the civilizations of the eastern Mediterranean at this period, the problem of the 'Sea Peoples'.

The Bronze Age crisis and the Sea Peoples

Life in the eastern Mediterranean was characterized during the Early and, especially, Middle Bronze Ages by the almost permanent stress of endemic war. Land, resources and people were caught up in an ever moving situation of violence and conquest. From minor wars against weaker neighbours or insubordinate vassals to those between power-ful kingdoms (Egypt versus Hatti; Hatti versus Mitanni; Egypt versus Mitanni; Hatti versus Babylon) no country was ever at rest. A degree of equilibrium, precarious as it was, did emerge, and it permitted the creation of those extraordinary kingdoms which still today prompt awe and admiration for their achievements. Such equilibrium was held in balance by a serious and professional diplomatic network, using Akkadian as a lingua franca, that linked these countries and produced most of the written documents available for study. Then (in the traditional view very suddenly), this entire world collapsed in the twelfth century BC, bringing to an end the eastern Mediterranean Bronze Age: this is what we have learned, and taught, for the past hundred years or so, thanks to some of the most prestigious scholars of their day, such as Emmanuel de Rougé, Gaston Maspero, William Flinders Petrie and R. A. S. Macalister, writing either side of 1900.

To these scholars we owe the first modern explanations of the turmoil that rocked the eastern Mediterranean during a crisis in the history of man of such a magnitude that it has been compared with the fall of the Roman Empire. Their reasoning was constructed out of a mixture of written records (especially Egyptian and Hittite), Greek legendary traditions (with a special focus on Homer's epics) and iconographic material (mainly Egyptian). From then on, scholars took sides, enthusiastically defending one or another 'cause' of such an abrupt ending of a period in history. Several possibilities have been put forward, studied and disputed in many a forum of academic research: cataclysms, crop failure, drought, famine and mass migra-tions. One important perspective concerns the Sea Peoples and their overwhelming destructive power, with their consequent responsibility for the ending of Bronze Age high civilization in the area. As soon as new documents came to light, they were immediately inserted into the established theories or used to build up fresh ones. However, different translations, different interpretations, different dating, all tangled up together, have made this period a dangerous scholarly minefield.

The written records, mostly in Egyptian hieroglyphs and Hittite, but also in Linear B and Akkadian, not to mention the Bible, have raised the crucial question of dating, and the equally difficult one of the place names that different countries give to each other in different languages. Some of these attributions, after lengthy discussions, are now generally accepted as sound, such as the Keftiu/Kaftor/Caphtor (Crete), Kati/Kitti/Ketta (Hatti or Khatti), Peleset (Philistines), Lukki/Lukka (Lycia), Millawatha/Millawanta (Miletos), Alasiya/Alashiya (Cyprus or, at least, its main city), whereas others are still slightly contested, such as (Ahhiyawa/Akkaywoi/Achaeans) or heavily disputed (Danuna/Danaans/Danites; Teresh/Tursha/Tyrsenoi/Tyrrhenians/Etruscans; Taruisa/Truisa Troia; Shekelesh/Shekels/Siculi/Sicilians; Sherden/Shardana/Sardinians) to mention just the main ones.

This is not the place to examine the substantial historiography of the Sea Peoples since de Rougé started to use the term in 1867, nor to retrace the discussion over each of these Sea Peoples, their origin or their later destiny. It is enough to mention that the linking of the Sherden to Sardinia, the Shekels to the Sicilian Siculi and the Teresh to the Etruscans goes back to the beginning of research on the subject, and there is still no conclusion to the debate. Similarities in descriptions of sea raids in the Homeric poems and in Egyptian sources have been explained either as coincidence or as hard evidence of the nature of these attacks. Further evidence can be expected from DNA testing, linguistics and other newer research tools. At the moment, however, we are still bound to do the best we can with the known documents and new archaeological data which are increasing year by year, especially from research in Israel, Syria and Turkey.

However, there are a few problems to be cleared up at the start, the first one being the very definition of Sea Peoples and their arrival from 'islands' on the Great Green. Some authors have pointed out the inappropriateness of such terms, trying to see the 'Great Green' not as sea but as marshlands at nearby Punt or suggesting that 'island' was a mistranslation, since the Egyptians, not having islands, would have no word for them. But these objections can be confidently dismissed. 'Great Green' often meant the Mediterranean and the Egyptians had certainly heard of islands (notably Keftiu/Crete). At present, the earliest written references we have to these seafaring warriors – as mercenaries with the Egyptians at Byblos and raiding areas in the eastern Mediterranean – are contained in the cuneiform Amarna Letters, dated to the fourteenth century BC. There is also a stela celebrating Pharaoh Seti I's victory over marauders from the lands to the east of the Jordan in 1300 BC. This situation was not new to Egypt: Asiatic marauders or perhaps just thirst-stricken herdsmen were known in and around the Delta from the VIth Dynasty. The so-called 'hapiru' (a word some link to the term 'Hebrew', though it had a broad meaning) and the 'hubshu', landless outcasts, were a concern to Egypt, whereas mercenaries, called 'mariannu', such as the Sherden/Shardana were normally used in the Egyptian army.

From Egypt we have three sets of important documents: (a) the inscriptions and pictorial depictions of the battle of Qadesh (1274 BC), especially those from the Temple of Abu Simbel; (b) the accounts of the attacks by the Libyans and their allies on Egypt during the reign of Merneptah (1236–1223 BC) – the great Karnak Inscription, the Athribis Stela, the Cairo Column, the Hymn of Victory; (c) the accounts of the attack on Egypt by a coalition of peoples during the reign of Ramesses III (1198–1166 BC) – the Harris Papyrus and the Medinet Habu Theban temple reliefs. From these sources most scholars derive their knowledge of 'the peoples of the sea', in spite of references to the presence of 'northerners coming from all countries' (Hymn of Victory) travelling with carts, tents, wives and children, cattle, pottery, and so on. According to the Karnak Inscription, they were Ekwesh, Shekelesh, Teresh/Tursha, Meshwesh, Lukka and Sherden/Shardana, all under the leadership of the Libyan chief Meryey, son of Ded. They were repelled and Meryey was killed in battle. Whereas the Medinet Habu reliefs depict Ramesses III's victory over Peleset,

Shekelesh, Weshesh, Denyen and Sikala, the Harris Papyrus adds the Sherden/Shardana to the list and states that they arrived by land, from the north, and by sea. The Medinet Habu inscription is the classic reference to them:

> The foreign countries made a conspiracy in their islands. Removed and scattered in the fray were the lands, at one time. No country could stand before their arms, from Hatti, Kode (Kizzuwatna), Carchemish, Yereth (Arzawa) and Yeres (Alashiya). They were cut off. A camp was set up in Amor (Amurru). They desolated its people and its land was like that which has never come into being. They were coming while the flame was prepared before them, forward towards Egypt. Their confederation was Peleset, Tjeker, Shekelesh, Denyen and Weshesh, lands united. They lay their hands upon the lands to the very circuit of the earth.

These Egyptian sources, apart from helping us to make sense of the Pharaonic ideology and propaganda, present us with some interesting questions that are finally leading to a better understanding of the period known as 'the Bronze Age collapse'. First of all, the Lukka, mentioned in the Amarna Letters as attacking Egypt and seizing villages in Cyprus, sided with the Hittites against Egypt in the battle of Qadesh, and do not appear with those peoples attacking Egypt under Merneptah and Ramesses III. The Sherden, on the contrary, who fought with Ramesses II at Qadesh, attacked Egypt under Merneptah and Ramesses III, which suggests that, at least during these 200 years, there were no clearly drawn, long-lasting allegiances. The reliefs of the battle of Qadesh and the Medinet Habu reliefs present a rich variety of the personal features of the Sea Peoples, including hairstyles and weaponry; scholars have been able to make intelligent guesses about their ethnic affiliations. Taking these data into account, how is it possible to reconcile tales of fierce sea raiders with references to uprooted farmers, their families and livestock?

The Ugarit Archives emphasize the sea, mentioning 'the Sikala/S-K-L/Shekels who live on ships', and the city's final requests for help from the King of Alashiya in relation to 'seven enemy ships arriving'. The traditional view of the Sea Peoples' movements as being a consequence of the destruction of the Mycenaean palaces at the end of the thirteenth century is still largely accepted. These wandering peoples, warlike and seeking new lands to plunder or settle, are still considered by many as reminiscent of the state of affairs after the Trojan War in the literary sources. However, it remains clear that the Sea Peoples were a very important element in the break-up of the eastern Mediterranean Bronze Age System and were even more important in the establishment of the new economic and political order which gave birth to the classical world. The natural reasons for the collapse which is simply called the 'catastrophe' by many, have been exhaustively discussed and nowadays only drought and consequent crop failure and famine are still regarded as important factors in the fall of the Hittite Empire, even though this barely explains the total collapse of an economic system that linked so many powerful states to one another.

It is interesting to note that scholars are finally reconsidering the ways in which the history of this period has been written, before tackling the manner in which it might have happened. This reconsideration follows two parallel lines. The first simply focuses on the historical validity of the Egyptian sources, and the second discusses the way these sources have been used by modern historiography.

Although still taken as the main reference by many, the validity of the Egyptian sources as truthful narratives regarding the Sea Peoples has being strongly contested, on the grounds that Ramesses III sought to emulate his famous namesake by claiming similar glories. Recent studies alert us to the danger of using the Egyptian iconographic sources as 'historical' documents, since the physical making of the reliefs and their use during the Napoleonic invasion of Egypt in 1798, and by de Rougé in the imaginative creation of the identity of what he called 'the peoples of the Mediterranean Sea', loosely seen as Danaans, Achaeans, Sardinians, Etruscans, Lycians, Sicilians etc., engaged in the search for the Promised Land as a rolling wave of conquering people, later substantiated by the archaeological discoveries of Flinders Petrie and others. What is particularly impressive is the long-lasting use of these rather dated explanatory models and the fact that, more than a century later, their substitution with new explanations is still in its infancy. Indeed, during the past two decades or so, we have seen the revival of one of the Victorian interpretations of the Sea Peoples, that of their creative and 'civilizational' role, put forward by the excavator of Gezer who saw the Philistines (assumed to be the same as the Peleset of the Sea Peoples) as the 'only cultured or artistic race who ever occupied the soil of Palestine'.

Based on archaeological research in Cyprus and Israel, outstanding scholars such as Avner Raban, Amihai Mazar, Lawrence Stager, and Moshe and Trude Dothan, have 'rehabilitated' the Sea Peoples, shifting them from their role as nomadic sackers to that of city builders, not the 'cause' of the Bronze Age system collapse but the stimulus and revitalizing force in a collapsing world. The constructive role of the Sea Peoples in the Levant and their contribution to civilization is heavily based on the belief that ashlar architecture (using squared trimmed stones) and Mycenaean IIIB and IIIC wares were carried to Canaan, via Cyprus, by Sea Peoples of Aegean origin: the P-L-S, or Peleset, or Philistines. Such a hypothesis is backed up by the equation with the biblical Philistines, among whom can be found observable traces of Aegean material culture. New DNA evidence from skeletons excavated in Israel confirms that the Philistines were Aegean warriors, most probably displaced Mycenaean warriors, who then intermarried with the Semitic population of Canaan. The biblical tradition records, too, that God brought the Philistines from Caphtor (Crete) just as He brought the Israelites from Egypt. At the very least, we can see here impressive evidence for the disruption caused by the invasions of the Sea Peoples.

The collapse of the Bronze Age system as a Mediterranean chain reaction

There is at least one thing modern scholars agree about, that the social and economic system of the Bronze Age – state-controlled, intertwining the great and small states of the eastern Mediterranean – collapsed and was replaced, almost immediately, by a new social order, with the state retreating in the face of a much more open, indeed entrepreneurial, economy. Most scholars see the collapse as a result of a number of circumstances – the dismantling of the palace-based civilizations, or natural disasters, or the Sea Peoples' invasions, or changes in warfare, or a combination of several of the above. However, if one interprets these 'reasons' as, on the contrary, the very *product* of collapse, the questions have to be formulated differently, and one starts to obtain another and very exciting set of answers. Some of them seek to explain the collapse as the result of internal factors within these societies, but here we will look at the explanatory models that go beyond events and that help to describe the overall structure into which they were inserted. Therefore, setting out in a critical way from the idea that the collapse of the Bronze Age system only happened because of its internal weaknesses, we shall try to suggest where such weaknesses resided and how they contributed to the final outcome.

In 1977 Paolo Pereira de Castro regarded the rupture of the suze-rain states, for long responsible for the flow of the long-distance trade palace-based economy, as the main factor in the dismantling of the Bronze Age system. One such rupture took a while to develop, having as one of its triggers the growing independence of the Urnfield cultures in the European interior, which moved from an ore-selling to a metal-producing social and economic structure. The first centre to be affected would have been the Aegean, which had to begin importing copper and tin from Near Eastern countries in order to continue its own metal production. The wreck of the ship found at Cape Gelidonya, which had been heading for the Aegean with a full cargo of tin and copper from the Levant, helped Pereira de Castro to elaborate on this hypothesis. In this setting, the western Anatolian vassal states became restive and started shaking off their submission to Hatti, fostered by Ahhiyawa. The rupture of economic dependencies would have been further widened by the availability of iron, which would have rendered obsolete the long-distance trade network carrying copper and tin. Childe believed in the 'democracy' of iron technology, spreading fast and dispensing with the palace organization needed for Bronze Age economic trade. Some have contradicted him by insisting that iron technology began after the collapse of the Bronze Age system. Apart from the fact that the idea of a Hittite monopoly on iron technology has been proved unsound and that iron objects are found throughout the eastern Mediterranean as early as the fourteenth and thirteenth centuries, we now have important data establishing Cyprus as one of the main centres for the production of iron in the period as well as evidence of molten iron in fifteenth century BC north Balkan sites.

The archaeological data from Cyprus have given support to a very interesting explanation by Susan Sherratt of the end of the Bronze Age system: Cyprus hosted polities that produced bronze from scrap metal, utilitarian iron and pottery which were traded below the élite level of state-controlled commerce, therefore functioning as a subversive factor unbalancing the economic network of the great empires and helping to drive them to final collapse. Operating this underground, subversive economic network were none other than the so-called Sea Peoples, based in Cyprus, an island, as far as is known, with no palace structure. Such an explanation can be beautifully supported by one of the Amarna Letters, precisely the one in which Pharaoh complained to the king of Alashiya about the Lukka and the Alashiyans attacking Egypt together. For the Alashiyan king answered that this was not true, since the Lukka had been taking one Alashiyan town after another during the previous years.

However, although Pereira de Castro and Sherratt agreed, as most scholars do, with the theory that the Sea Peoples came from somewhere in western Anatolia, they do not explain why these peoples began moving. I would therefore like to suggest a closer look at the history of Hatti. It is quite clear that the Hittite empire could not extract great riches from its meagre agriculture and from animal husbandry. Its wealth came from trade – mostly as an intermediary – and from an incessant process of conquest: new lands, new subjects, new tribute, a new workforce, new warriors to enforce the existing cultural network of expropriation. The *King's Deeds*, or memoirs, of the main Hittite Great Kings (sometimes written on their behalf by their heir) proudly describe such conquests, the violent reduction of enemy lands or restless vassal territories, by destruction, pillage, fire and the enslavement of men, women and children.

That human beings were a precious commodity during the Bronze Age is attested in the Pylos Tablets (with their long lists of women slaves of very diverse Mediterranean origins), in the Hittite administrative documents attributing work in the mills to enslaved prisoners (specially blinded for the task) and the Homeric descriptions of raids whose main outcome was the capture of natives, as Odysseus did in the Egyptian delta. However, what should particularly be stressed is the obsessive attention to prisoners, fugitives, deportees and escapees that is to be seen in all Hittite treaties. I would like to suggest that the very growth and development of the Hittite empire produced, alongside 400 years of endemic war and ruthless conquest, a mass of uprooted people, landless outcasts who managed to escape from the yoke, probably 'living on ships', as the Ugarit tablet informs about the Shekels/Shikala, who set up bases in deserted areas of Cyprus, out of the reach of the palatial structures (which are not in any case known in Cyprus), from where they produced their goods and traded outside the established official network, loosening ties of vassalage and reciprocity, subverting and finally helping to unbalance and destroy the old system.

If one looks at the period from this new perspective, one might understand the different pattern of destruction and abandonment (the Aegean, most of Hatti, parts of the Syrian coast, the kingdom of Ugarit), destruction and reconstruction (parts of the Levantine coast, parts of Cyprus) and lands left untouched (parts of Cyprus and of the Syrian coast and southern Anatolia) as the possible result of the Sea Peoples' long-lasting resentment or links of friendship with them, as the case may be. The sheer fact that Cyprus presents no uniform level of destruction and that Mesopotamia passed the catastrophe unharmed seems to strengthen this interpretation. As a matter of fact, Mesopotamia had no iron ores and continued to depend on long-distance trade to obtain the metal.

One must, therefore, look at Cyprus and the Levantine coast in order to understand the opening of the new era of iron, the dominion of free merchants based in city states at Tyre, Byblos, Sidon, but also scattered in small villages and rural settlements. These men spoke Ugaritian, Moabite, Hebrew, Aramaic and other Semitic dialects, and developed the script which is the ancestor of the modern alphabet. Thanks to Herodotus they came into history as the Phoenicians, but they called themselves *Cana'ani*, Canaanites. Western scholarly tradition was in the habit of looking for the history behind the Homeric epics and failed to see it as a part of a repertoire that belonged to wider eastern Mediterranean culture. In fact, it was not just Helen, but also Sarah and Hurray who were abducted, to the palaces of Pharaoh and to the Philistine town of Gerar (Genesis 12:15 and 20:2) and King Pbl's in Udum. The three of them were retrieved by their husbands: Menelaus, Abraham and King Kret (Keret).

It never ceases to amaze just how small the Mediterranean basin was. One of the main figures of the Classical Greek pantheon is associated with the eastern deity Ishtar/Astarte/Ashdoda: namely, the goddess Aphrodite, linked to fertility, protector of sailors and fishermen, born from a shell, in Cyprus, married to Hephaistos, the god of metalworking: a many-faceted Eastern Mediterranean Goddess, the spirit of the Mediterranean.

The fluxes of empires, the voyages of the first merchant venturers, the diffusion of Egyptian and other Oriental cultures through the eastern and eventually the western Mediterranean – these were the great themes that have struck observers since Herodotus and Thucydides began to write their histories, and which are amply reflected in the archaeological record as well. They are recorded, with an extensive overlay of myth and fancy, in the works of Homer: the Mycenaean empire in its latter days, wasting its energy on the siege of Troy; the wanderings of Odysseus aboard ship across the Mediterranean. Other cycles of legend told of Jason's adventures in the Black Sea. Both Etruscan and Roman traditions recorded migrations from the East: the voyage of Aeneas, the Trojan, to Latium by way of Carthage, seems also to have been a favourite of the Etruscans, while Herodotus mentioned how a Lydian prince, Tyrsenos, led half of his people in a great migration away from famine-stricken lands, to found the Tyrrhenian cities of Etruria.

Even though scholars have long doubted whether all or any Etruscans were migrants from the East, rather than agile imitators of Eastern fashions in art and culture, what is important here is the powerful awareness that the Bronze Age came to an end with large-scale population movements. Centres of advanced culture such as the Nuraghic civilization of Sardinia went into decline, as did Crete, long the power-house of the Minoan and then of the earliest Greek civilization, that of the Mycenaeans, whether because of volcanic eruptions in the Aegean or because of internal and external political and economic crises. The late second millennium BC was recorded in Egyptian texts as the era of the Sea Peoples, whose names uncannily recall the names of territories and peoples in the late Mediterranean: the Shardana, whom some have connected to Sardinia, the Tursha, who may be connected to the Trojans and the Tyrrhenian inhabitants of the Aegean, of whom more will be said in the following chapter, the Peleshet, whose name recalls that of the Philistines (Mycenaean migrants) and of the

'Pelasgians', a term used by classical Greek writers as a catch-all
to describe the early non-Greeks of the Aegean region. There
were certainly such non-Greek peoples in the Aegean in classical
times, as a famous sixth-century inscription from Lemnos in a
language related to Etruscan, but apparently different from it,
reveals: almost the only evidence that Etruscan had any relatives
among the languages of the ancient Mediterranean. In fact,
we should not be surprised to find that the Mediterranean
contained plenty of ethnic and linguistic pockets, the product
of centuries of migration, warfare, resettlement and pilgrimage
to religious shrines. This was still how it appeared in medieval
and early modern times; ethnic and linguistic homogeneity has
arrived late, as far as it has ever been achieved.

One migration made little impact on the writers of
official inscriptions in Egypt and neighbouring lands, but
was destined to have far greater impact on the civilization of
the Mediterranean and the entire world than the movement
attributed to Philistines, Tyrrhenians and others: the arrival of
the Israelites in the land of Canaan. Modern research tends to
treat the Bible stories more as literature than as history, and the
archaeological record is not capable of demonstrating exactly
where Abraham, Moses and other biblical heroes trod. By the
early Iron Age, however, the Semitic inhabitants of the highlands
of Canaan did identify themselves with twelve tribes who had
escaped slavery in the land of Egypt, with the help of one true
God who was the creator of the universe. Again, there is plenty
of debate about when the Israelites began to understand this
one God as the only God in the entire universe, although early
tales of Elijah and other prophets were certainly scathing about
false gods, in a manner that hardly suggests any belief that they
existed. Debate also rages about how important the kingdoms
established by these tribes actually were: the Bible texts no
doubt exaggerated the size of David's realm, but the accounts
of day-to-day conflict between bronze-wielding Israelites and
iron-wielding Philistine invaders, while Egyptians, Assyrians and

other great empires also attempted to establish dominion in the region, are real enough. So too are the accounts of diverse cult centres, such as that at Shiloh, and of the attempts to centralize the worship of God in the new sanctuary at Jerusalem around 1000 BC. This was accompanied by the emergence of a literate élite, who adapted the Phoenician alphabet; by the time of the Babylonian exile in 586 BC the prophet Jeremiah and the scribe Baruch were active in collecting and collating the traditions and laws of the Hebrews. Although religious tradition attributes the first five books of the Bible to Moses, who was said to have received them from God, the overwhelming tendency of modern scholarship, Jewish as well as Christian, has been to see them as a late compilation, pieced together from a variety of priestly traditions, and finally edited by Ezra the scribe at the end of the sixth century, when the Jews (as they can now be called) returned to their homeland after a brief but painful sojourn by the waters of Babylon.

The land the Israelites inhabited provided livelihoods for wheat and barley farmers, for shepherds and goatherds; its material remains, except for occasional luxury items that may have graced a princely court, suggest that this was a land in which life was lived simply. What it produced were religious and social ideas, not luxury artefacts. Although some of the moral themes present in early Hebrew literature have points in common with neighbouring cultures (comparisons have often been made between the Babylonian Code of Hammurabi and the law codes of the Pentateuch), the double emphasis on service to one God and on God's demands for living an ethical life were unprecedented.

Thus, tossed between Egypt, Assyria and Babylon, the Hebrew religion and indeed the Jewish people were forged in the eastern Mediterranean crucible. Though the Hebrews sought to reject Pharaonic Egypt and the temptations of Babylon, their experiences of Egypt and Mesopotamia lay at the root of the experiences which led them to see the working of the hand of God in history.

THREE

The battle for the sea routes: 1000 – 300 BC

MARIO TORELLI

During the second half of the second millennium BC, we can observe particularly intense and profitable navigation back and forth across the Mediterranean, which constituted an 'inner lake' of immense proportions linking southern Europe, North Africa and the Near East. The protagonists were the Aegean peoples, first of all the Minoans of Crete and then the Mycenaeans, who were in the first instance interested in the Near East, which was a source not only of precious goods, particularly the textiles and prestige objects produced by the great civilizations of Egypt, Mesopotamia and Anatolia, but also of raw materials, such as the copper that came from the rich mines of Cyprus and the precious stones that came from the Fertile Crescent. The Aegean navigators remained, as far as can be seen, undisturbed in their mastery of Mediterranean navigation between the fourteenth and the twelfth centuries BC; and they interested themselves both in the supply of goods to the courts of the great lords or *wanakes* of the mainland and the islands, and, above all, in the trade between the Aegean and the coasts of Syria and Palestine, linking these regions to the central Mediterranean, and even occasionally reaching as far as the Iberian peninsula.

In the last fifty years or so the evidence for a Mycenaean presence on the coast of southern Italy, in Sicily and in Sardinia has grown to such an extent that it is no exaggeration to speak, in many cases, of genuine settlements by groups or by individuals of Mycenaean origin.

Although the number of places visited by these navigators was not enormous, what is striking is the early date of their arrival, and even more so the quantity and quality of the Mycenaean goods often found there, whether inhabited sites or in tombs, all of which leads one to think of a permanent presence of Mycenaeans. The analysis of many thousands of Mycenaean ceramics found on the site of the future Greek colony of Metaponton in southern Italy, at Termitito in modern Basilicata, has revealed that alongside ceramics imported from the heartlands of the Mycenaean world, in particular the region of Argos, a significant quantity of pottery was in fact of local manufacture.

These distant enterprises are often linked by modern observers, without a great deal of evidence, to stories of Greek heroes that spread among the native inhabitants of the newly settled lands as a means of legitimizing Greek territorial conquests and the creation of diplomatic ties with barbarian peoples. However, the enterprises can also be regarded as an essential foundation of those features that would come to characterize the commercial traffic of the Mediterranean throughout the pre-Roman age: the combination of mercantile contact and colonial settlement. For the routes followed by Phoenician and then Greek merchants would replicate to a large extent those of the Mycenaean traders, extending them further in ways that were to some degree predetermined by those traders. And, just as in the Bronze Age, these merchants were able to supply the more highly evolved civilizations of the Near East with the raw materials and other goods that they needed, receiving in exchange luxury goods that were much esteemed by the indigenous cultures further west.

At the same time, however, the relationships fostered by the merchants with the peoples of the western Mediterranean were never limited simply to commercial exchange, but rapidly gave way to developments that went beyond straightforward trade. Indeed, if conditions were right, that is, if the native population was relatively weak and yet there were rich agricultural resources, the transition from mercantile contact to colonial foundation became an almost natural one. But if the native population was militarily powerful and able to prevent the intrusion of colonial settlements, commercial contacts by themselves remained the principal vehicle for the transfer of technical know-how, with the arrival of individuals in possession of skills which were unknown locally but were highly prized.

In motives and methods, later contacts across the Mediterranean thus followed the pattern of those in the Mycenaean period, and this applies as much to the Phoenicians as it does to the Greeks. In fact, there is little difference between the way these two groups operated. Even if they followed different routes, they were all laid out in the Bronze Age by their Aegean precursors. Here we can look at the settlements on islands or peninsulas close to the land where trade was being directed: in the Bronze Age the islands of Vivara in the Gulf of Naples or the peninsula of Thapsos in Sicily, and in the first millennium the islands of Pithecusa (Pithekoussai), the first Greek base in the Tyrrhenian Sea, of Motya and Ibiza, which were Phoenician outposts in Sicily and in Spanish waters, as was the promontory of Cádiz, isolated by its surrounding marshes. Like the Mycenaeans, both Phoenicians and Greeks were interested in sources of metals, and like them the main commodities they carried were luxury goods, which were as much in demand in the first millennium BC as they had been in the second.

Trade at the start of the first millennium BC: Tyrrhenians, Phoenicians and Euboeans

The end of the Bronze Age and the start of the 'Dark Age' was marked by profound changes in the entire eastern Mediterranean. Several large and powerful states in Greece and Anatolia, the Hittite Empire and the Mycenaean kingdoms, collapsed, and a new political and ethnic order emerged in continental Greece, in the islands and in Asia Minor. The Mycenaean voyages, which had linked Greece and the Aegean to the Near East for much of the second millennium, without much sign of disturbance, suddenly ceased between the twelfth and the eleventh centuries BC. From the evidence, trade between the eastern and the western Mediterranean seems to dry up: one no longer finds eastern goods on archaeological sites on the Italian peninsula and on the large islands of Sardinia and Sicily. In the turbulent setting of the Mediterranean at this time it was not simply the much discussed 'Sea Peoples' who rendered the seas unsafe and impeded the formerly regular commercial contacts between East and West.

The so-called 'List of Thalassocracies', a time-worn inventory of the phases of sea power transmitted to us in the chronicle of Eusebius of Caesarea, deals with this obscure period between the millennia, and in particular the time between 1174 BC and 961 BC; here Eusebius refers to the successive sea dominion of the Lydians and of the Pelasgians, in other words with two legendary nations linked to the Tyrrhenians or Etruscans. These two groups of people identified by a common language (the Tyrrhenian tongue spoken in Lemnos, Imbros and the eastern part of the Chalcidian peninsula on the one hand, and the Etruscan language spoken in Etruria on the other) appear to have introduced significant innovations into the commercial networks established in times past. They are mentioned in Egyptian sources as participants in the raids of the 'Sea Peoples' with the specific name of *Trshwa* or *Tursha*, and with them we see the emergence of a new mercantile element experienced in metalwork. Indeed, both the Tyrrhenians of the Aegean and those of the Italian peninsula possessed a special vocation for metalwork, amply confirmed by archaeological evidence. The location of the two branches of the Tyrrhenians speaks for a careful choice of place of residence, probably determined by access to sources of metal and by the commercial routes directly or indirectly connected to it: the 'Tyrrhenians' of the West, as Ephoros attests, were active in piracy before the arrival of Greek colonists in Sicilian waters, while the 'Tyrrhenians' of the Aegean appear to be linked strategically to the sources of metal in the Caucasus, sources which are recalled in the myth of the Argonauts.

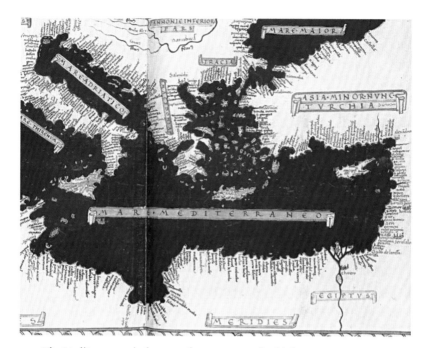

1. The Mediterranean is the sum of many seas, each with its own character, each feeding and being fed by the one 'Great Sea'. The Black Sea was only united with the rest geologically recently. This map dates from the mid-fifteenth century.

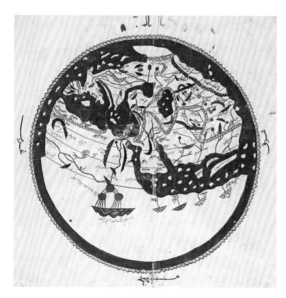

2. With its unmistakable outline, the Mediterranean occupies a pivotal position between three great landmasses, making it a crucible of history. The map of Al-Idrisi, drawn in 1456 but based on a twelfth-century original, is reasonably reliable, though the British Isles have gone astray.

3. Lemons were first grown in Europe in Muslim Spain. In this work by the eighteenth-century Spanish artist Luis Meléndez, lemons occupy the foreground, while the barrel on the right probably contains olives, the jar olive oil and the bottle wine.

4. The luxuriance of Mediterranean vegetation made a deep impression on Jan van Eyck when he visited Portugal in 1428. In the background of one panel of the Ghent Altarpiece he vividly conveyed these exotic plants, so different from those he was used to in northern Europe.

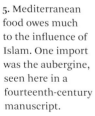

5. Mediterranean food owes much to the influence of Islam. One import was the aubergine, seen here in a fourteenth-century manuscript.

6, 7. The grape is the major crop in many Mediterranean countries, to be eaten fresh or dried and above all its juice to be drunk as wine. In Francesco del Cossa's *Autumn* (mid-fifteenth century), a sturdy peasant stands like a pagan goddess of fertility. In the biblical Book of Numbers grapes are taken as a sign of the overflowing abundance of the Promised Land, as seen in a miniature from the Alba Bible, painted in Spain *c.* 1422–30.

 tan bien tomaron delas granadas

8. Three worshippers bring tribute – model oxen and a boat – to the statue of a god or the deceased in front of his tomb in a scene painted on a Minoan stone coffin dating from the middle of the second millennium BC from Hagia Triada in southern Crete.

9. In the centuries before the rise of Rome, the Etruscans were one of the dominant powers of the western Mediterranean, with a culture under strong Greek influence. This fresco from Tarquinia shows a couple at a funerary banquet.

10. The Greek imagination constantly outstrips expectation, combining influences from many seemingly irreconcilable cultures, as seen in this gold earring representing a harpy or siren. The upper half is a beautiful winged woman playing a kithara, the lower a bird of prey, her legs ending in vicious claws. It probably comes from the eastern Mediterranean and dates from the fourth century BC.

11. A striking lion-headed perfume flask with painted scenes showing warriors and a hunt. In the Proto-Corinthian style and found at Thebes, it dates to the mid-seventh century BC.

12. A collar of beaten gold (second millennium BC) from Byblos dates from a time when Phoenicia was subject to Egypt. The Horus hawk in the centre is typically Egyptian but the egg-and-dart along the bottom border is a Phoenician motif which passed into Greek art.

13. A trading galley brings merchandise, probably metal bars, to the shore, where it is unloaded and weighed, in a mosaic in a Roman tomb in Tunisia, *c.* AD 250.

14. Mediterranean winds could be predicted up to a point, allowing for regular seasonal patterns of sailing. The prevailing wind between southern Italy and Egypt, for instance, was northwest, so the voyage out was four times faster than the return. This mosaic personification of the wind is from Merida in Spain.

15. The Ostrogoths, under their king Theodoric, entered Italy in 493 and established their capital at Ravenna. This detail from S. Apollinare Nuovo shows their fleet at Classe, the port of Ravenna.

The collapse of the Mycenaean kingdoms, accompanied by the population movements within the Balkans known in the sources as 'the return of the Heraklidai', brought a new ethnic order on the Greek mainland, and, most notably, the definitive settlement of the coasts of Asia Minor by Greeks. This would have great importance for the future of maritime trade. The 'return of the Heraklidai' is closely connected with major changes in material conditions, notably the spread of iron and the alterations in the system of production that followed the dissolution of the power of the Mycenaean *wanakes*; one should also take into account the movements of groups speaking the Ionic form of Greek into Asia Minor, entering areas already penetrated in the second millennium by carriers of Mycenaean culture, movements which were described in the sources as 'migration' or 'colonization', and dated to the mid-ninth century BC. This 'Ionian colonization' has to be viewed in close conjunction with the birth of the political institution that characterized Classical Greece, the *polis*, whose first stages can definitely be located in the Ionian setting of Asia Minor.

Alongside the population dispersal that Ionian colonization of Asia Minor provoked, and probably in conjunction with the appearance of new mercantile elements (such as the 'Tyrrhenians' and the Phoenicians, of whom more shortly), we can identify one further element which played an important role in the Greek emporia of the early first millennium: the Euboeans. The island of Euboea was not directly affected by the 'Dorian migration', and seems to be less important in relation to the Ionian expansion into Asia Minor; and yet Euboea, with its two major centres at Chalcis and Eretria, took a leading role in the recovery of Greek trade. Euboean pioneers took a special interest in the northeastern Aegean, around the Chalcidian peninsula, in open rivalry with the Tyrrhenians of that region. The Euboeans would also be the first to enter the Tyrrhenian Sea in the West, creating a symbiotic relationship (which was also a tense one) with the Etruscans, and they made an appearance on the coasts of Syria and Israel, an area which was the focus of Phoenician navigation. It was no coincidence that Chalcidia had the double function of a barrier that controlled access to the Aegean from the Black Sea and a link with Thracia, which throughout the whole of the first millennium BC would represent a principal, if not the principal, source of precious metals and other significant commodities such as slaves and wood required by the more developed centres in the Mediterranean. Euboean sailings to the coasts of Italy and Sicily go back to the ninth century BC, as shown by the presence of Middle Geometric II ceramics on Etruscan, Campanian and Sicilian sites.

This was also the time when contacts with the coasts of Syria and Palestine began to develop, by al-Mina in the mouth of the Orontes. The start of the first millennium BC was thus marked by a new wave of trading contacts on the ruins of those established in the Mycenaean epoch; it was a phase in which the dominant powers were the Tyrrhenians of the Aegean and of Etruria, the Euboean Greeks and the 'red' *Phoinikes*, or Phoenicians. This revival of long-distance trade, with the entry of iron into manufacturing and trade, with navigation across the Mediterranean and the growth of piracy (the other side of the coin as far as trade is concerned), has to be examined alongside the key moments in the history of Dark Age Greece – the Dorian migration and the Ionian colonization – and alongside the initial conflict and subsequent integration that took place with the pre-Dorian or 'Achaean' element indigenous to Greece and indigenous inhabitants of Asia Minor. This is the setting for the emergence of the Greek city-state, the *polis*, which was to become the central pillar of classical civilization.

The old routes of the Mycenaean era were not simply renewed but extended, even beyond the Strait of Gibraltar. Along the maritime routes towards the sources of metal in the Caucasus and in Italy two groups confronted one another: one was the Tyrrhenians of both the Aegean and of Italy, whose destinies were soon to evolve in very different ways (those of the Aegean going into a rapid decline and those of Italy into an irresistible ascent); the other, the Euboeans, whose role was to be the opening up of Greek colonization in the West. The efforts of Pentathlos of Knidos (*c.* 580 BC) and Dorieus of Sparta (510 BC) serve as a reminder that the Greeks would try to use their colonial settlements to interrupt the trade routes of the southern Mediterranean that were under the control of the Phoenicians. The latter maintained a strong interest in the mines of Sardinia, in African luxury goods and in Spanish precious metals, and therefore gave priority to routes across the southern span of the Inner Sea, routes which would remain their special preserve until Rome made headway in these waters. In order to achieve these ends, the Phoenicians created trading settlements which soon developed into colonies: Carthage and the ring of emporia in Libya, along with Motya in western Sicily, appeared to be able to bar entry to the Sicilian channel; Soluntum in Sicily and the many harbours they used in the Sardinian region of Sulcis also formed a formidable barrier blocking access into the southwestern Mediterranean, an area the Phoenicians saw as effectively their private domain. Their position was further strengthened by bases in the west: at Ibiza in the Balearic Islands, at Cádiz beyond the Strait of Gibraltar and in the trading stations they established on the Moroccan coast.

By contrast, the central and northern parts of the western Mediterranean would long be dominated by the Etruscan navies: the diffusion of Etruscan trade from Liguria to Provence between the seventh and the fourth centuries BC is well documented in the archaeological record that has been recovered from the Ligurian and Celtic *oppida* along the coast and on the lower reaches of the Rhône. This network was copied only somewhat later by the Greeks. Eventually they took complete control of navigation in the Adriatic, and were able, with the occupation of the Strait of Messina, to block Etruscan pirates from gaining access to the Ionian Sea. Earlier, however, the Chalcidean bases established at Pithekoussai and Cumae, which had no immediate follow-up before the expansion of Sybaris at the end of the seventh century, provided only a weak presence in the lower and middle Tyrrhenian Sea in the face of Etruscan raids, at least until the Syracusans demonstrated their naval power at the battle of Cumae in 474 BC.

Even later, at the end of the seventh century BC, this Etruscan hold over the central and southern Tyrrhenian was challenged by Phocaean trade aimed at the same region. In this way, the Etruscan-Phoenician axis came into being, setting them (and the Carthaginian successors of the Phoenicians) against the Greeks of Magna Graecia (southern Italy) and Sicily. This confrontation would last until the end of the fourth century BC, when not merely the power relationships would alter, but so would the needs, the style of living and the economy of the Greeks, Etruscans and Carthaginians, with resulting effects on economic and political ties between these groups.

Navigation and exchange in the Archaic period: the Phoenician model

We can now see that the form Phoenician commercial exchanges took around 1000 BC and during the following 200 years constituted a model for the way the Greeks and the Etruscans would conduct their Mediterranean trade. Santo Mazzarino argued in his classic study *Between East and West*, of 1947, that the *Phoinikes* of the second and of the first millennium BC should not be confused with one another, in a way that masks the memory of the Mycenaean navigators from the time that they too operated along the same trade routes and established ties with native peoples whom they visited in the second half of the second millennium. However, it goes without saying that the *Phoinikes* of historical record are unquestionably the Phoenicians. From their places of origin in Byblos, Tyre and Sidon, and from the lands in Cyprus that fell under their sway, the Phoenicians radiated across the entire Mediterranean, to Spain, Africa, Sardinia, Sicily, at least from the eleventh century BC onwards; at this point Egyptian documents already recognize them as merchants, and they remained a force until the end of the eighth century, when

Assyrian expansion and the growing Greek presence threatened their monopoly.

For several reasons, the Phoenician presence in the West has great historical importance. For the Greeks first of all but also for the Etruscans, the Italic peoples, the Libyans and the Iberians, the Phoenicians represented a powerful model for the conduct of trade and also contributed to the spread of cultural models, social institutions and indeed a whole way of life. The spread of luxury goods took place through many complex channels, closely tied to the exchange of raw materials, especially metals, from lands rich in natural resources. The varied interests of the Phoenicians are well documented in biblical texts, such as the references in Ezekiel and the Book of Kings, not to mention classical authors such as Herodotus (on wine), Pseudo-Aristotle (on oil) and Silius Italicus (on wood). The luxury goods that they transported also functioned as a channel by which ideologies were transmitted, as we shall see shortly. But the very structure of exchanges, rooted in eastern models, was then faithfully reproduced in the areas where the Phoenicians met the native peoples of the Mediterranean, and became a powerful source of diffusion for eastern culture.

The Phoenicians were in fact the bearers of a strong and special-ized tradition of artisan production which originated in Phoenicia itself, or at least in the area of Syria-Lebanon-Cyprus, but which also brought in objects and models from Egypt, Anatolia, Meso-potamia and Urartu. A brief list of goods would include products made of precious materials, whether metal, ivory or fine wood, drinking vessels made of bronze, silver and gold, large ceremonial containers such as incense burners, carts, cauldrons and tripods, perfume flasks in faïence, glass or alabaster, items of furniture with fittings made of metal or ivory, and also *athyrmata*, 'crockery', the ostrich eggs transformed into animal shapes by adding a collar, a mouth and ivory feet, or the seals and scarabs of faïence or semi-precious stone.

The acquisition of such items by those at the top of society, who had contact with the Phoenician merchants, resulted in a profound mutation in the habits of these élites, which ended up not merely imitating the social customs of the élites of the Fertile Crescent (such as ceremonial banquets, or the boiling of meat in vast cauldrons), but also adopting a whole style of life that presupposed an ideology of power similar to that exercised by the great monarchies of the East. In full accord with this, there appear among the manufactured articles imported from the East objects that were intended to indicate quite unequivocally the ceremonial image of the King as it was elaborated by Eastern courts, with thrones, footrests, sceptres, whisks, breastplates, bracelets, cloth of gold and purple vestments and so on. Thanks to the uninterrupted transmission of these symbols from the Etruscan world to that of the Romans, and then from the Romans to the Middle Ages, many of these objects would remain symbols of the power of kings and magistrates well beyond antiquity.

The Tartessian élites of the Iberian peninsula were one group who assimilated into their traditional Bronze Age culture, in which the cult of ancestors had had a particular importance, many features of Phoenician culture, thanks to their close and constant contact with the Phoenician settlements in southern Spain. In the Greek and colonial Greek setting, as in the Etruscan and Italic one (whence it would be diffused through much of Europe) the Orientalizing culture brought by the Phoenicians was rapidly imitated at a local level, as one can see from the Celtic princely tombs at Vix in France and at Asperg and Hochdorf in Germany; this culture became an indispensable instrument for the exercise of power in the archaic societies that were evolving from primitive ideas of royal power towards domination by aristocratic élites whose authority was based on some sort of servile dependence. We see first Eastern-type ceremonies of royalty based on the rites of priest-kingship, then all the opulence and exhibitionism of rituals modelled on Eastern modes (including also sometimes the use of writing). This proved compatible in the long run with the beginnings of shared power among the emerging aristocratic élites, and became the model for the further reproduction of these societies which were influenced by the cultural model imported from Phoenicia.

The spread of an Orientalizing culture depended, therefore, on the forms of contact between peoples that had already been established in the Phoenician trading networks, even though the trading centres (as one can see from their relatively marginal location) stood on the edges of mainstream society. Here what mattered was the nature of the exchanges that took place and the social organization of the native societies with whom the traders came into contact: in the case of occasional contacts with very undeveloped social structures, the standard model was that of 'silent trade', without face-to-face contact, of the sort attested when Phoenicians traded with Libyans.

Where one examines more stable relationships with complex societies, the presence of Phoenician businessmen, by agreement with the native leaders, was founded on the control of safe havens on the coasts and in particular on island bases, where they established emporia. This is plain from the evidence for Sicily before the coming of the Greeks and from the case of Cerne (probably the modern Essaouira or Mogador in Morocco); archaeologists have identified genuine trading settlements with metal workshops and artisan quarters attached to them, for instance, at Toscanos and Trayamar in Spain. These were the support centres from which Phoenician merchants developed their relations with local rulers. This seems to be reflected, though a few centuries later, in the relationship between the Phocaean traders and the Tarquins of Rome, attested by a famous passage of Justinus which derives from Pompeius Trogus, a historian from Marseille who was well informed about Phocaean colonization and settlement.

On the lines of the description by Thucydides of how Amphipolis developed from an emporium into a polis or city, these supply bases developed into true colonies, always characterized by a strong maritime vocation, and always set apart on islands, peninsulas or coastal areas which were easy to defend because they were surrounded by lagoons or marshes, as at Cádiz in Spain, at Lixus, Utica and Carthage in Africa, at Motya, Soluntum and Palermo in Sicily, at Nora, Cagliari, Bithia, Sulcis and Tharros in Sardinia. The massive influence of these colonies can be measured from the constant seep and penetration of Punic culture among the native peoples of Spain, Africa and Sardinia (though rather less in Sicily), to such an extent that it was still visible in the period of the Roman Empire, as in Numidia and the Libyan-Berber areas.

The Phoenician emporia, whose prestige spread throughout the Mediterranean (as the *Iliad* and *Odyssey* bear witness), were organized around sanctuaries which, even if controlled by native inhabitants, were dedicated to Phoenician deities and were characterized by the traditional rituals of Syrian Phoenician religion. Ancient sources, together with modern research, attribute to the arrival of the Phoenicians the foundation of several important and prestigious shrines of the classical period, such as those of Ishtar/Aphrodite at Kythera, Corinth and the Etruscan port of Pyrgi, of Sid/Sardus Pater in Sardinia and of Melkart/Hercules at Gades (Cádiz) in Spain and at the Tiber port of Rome. From these and similar sanctuaries important features of religious ritual were adopted by the local inhabitants, thus contributing to the further diffusion of ideas intimately connected to oriental power structures. We see this in the case of the sacred marriage rituals linked to Adonis, which traced their origins back to the Phoenician city most closely linked to rituals of kingship, Byblos, and which then spread throughout the Greco-Roman world, flourishing there right up to the end of antiquity.

The model of the Phoenician emporium was rapidly imitated by the Greeks, who followed many of the trade routes already laid out by the Phoenicians, and maritime routes previously less intensively utilized; the Greeks also acquired from the Semitic language of the Phoenicians technical terms concerned with trade, as well as borrowing from the Phoenicians an alphabet which further facilitated the conduct of business. Thus in the footsteps of Syrian trade, at times (certainly in the earliest phases) mixed up with the Phoenicians and with every intention of imitating their methods, the Greeks began to penetrate the Levant: first of all Euboean merchants, in the ninth to seventh centuries BC, and then in the seventh and sixth centuries traders from Ionia and the island of Aigina, they established important emporia on the Phoenician coast, between Tell Sukas in the kingdom of Hama, and Bassit (the ancient Posideion), at al-Mina at the mouth of the Orontes, in Egypt at Naukratis. Thence the movement of Greek merchants moved westwards, towards the coasts of Italy, France and Spain, in sharp competition with the Phoenicians who were after the same goods, exchanging not just Eastern goods but also Greek products, above all pottery, so that Greek items became the most widely diffused trade goods in the Mediterranean between the end of the seventh and the fourth century BC.

The imitation of the Phoenician trade counters, normally on island bases or surrounded by a wall (*teichos*), is apparent in the most ancient of the western emporia, Pithekoussai; the model was widely diffused throughout the Mediterranean, from the coasts of the Black Sea and southern Thrace to southern France (Marseille) and southern Spain, where we find a settlement which, even though it evolved into a real town in its own right, took the name of Emporion, the modern Ampurias or Empuries. This model was developed with the clear intention of guaranteeing the political and fiscal autonomy of the emporia in their relations with the native population. When, on the other hand, emporia were created in areas under the direct or indirect control of the local inhabitants, the Greeks, like the Phoenicians, organized their systems of exchange in close relationship to the nature of the social structures with which they were entering into economic ties. Thus, in the instance of societies with a tribal structure, commercial exchange was controlled directly by the local traders; but when, as in Etruria and Latium in the seventh and sixth centuries BC, the native social structures were more complex (with local princes who were the heirs of pre-historic monarchies, and the formation of urban centres), then the emporium tended to follow the classic Phoenician model, or in particular that of Naukratis. Here the focal point was a sanctuary with rights of asylum, thus assuring the safety of business partners and of the administrators of the funds donated to the temple, which constituted the earliest type of taxation. There are good examples of this type of emporium in the sanctuaries of Uni/Ishtar at Pyrgi, the port of Caere, and those of Aphrodite, Hero, Demeter and Apollo at the port of Tarquinii, Gravisca, where the willingness to appeal to Phoenician models is abundantly plain.

We can link to these cult centres a whole series of sanctuaries in Italy in which commercial exchange was taking place, including also the formation of marriage ties, which furthered social and cultural integration. This tendency to collective control of exchange would be further underlined in the Etruscan cities with the creation of republican forms of government, and thus the end of the old personal relationship between the traders and the King/tyrant, a point made plain in the clauses of the Roman-Carthaginian treaty of 509 BC recorded by the Greek historian Polybius: as in the Greek cities, trade moved from the sanctuary to the agora or forum and was placed under the control of public officials, while the merchants themselves were forbidden to stay any longer than was necessary 'in order to complete their sacrifices and load water for their journey'.

The model of the sanctuary emporium, as a centre either of 'colonial' trade or as the commercial centre servicing an entire region, thus acquired new life as a result of the emergence of the marketplace controlled by the city itself, and was perpetuated in the regular fairs and *nundinae* linked to religious festivals, a system which we find throughout Europe beyond the end of the ancient world. It was a particularly tenacious system, too, for we have the evidence of Strabo that he visited the site of the Latin colony of

Fregellae a century and a half after it had been destroyed, only to find that the inhabitants of the neighbouring towns on the Via Latina 'meet at Fregellae to hold a market and to celebrate certain religious rituals'.

From Euboean predominance to the rise of Great Ionia: seventh to sixth centuries BC

As has been seen, the forms of exchange created by the Phoenicians between the eleventh and the eighth century BC provided a model for their main rivals, the Greeks, who created their own trade counters in easily defensible positions that also functioned as cult centres. The increasing complexity of trade reflects the growing socio-political organization of the Greek world. Both in Greece proper and on the Ionian coast, the definitive expansion of the cities and of urban institutions between the eighth and the seventh century BC was reflected in military organization, around the hoplite soldiers, and in political organization, as aristocrats took power from kings. This occurred among the Euboeans, Corinthians, Achaeans, Spartans, Cretans, Olazomenians, Lesbians, Phocaeans and others who occupied the Ionian shore and the coasts of the southern Tyrrhenian Sea, as well as eastern Sicily, the southern Aegean and the coasts of the Black Sea; they also established isolated advance positions in Cyrene, in Africa, in Ampurias, in Spain and in Marseille, in Gaul, as well as along the eastern coasts of the Adriatic.

Thus the trading world of the Greeks rapidly became much enlarged. Already in the eighth century we can see that Corinth occupied a dominant role. In the first place, we find its Geometric pottery spread very widely along the western-bound trade routes of the Euboean merchants, a quite astonishing phenomenon. Thucydides in a famous passage comments on the special position acquired by the Corinthian emporia, not solely in the direction of Thrace, a sort of El Dorado where they founded Potidaia in the early sixth century, but above all on the routes towards the Adriatic, where we observe first the foundation of Corcyra (Corfu), taken by the Bacchiads from the original Euboean settlers, and then of Epidamnos (Durazzo, Dürres) in 625 BC, followed soon by Ambrakia, Leukas, Anaktorion and Apollonia. These centres helped consolidate the control over trade exercised by Corinth, particularly over the quiet passage from the Balkan shores of the Adriatic towards Italy. Corcyra was the nodal point in the dominion that Corinth sought to create along the trade routes of the Adriatic and Ionian seas; evidence for this can be found in the fact that the first naval battle recorded in ancient Greek history, dated by Thucydides to 674 BC, saw Corinth ranged against Corcyra, which clearly was trying to establish its own sphere of influence at sea.

In any event, a bitter rivalry soon made itself public, setting apart Corinthians and Euboeans, though the special geographical position of Corinth allowed it to benefit greatly from trade conducted on its behalf by other powers (notably its long-distance trade), among whom the eastern Greeks of Ionia figured prominently from the late seventh century. These circumstances help explain the impact of the colonization of the Ionian coasts of Italy and Sicily, which reflects closely the conflicts that broke out within the Greek world for control of the trade routes heading towards the central Mediterranean. The Chalcidians exercised control of the Strait of Messina, essential for access to the Tyrrhenian Sea; Thucydides explains how, first as pirates and then with their colonies at Rhegium (Reggio di Calabria) and Zankle, they colonized the whole of the southern stretch of the eastern Sicilian coast along with the men of Nassos, an area stretching from Zankle to Leontinoi. Corinth, on the other hand, was assured of dominion over the central part of the same coastline, and founded its sole colony in Sicily, that of Syracuse; flanked by its neighbours from Megaris at Megara Hyblaia, Corinth was able to draw into its web the entire Ionian Sea coast from the Gulf of Taranto to Reggio by making use of its allies from Achaia, Lokris and Lakonia, in other words from regions in the Peloponnese or around the coastline of Corinth. This formidable colonizing drive under Corinthian auspices lay at the root of the decline of Euboean influence, which we can detect from the mid-seventh century.

While Euboean commerce seems to have concentrated on the exchange of luxury items, after the manner of the Phoenicians, and on the sale of Corinthian prestige pottery, the trade of Corinth and its satellites had a different character, adding to its own pottery the export of wine and of oil from Attica (first of all) and from Corinth itself (later on). The export traffic targeted Etruria, where we can observe the arrival of Attic amphorae of the type known as 'SOS', followed by a surge in the export of Corinthian amphorae throughout the sixth century BC.

However, we can understand better the meaning of this apparent Corinthian mastery over Greek commerce in the seventh and much of the sixth century BC by taking account of the role the Greek cities played in the foundation of Naukratis; this was the sole port in the Nile Delta that was conceded to the Greek merchants by the Pharaohs, and was possibly already active in the mid-seventh century. Those cities that became involved in Naukratis were all, in fact, eastern Greek cities, apart from Aigina (of which more shortly). The towns with the greatest role in the trade of Naukratis were certainly Miletos and Samos; archaeological evidence from the first half of the sixth century confirms the importance of these towns as eastern Greek suppliers of the Italian markets, bringing pottery suited to the dining table: the so-called 'Trader Complex', which may be a sanctuary dedicated to Aphrodite of the late seventh century BC, discovered to the north of the marketplace in Corinth, along the road to the port at Lechaion, is very rich in eastern Greek goods, Lakonian goods and Etruscan bucchero vases in their distinctive black garb, alongside fine Corinthian ceramics. This site thus looks quite similar to other emporia used by the eastern Greeks, from Naukratis to Gravisca.

Corinth was in an especially powerful position sitting astride the isthmus separating the Ionian and Aegean seas, and was able to offer both sea and land transport, making use of eastern Greek sailors as intermediaries. It could offer them technical support, as in the case of Aminokles of Corinth, who built ships for the Samians (as Thucydides relates); and it could also offer rare opportunities to develop valuable trading links. The Greeks of Ionia were, for their part, assured of ready access across the Aegean to primary goods of fundamental importance, thanks to the great success of Miletos as a sea-power. Increasingly, too, the precious grain of Crimea and the Sarmatian plain filtered through to their region, laying the groundwork for the Black Sea trade linking Thrace, Crimea and the Caucasus; this would have especial importance in the classical, Hellenistic and indeed Byzantine periods, given the lack of ready food supplies in the cities of Greece proper.

Another aspect of trade and economic activity with great cultural significance is connected to the Corinthian and eastern Greek period of predominance: the arrival in barbarian lands of skilled labour and of new technologies, which entered these lands often alongside displaced aristocrats who were the major protagonists of the early trade links. In fact, from the very first contacts with the Euboeans and subsequently with the cities of Magna Graecia and Sicily, we find evidence of the arrival (particularly in Etruria) of Greek immigrants with essential know-how that could be applied to the taste for luxury of the Etruscan élites. A prime example is the career of Demaratus, a Bacchiad from Corinth, active in trade, who was said to have been expelled from Corinth and who established himself in Tarquinii where he married a noble Etruscan lady and became the father of the future Etruscan king of Rome, Tarquinius Priscus. Demaratus is supposed to have brought along with himself painters and specialists in roof decoration, thus founding a significant branch of the applied arts, if Pliny the Elder's sources are to be believed.

Thus the Greek emporia were vectors not solely of commerce but also of men, ideas and techniques, thanks in part to the pro-tected sanctuaries that offered safe haven to those who arrived from overseas. One of the first innovations of the Greeks was certainly the introduction of fine wines, perhaps the most important feature of the luxury trade of both Phoenicians and Greeks, for with wine came the rites associated with its consumption, above all the symposium or feast. The arrival among the barbarians of wine and of social practices connected to its consumption has parallels: the diffusion of olive cultivation is dated by the Roman author Fenestella to the end of the seventh century BC; and we can also see how the Hellenizing ceramics of both Anatolia and Etruria bear witness to these social, cultural and economic ties.

Technologies travel with people: the transformation of agricultural and industrial production according to Greek models was closely followed by the assimilation of elements of Greek culture, reflecting the nature of archaic trading contacts. Even the most venerable Eastern civilizations, such as that of Egypt, recognized in the archaic Greeks distinctive skills that could be put to use in building their own political and social framework; as Herodotus relates, the Pharaohs of the sixth and seventh centuries BC showed great respect for Greek civilization, despite their conviction of their own superiority, and sent gifts to the great Greek shrines. They also showed great appreciation of Greek military skills, using Greek mercenaries, whose presence is well recorded in surviving inscriptions. Artisans and merchants of Greek origin were active at the Lydian and Persian courts.

But what is really important is the role of Greek technology in the development of the 'barbarian' societies of the West, which became increasingly Hellenized. This phenomenon was so widely diffused in time and space that it is hard to draw up a precise list of objects, peoples and places; but part of this process originated in the contact between the Greek elites and the 'barbarian' ones, while Greek artisans penetrated deep into 'barbarian' societies, forming the basis for localized production of all those goods that indicated the spread of Greek habits and customs.

It would be impossible to overestimate the importance of these Greek commercial connections in the diffusion of Greek culture beyond Hellas: the rich evidence from Gravisca, archaeological and epigraphic, reveals the impact of Greek merchants very far from their homeland, as does humbler evidence from the lead-inscribed lettering found at Berezan, Ampurias and Pech Maho; here we find evidence that elaborate lending systems and personal guarantees had come into existence, binding the native inhabitants to Greek and Etruscan businessmen. This growing Hellenization, even if it varied in intensity, was a powerful force among the 'barbarian' peoples of Anatolia, the Balkans, Italy, the Punic areas, Iberia and certain Celtic areas as well, long before the great wave of Hellenization that accompanied the creation of the Hellenistic world in the fourth century BC.

The growing prestige of the economic and social system of the Greek city-state was one factor in the spread of Greek culture; but so was the constant, lasting nature of the commercial ties and the diffusion of Greek skills in remote areas which were desirous of obtaining goods produced by able Greek artisans. Here the advantages of obtaining such goods cheaply rather than relying on the thousand dangers that buying them from Greece involved was also a consideration. It is important to recall that, with the often total silence of sources relating to navigation and exchange, it is frequently archaeology which provides the best evidence for the movement of goods and men.

The nature of trade in the late Archaic and Classical periods
The main novelty to be observed at the start of the sixth century BC is the entrance on the scene of a new type of ship, which replaced the slower boats with a pronounced bow, the *strongylon*, which had served Mediterranean mariners since prehistoric times. The new vessel was the fifty-oared fast warship known as the *pentekontura*, which, according to Herodotus, was first adopted in Phocaea. There

were many important results of this innovation. The ships were well suited to use by bold pirates, and piracy, already endemic in the Mediterranean, became even more widespread, as the earliest sources make plain. The smaller amount of space on board the new ships rendered several changes in the character of trade necessary, favouring the carriage of high-value goods of small size. The only significant example to survive, that found off the island of Giglio in the Tyrrhenian Sea, contained arms and a limited range of goods, underlining the fact that trade had become less safe and that there had been a shift towards commerce in luxury items. Important in these developments was the role of the Phocaeans in the foundation of Marseille (600 BC) and then of Emporion/Ampurias (around 520 BC), in areas traditionally dominated by Etruscan and Phoenician shipping.

But this phase was of relatively short duration. By the mid-sixth century, the pressure of the Lydian rulers on the coast of Anatolia brought about a decline in Ionian navigation along the routes that had traditionally been controlled by the Greeks. The exodus of the inhabitants of Phocaea in 542 BC symbolizes the changes taking place in trade and navigation. The Phocaeans, forced out of their home town, tried to establish themselves among the western Greeks with whom they had close relations (particularly with their cousins in Marseille). But they were repulsed, and then tried to settle in Corsica at Alalia (Aleria), threatening the Etruscans, for whom nearby Elba was a major source of wealth and for whom trade along the coast from the Arno to the mouth of the Rhône (inhabited by Ligurians) was also important.

The Etruscans did not hang back; the rival fleets met in the sea off Sardinia. The Etruscans had the support of their traditional allies the Carthaginians, who not long before had begun to take over the Phoenician colonies in Sardinia and Sicily, and were anxious to preserve the status quo in the western Mediterranean. The Etruscans suffered severe losses, but they forced the Phocaeans to abandon

Corsica forever and to flee to Campania, where, with the support of the men of Poseidonia who had been established there under the aegis of Sybaris (a traditional ally of the Ionians), they founded the colony of Elea.

The intensification of pressure on the Ionian cities that followed Persian advances into the region set off a revolt among the eastern Greeks against their new masters. This reached a rapid conclusion with the naval defeat of the rebels at Ladis in 494 BC, after which the maritime achievements of the eastern Greeks became only a memory. But from the first half of the sixth century BC two cities, Aigina and Athens, became significant powers at sea. Indeed, they had both been members of the ancient Amphictyonic League of Kalauria, but both places had played little part in the great colonizing movements of earlier centuries and had a somewhat marginal role in the sharing out of markets and trade routes during the eighth and most of the seventh century BC. But their rise in the sixth century BC was very rapid.

Aigina already had a sanctuary at Naukratis, and in the sixth century began to take over the routes previously followed by the eastern Greeks; it soon imposed its own money, the most ancient in the Greek world, on the markets it served. It took over the role of Samos in the trade of Kydonia, on the Cretan coast, in 510 BC, after the former fell under Persian sway. At the end of the sixth century BC Herodotus described Sostratos, the son of Laodamus of Aigina, as 'the greatest merchant of all time'; he is known also from archaeological evidence and from inscriptions as the patron of the shrines in Naukratis and Gravisca and as the agent for the transport to Etruria of previously unheard of quantities of Attic pottery. Athens in the years after Solon's rule in fact developed a ceramic industry which, making use of pre-existing networks, imposed itself on all the Mediterranean markets by the middle of the sixth century. The development of an Attic coinage, the so-called *Wappenmünzen*, in the same period, found most plentifully in the *naukrariai* (the areas traditionally inhabited by the sailors), also reveals the peaceful progress of Athenian shipping on the high seas. At the start of the fifth century BC the rivalry between the cities of Aigina and Athens became quite bitter, taking the form of battles and armed encounters.

By 458 BC Athens had seen off Aigina for good, and began an apparently irresistible rise to power; the positive ending of the Persian wars and the creation of the Delian League gave Athens undisputed primacy at sea along with its Attic allies. This Athenian hegemony permitted the intensive movement of Attic ships (notably those of Athens' allies) across the Aegean and the eastern Mediterranean, carrying Thracian gold, Macedonian wood, Black Sea grain, to mention the most significant items in a vast trading network whose basis had been founded in previous centuries by the Greek cities and their colonies.

But change took place not merely in the Aegean marketplace. In a manner that was even more decisive than in the Archaic period, the beginning of the fifth century BC and the end of the Persian peace, which had been crucial in the development of central Mediterranean traffic, saw a new role for the colonies of Magna Graecia and Sicily (especially Syracuse). The severe defeat suffered by the Carthaginians on land at Himera (480 BC), and that off Cumae by the Etruscan navy (474 BC), demonstrated both the decline of traditional Etruscan sea power and the entry into Tyrrhenian waters of a powerful Syracusan navy. The subsequent Syracusan occupation of Pithekoussai, followed by the raids of 453 BC aimed at Elba and Corsica, helps one understand how the old, increasingly fragile, equilibrium of the Archaic period had been fractured, and how a new set of relations was coming into being.

The far West remained the uncontested sphere of influence of Carthage, as it would be until the collision with Rome in the third century BC. However, the routes across the central Mediterranean, leading to the important markets of Etruria and the Gulf of Lions, which had previously been controlled first by the Euboeans and then by the Ionians, became the focus of a contest between the Athenians and the Syracusans. This is demonstrated not merely by the close alliances between the Athenians and the colonies of Magna Graecia (including the foundation of Thourioi in 444 BC), but also by the partly diplomatic, partly military expedition of Diotymas to Naples in 433 BC, on behalf of Athens.

At the same time, thanks to a firm alliance with Corcyra, trade up the Adriatic towards the Po delta fell under Athenian control, inundating the rich Etruscan colonies of the Paduan plain with its vases, including the style known as Corinthian B which was used to bring wine from the former Corinthian colonies in Ionia and Illyria. The Etruscan maritime cities turned into backers of Athens against Syracuse, supporting the former in its Sicilian adventure in 415 BC. The outlook of Corinth was linked to the fortunes of its former colony of Syracuse, while its own money, which had taken over from that of Aigina as the principal form of cash circulating in the western Greek cities, competed with that of Athens in the disputed markets of the Tyrrhenian Sea.

Against the background of the Peloponnesian War, and above all of the disastrous Athenian expedition against Syracuse, we can observe the rivalries which had been born out of competition for control of the trade routes linking East and West. The results of increasingly fine analysis of the ceramic evidence, above all the examination of amphorae discovered in excavations throughout the Mediterranean, enable us to perceive more clearly the panorama of trade routes existing in the fifth and fourth centuries BC, trade routes which (by comparison with the Archaic period) seem reasonably stable.

The presence of Carthage beyond the traditional Phoenician sphere of influence was quite limited; however, the quantitative data recovered for the sixth century BC from the amphorae found at Etruscan Gravisca reveal that a tenth of the amphorae were of a

Punic type, hardly a negligible proportion of the trade conducted in the vital marketplace of the central Tyrrhenian region.

A similar picture presents itself of the Etruscan trade routes towards Liguria and southern France in the fifth and for much of the fourth century BC, including occasional visits to northern Spain. The wide diffusion in the Archaic and Classical periods of amphorae of the Corinthian B type is a sign of the henceforth independent policies of Corcyra, which was now in full competition with its mother city of Corinth and had become an ally of Athens. At Spina in northeastern Italy almost all the amphorae of the fifth and fourth centuries were from Corcyra; thus its alliance with Athens gave the former Corinthian colony a great boost.

The role of Magna Graecia and Sicily is more uncertain. The similarities between the so-called Ionic-Massaliot amphorae, which were quite widely diffused in the Archaic period and which can probably be attributed to the western Greek colonies, and the amphorae from Magna Graecia and Sicily of the fourth century, is notable. Taking into account further similarities with Corinthian B amphorae, this material will enable scholars to set out the origins and development of the production of amphorae in Greek Italy, to make sense of links with Corinth and the Ionian world, and to describe the routes taken in western Greek trade and the extent to which it overlapped (as Archaic Ionian trade had done earlier) with the Etruscan and Carthaginian commercial spheres. However, it should also be borne in mind that Carthaginian conquests in fourth-century central and western Sicily gave a Punic flavour to the trade in wine out of the Carthaginian provinces in Sicily.

To a large degree the Classical period, by comparison with the sixth century BC, changed mainly the masters of the trade network, and only to a small extent the origin and destination of the goods carried. The true change in the routes, in the manner of production and in the exchange of those goods that lay at the heart of Mediterranean trade, occurred in the second half of the fourth century BC;

it was marked by the increasing preponderance of Greco-Italic amphorae in the markets, carrying the produce of Roman and Campanian vineyards whose wine was the fruit of an alliance between the Roman nobility and the aristocracy of the Campanian cavalry classes. But this is an event that belongs to the history of Roman imperialism which at this time was in a phase of slow, if inexorable, gestation – a true giant that emerged slowly, but no less fearsomely, from the mists at the heart of the Italian peninsula.

The Mediterranean described by Mario Torelli, in which
Phoenicians and later Carthaginians, Etruscans and Greeks
competed for control of the trade routes, changed character
decisively with the rise to power of Rome, a city whose origins
(setting aside the rich legends of Aeneas and Romulus) must
be traced back to the confluence of Etruscan and Latin culture
at the mouth of the Tiber. The depth of Etruscan influence on
Rome can be seen in the way that the names of many gods and
heroes were remoulded as they passed from Greek through
Etruscan speech into Latin: Persephone became Proserpina,
Odysseus Ulysses, while the Latin name for Athena – Minerva –
was shared with the Etruscans (Menrva). The demands of trade
led the Romans also to adopt their alphabet from the Etruscans.

Still, no one would have guessed that the future lay with
Rome: though the Romans destroyed their powerful rival and
close neighbour, Veii, in 396 BC, the Gallic invasion of 390 BC
suggested that the wars between Romans and Etruscans were not
the only source of instability. Three wars against another mighty
Mediterranean power, Carthage, were also fought before Rome
put an end to the threat posed by Punic power in the central
Mediterranean. Alongside these victories, the slow process of
colonizing lands which had fallen subject to Rome, of asserting
Latin culture within the ethnically and culturally diverse
Italian peninsula, and eventually of winning control of the
Mediterranean islands gave the necessary depth to this broadly
extended political authority. Yet Rome remained a culture that
looked up to Greek models, as the Etruscans had done before, so
that the earliest fragments of Latin literature include translations
of Greek drama, while Latin poets attempted to adapt the metre
system of Greek, well suited to such a sonorous language, to the
needs of the harder tongue they spoke.

These events in the West were paralleled by major changes
in the East during the fourth century. In the fifth century, the
Peloponnesian War illustrated the lasting importance of
the struggle for the control of trade routes linking Greece to

Italy and the Adriatic; it also marked a heroic moment in the assertion of Athenian political values in the face of the stark and uncompromising challenge posed by the dreary Spartans. But city-state politics were to change character forever. In the past Athens and its allies had fought off Persian emperors; but the real challenge was now more local.

The kingdom of Macedon, whose inhabitants were regarded as semi-barbarians by the inhabitants of the Hellenic cities, became a great power first within Greece, under Philip II of Macedon, and then on a world scale, as his son Alexander marched his armies into Syria, Egypt, Babylonia, Persia and the borders of India. Though he died young, and though his empire was then split between three rival warlords, Alexander left a legacy of absolutely fundamental importance. Greek culture, fused with the ancient cultures of Persia and Egypt, struck deep roots in the eastern Mediterranean; the Hellenistic period was one of active city building, flourishing trade, the spread of divine cults out of Greece and Egypt, providing the essential backdrop for the diffusion of a new religion that grew out of Judaism but rapidly came to lay more emphasis on its universal vocation: Pauline Christianity. Even the Roman conquest of Greece in the middle of the first century BC, and the establishment of Roman power in Egypt under Julius Caesar and Mark Antony, did not undermine the predominance of Hellenic culture.

The great symbol of this culture was a maritime city that was inhabited by people of hundreds of nations, but which still possessed a predominantly Greek character: Alexander the Great's foundation in Egypt, Alexandria, which was to house the greatest library of the ancient world. In Alexandria, the seat of a massive Jewish community, the weekly Torah reading was delivered in Greek, for seventy-two wise men of the city had closeted themselves away in isolation from one another to translate the Hebrew Bible, only to produce (so legend relates) seventy-two identical versions, the translation known as the Septuagint which remains in daily use in the Greek Orthodox

Church. It is not even clear if the great Alexandrian Jewish philosopher Philo could read Hebrew; his works were, again, preserved by the Greek Church.

Taken together, then, the expansion of Rome, which came to include Carthaginian territories in Spain as well as Italy, and the creation of the Hellenistic *oikoumene* ('community') transformed the Mediterranean by bringing to it increasing political and cultural unity. The distinction between a Latin West and a Greek East would persist for many centuries; but these two spheres were now gradually beginning to function in harmony with one another. It is true that the Ptolemies in Egypt, the Seleucids in Syria, and other warlords, continued to campaign against one another, perpetuating the rivalries of those lands in pre-Hellenistic times; their grasp of local problems could be woefully poor, as emerged in Judaea when Antiochus Epiphanes tried to introduce his cult into the Jewish Temple, leading to the Maccabaean revolt. But this was still a world in which the individualistic concerns of city-states such as Athens and Sparta were now subordinated to larger political entities.

Growing political unity brought prosperity to commerce, as piracy was restrained and as the long-distance movement of vital goods, such as Egyptian and Sicilian grain, was facilitated. The effects were visible, too, in the adoption of classical styles of architecture and sculpture throughout the Mediterranean. The Romans showed such strong affection for Greek classical art that the emperors and other great men filled their palaces with copies of the works of Praxiteles and Pheidias; indeed, many a great work of classical Greek sculpture is now known only through its surviving Roman copies. In the following chapter, Geoffrey Rickman shows how Polybius, the Greek historian of Rome, became aware that events around the Mediterranean were all interconnected. The Mediterranean was becoming one world.

FOUR

The creation of *Mare Nostrum*: 300 BC – AD 500

GEOFFREY RICKMAN

Alexander the Great died in Babylon in 323 BC. The enormous extent of his conquests, deep into Asia, and the place of his death, in Mesopotamia, might seem to indicate that not only had the world changed, but that its focus had moved eastwards, inland, away from the Mediterranean Sea.

This proved to be far from the case, as the rival successors to Alexander's empire, with their kingdoms strewn from Macedonia and northern Greece, through Asia Minor, Egypt and Syria, struggled fiercely for power by sea as well as by land. The Antigonid kings in Macedonia and the Ptolemies in Egypt in particular were in bitter conflict for control of the eastern Mediterranean.

The 'Hellenistic' world, as the period after the death of Alexander is termed by modern scholars, was indeed Greek, in language, culture and institutions, at least in the crust thinly overlaid on top of the multifarious peoples whom Alexander had overrun. Greek-style cities, equipped with temples, agoras and gymnasia, abounded, and there was community of attitude and outlook between them. But, with some exceptions, they were more units of administration than autonomous political entities, as in the past. The scale and resources of the old *poleis,* city-states, of the Greek world, even of such powers as Athens and Corinth, were now vastly exceeded by the new kingdoms. This allowed Antigonids and Ptolemies to indulge in a kind of 'arms race' at sea, where ever larger warships were constructed. Triremes, 'threes', the standard warships of earlier Athenian fleets, low, fast, strong vessels, used skilfully to ram their enemies, were replaced by 'fours', 'fives', 'eights', 'sixteens', 'twenties', 'thirties', and even a 'forty'.

How such ships were oared and rowed is a subject of controversy. It is unlikely that the number of banks of oars ever exceeded the three banks used on the triremes of the past. But the numbers of rowers for each oar, their position and their rowing motion probably all changed. Fortunately this age of 'gigantism' and conspicuous display by the Hellenistic kings did not last. From the mid-third century BC the commonest type of warship throughout the Mediterranean was the 'five', the quinquireme. Nor in the end were the ferocious struggles of the successors in eastern waters to decide the fate of the Mediterranean sea. For that we need to look further west.

In 273 BC one of the other aspirants to Alexander's power, Pyrrhus, king of Epirus in northern Greece, tried to intervene in the affairs of southern Italy and of Sicily to extend his influence and possessions – perhaps to be an Alexander in the West. His efforts were frustrated by Rome, a small republic in central Italy. That rebuff of a Hellenistic king, at the head of a considerable force, at a time when Greek military prestige was at its height, was a portent. It certainly brought Rome to the attention of a wider world.

But it was the clash in Sicily with the Phoenician state, Carthage, which propelled Rome firmly on to the Mediterranean stage, and into becoming a sea power. Later tradition exaggerated Roman ignorance and inexperience of the sea before the outbreak of the First Punic War in 264 BC. Rome had had links for generations both with Etruscans to the north, and Greek colonies to the south of her, each with fine seafaring traditions. Carthage itself, a Phoenician colony in North Africa, set magnificently on the north coast of what is now Tunisia, and with aspirations to control Sicily had maritime connections all over the western Mediterranean and back to the Levant. From perhaps the sixth century BC Rome had had a series of treaties with Carthage, which defined among other things where

Roman ships might and might not go. By 311 BC Rome had created the office of *duumviri navales,* 'to repair and equip the fleet', probably for coastal defence, and added in 267 BC the *quaestores classici,* 'quaestors of the fleet', stationed in various coastal towns, such as Ostia at the Tiber mouth.

Nevertheless it was the realization that the conflict with Carthage in Sicily could not be won by land alone, but demanded the cutting of the sea links with Carthage itself, which put the naval efforts by Rome on a new plane. A bigger war fleet of quinquiremes than Rome had ever possessed was needed. In fact in a war which lasted twenty-three years, with prodigious losses on both sides, the creation of fleet after fleet, of hundreds of vessels each, was to be demanded. The Romans improvised at the start, to counter the greater maritime skill of the Carthaginians, turning sea battles into land battles. Boarding bridges with a spike at the end (*corvi,* 'crows'), grappled the enemy fast, and allowed soldiers to pour across. Later these devices were abandoned, and with growing naval skill, and unrivalled supplies of manpower, Rome outlasted and outfought her enemy.

The secret of Rome's strength lay in her system of alliances within Italy. Instead of taking tribute from her allies she required troop contributions. The allied troops took part in her campaigns, and benefited from the success and booty won. Carthage by contrast had a tribute-paying 'empire', held down by repression, and a mercenary army who served for pay. The point was reinforced when the war ended in 241 BC with the Roman victory at sea in the battle of the Aegates (Egidi) islands off western Sicily. The major part of Sicily was ceded to Rome, and to that were rapidly added in 238 BC Corsica and Sardinia, where unpaid mercenaries were in revolt from their defaulting Carthaginian paymasters.

Carthage's humiliation and losses led to her seeking compensation in southern and eastern Spain, an area of great agricultural and mineral wealth. A remarkable family of Carthaginian generals, of whom Hannibal is the most famous, were very successful in extending her power and influence in the area. Hannibal's attack on Saguntum, a town on the east coast of Spain, and an ally of Rome, became the pretext for the second great war between Carthage and Rome, which lasted from 218 to 201 BC. Rome had every intention of fighting this war, as she had the previous one, away from Italy, in Spain and in Africa. But Hannibal made his famed pre-emptive strike, invading Italy itself over the Alps. Initially he won a series of stupendous victories in the peninsula but the invasion ultimately failed. After a decade he was forced to withdraw to Africa to look to the defence of Carthage itself. Crucially he had failed to shake the loyalty of the majority of Rome's allies in central Italy, who had a vested interest in Rome's success. They helped Rome to continue to field multiple armies to fight campaigns in Spain and to invade Africa, while still dogging Hannibal's heels in Italy. But what ultimately doomed Hannibal's invasion was what also had helped to cause it, namely Carthaginian weakness and lack of confidence at sea – a legacy of the First Punic War. Hannibal could not easily be reinforced from either Spain or Africa by fresh troops. With Hannibal's final defeat in Africa and the end of the war, Carthage's Spanish possessions along its southern and eastern coasts were ceded to Rome. The shores of the western Mediterranean, not just the Tyrrhenian Sea, were beginning to pass into Roman control.

Polybius, the Greek historian of Rome who wrote in the middle of the second century BC, and was an acute and privileged observer of Rome's rise to power, since he spent time as a hostage-cum-guest with the family of Scipio, the victor over Hannibal, made a famous comment on the Hannibalic War. 'Previously', he said, 'the doings of the inhabited world were held together by no unity ... but ever since this date [the 140th Olympiad, 220–216 BC] history has been an organic whole, and the affairs of Italy and Africa have been interlinked with those of Greece and Asia – all leading up to one end.' Polybius' story is, then, about the way the Romans became lords both of the land, and of what he called 'our sea'.

It was a very perceptive remark, and he was of course right. But why? The answer lies in the consequences of the Hannibalic War. Philip V of Macedon had become an ally of Hannibal while the latter was in Italy. Rome determined that he had to be punished, and became involved in war with Macedon, the ancient kingdom of Alexander himself. There seems to have been no desire by the Romans for acquisition of new territory in this area, unlike the West. There was even the rather theatrical gesture of declaring Greece 'free' in 196 BC. This simply acted as a temptation to the Seleucid king in Asia, Antiochus, to interfere in Greek affairs. He too had to be punished, driven from Greece, and pursued into Asia Minor (modern Turkey). It was the first Roman crossing into the East. The great Hellenistic kingdoms were proving no match for Rome, and Rome was becoming inextricably entangled in the affairs of the East, despite earlier attempts at withdrawal.

By 146 BC Roman attitudes were hardening, and there occurred two atrocities which shook the Mediterranean world – the destruction in the same year of the ancient cities of Carthage in the west and Corinth in the east. Carthage's obliteration had been preceded by a short war from 149 BC, triggered by a Roman demand that Carthage transplant herself away from the sea altogether. There was a bitter siege followed by the razing of the city. Corinth's fate was more sudden, a terrible example to the rest of Greece to behave itself while enjoying its 'freedom'. Both were states of great antiquity, both were maritime to their core, and both were to be refounded by the Romans themselves later, but the message was clear. Rome would brook no rival in dominance of the seas, and of the world connected by the seas.

Rome's intolerance of rivals at sea, however, did not result in the maintenance of any great war fleet during the second and first centuries BC such as she had developed in the third century BC during the First Punic War. Increasingly she relied on the ships of her naval allies among the Greek states of southern Italy, and as campaigns in the East developed, under generals like Lucullus and Pompey, on the ships of her allies in the Aegean and the Levant – the traditional maritime states of the East. The result of this lack of proper Roman naval fleets, and of arbitrary Roman policies, such as the slighting of the power of Rhodes, which had maintained some sort of policing of the seas, was the increasing growth of piracy. Roman efforts at suppression of the main pirate bases in Cilicia in southern Turkey were half-hearted, or incompetent, and piracy had become a menace by the first century BC. Even in Italy, Ostia at the mouth of the Tiber, only 20 km (12 miles) from Rome itself, had been attacked by pirates in 87 BC. The situation was not to be tolerated. In 67 BC Pompey was given comprehensive special powers to sweep the Mediterranean clear of pirates. Within sixty days he had finished his task, and, although it never completely disappeared, piracy on a significant scale was not to be seen again in the Mediterranean for hundreds of years.

By this time, of all the Hellenistic successor kingdoms only Ptolemaic Egypt, perhaps the richest of them all, remained outside the circle of Roman annexation or control. With Cleopatra, the last of the Ptolemaic rulers, intriguing to restore the full power of her kingdom and its outlying possessions, and hoping to use first Julius Caesar and then Mark Antony for her purposes, Egypt was drawn fully into the centre of Roman politics. The circle of Roman control of the Mediterranean was about to be completed.

The possibility of direct Roman intervention in Egypt, was a tantalizing prospect for all the major political figures during the last decades of the Republic. But it finally came about as the result of the struggle for power between Mark Antony and Octavian, the future Emperor Augustus. That struggle was finally settled not by land but by sea, in what was to be the last great sea battle in ancient history, the battle of Actium off the west coast of Greece in 31 BC. That victory and the subsequent seizure of Egypt was a significant personal coup for Octavian. Its annexation put into his hands great accumulated wealth, and enormous natural resources, particularly grain, of which Rome and the Mediterranean world had great need. It also yielded a great port, Alexandria, which was an outlet not just for the resources of Egypt, but for the luxury and other goods of the East from Arabia, India and China. It is not surprising that Egypt, though a Roman province, always remained peculiarly bound to the personal control of the Emperor.

Octavian gradually, and with great guile, transformed himself from the last of the rival dynasts of the late Republic into the first Roman emperor, Augustus. While he pretended always that the Republic and republican forms of government still continued, the realities were changing, and not least at sea. After collecting together the remnants of the various battle fleets for a period at Forum Iulii (Fréjus) in southern France, he established new permanent naval bases at Misenum on the Bay of Naples, and Ravenna on the Adriatic. Smaller naval detachments were placed elsewhere, for example on the coast of North Africa and on the Black Sea, so as to maintain a permanent naval control. Not least among Roman aims was, of course, to secure the safety of the Emperor himself by controlling all the approaches to Italy; as the Roman historian Tacitus tartly pointed out: 'Armies, provinces, fleets, the whole system was interrelated.' But a permanent navy also helped to inhibit piracy, sea raiding and general lawlessness at sea.

Whatever the new Emperor's motives might have been and the political sophistries he adopted, the result was an unchallenged Roman domination, and imperial control, of the Mediterranean Sea. Men knew that and were grateful. A touching story, preserved in the Roman biographer, Suetonius, illustrates the point. During Augustus' final illness in AD 14, his ship with the old emperor on board passed one of the great grain ships from Alexandria arriving at the port of Puteoli on the Bay of Naples. The passengers and crew, recognizing him, put on white robes and garlands, burned incense and showered him with blessings and thanks for the safety of the seas. A great age had begun.

Our knowledge of this age of sea traffic has now been greatly increased by the discipline of underwater archaeology. The invention of the aqualung, and its development, by Jacques Cousteau, in the period after the Second World War, allowed for the first time the proper investigation of the sea bed, at least in shallower waters. The ability of divers to stay under water for a length of time, relatively unencumbered, meant that not only was it possible to recover individual objects such as amphorae, jars for carrying oil and wine, but to carry out proper underwater excavations of wreck sites. Such excavations have given increasing precision to our knowledge of ship-building techniques, the size of ships, cargoes carried and routes taken. Caution has to be exercised in drawing conclusions and making generalizations, because some areas have been more intensively investigated than others; some of the excavations in the early days were less expert than they might have been; and deep-sea areas of the Mediterranean are beyond the reach of the aqualung. But even so, more than 1,000 wrecks have already been discovered. From them it is clear that in the period from 200 BC to AD 200 there was an intensity of traffic by sea which was not to be matched again for a thousand years. There can be no doubt whatever that the Mediterranean Sea was of the greatest importance to the world of Rome and its Empire.

The way in which the Romans themselves referred to the sea adds weight to this conclusion. Originally the Mediterranean seems, for practical purposes, to have been viewed as a series of smaller seas, whose names most often were taken from neighbouring coasts or islands – *Mare Tyrrhenum*, 'the Tyrrhenian Sea', *Mare Balearicum*, 'the Balearic Sea'. The term *Mare Mediterraneum* seems not to have been used at all until relatively late. The geographer Solinus appears to have used it in the second half of the third century AD, and our first direct knowledge of it is in Isidore of Seville in the sixth century AD. When the Romans wanted to talk about the whole sea, they referred to it as *Mare Magnum*, *Mare Internum* or *Mare Nostrum*, 'the great sea', 'the internal sea' or 'our sea'. The two latter terms are the most interesting for us. The Mediterranean sea did indeed provide Rome with the internal routes of expansion and empire. They were used by officials, soldiers, migrants, slaves, craftsmen, itinerant preachers – in fact all and sundry – no less than merchants as such. With control of all the lands around the sea in Roman hands, the Mediterranean became an internal lake, 'our sea'. The Greeks had used a similar term before, *he thalassa he kath' hemas* – 'the sea over by us', 'our sea', to be sure, but only in a strictly limited sense. For the Romans of the early Empire it really was *Mare Nostrum*, 'our sea', all of it, and with appendages in the Black Sea and Red Sea, and even beyond the Strait of Gibraltar. This complete political dominance, and use, of the whole Mediterranean by one power had never occurred before, nor has it happened – in quite the same way – since.

The Roman possession and enjoyment of the sea came ultimately to be expressed in the fullest possible way. Maritime villas, for example, in favoured areas like the Bay of Naples, flaunted the wealth and taste of their owners to the passing shipping, and with their towers and colonnades helped in turn to provide recognizable day-marks for navigation. Such villas had their own miniature harbours and mooring facilities, just as ordinary workshops, and craft industries in places like the Istrian peninsula in the northern Adriatic had jetties and moles for loading goods. Along the edge of the sea were areas of salt-pans, as at Ostia, and fish farms, as at Cosa in Italy, and especially along the south coast of Spain. The latter could be large – commercial establishments for the production of salt fish, and above all *garum*, fish sauce, which came to be exported all over the Roman world.

Roman sea trade was dominated, as it had been since time immemorial, by small-scale *cabotage,* tramping from port to port. The world of Mediterranean coastlines was interconnected in a way that their hinterlands, often cut by mountains or marshes, could not be. This interconnectedness was just as well since there was greater

variation in climatic conditions and productivity from place to place
– even those in close proximity – than sweeping generalizations
about 'Mediterranean climate' and 'Mediterranean crops' might
lead one to believe. Despite proclaimed ideals of 'self sufficiency',
mutual interdependence was very much the order of the day, if it
could be achieved, and the sea made it possible. The conditions of
navigation in antiquity, subject to wind and weather, dependent on
human muscle, and how much could be carried by way of drinking
water and food, demanded anyway that there should be ports, harbours, refuges or at least landing beaches at regular intervals, say
every 50–70 km (30–45 miles). So *cabotage* was the natural way the
world worked from every point of view.

But with the coming of complete Roman dominance came
also other navigational patterns. It had always been the case since
the days of the Phoenicians, if not earlier, that long voyages could
be undertaken, if need be. Phoenician trade and colonization had
stretched from the Levant to the coasts of Africa, Spain and beyond.
The Greeks had sent colonizing expeditions to Sicily, southern Italy
and the western Mediterranean. But with the Roman Empire came
long-distance, high-seas trade in major commodities, with regular
rhythms which, as it were, ploughed the seas in an annual cycle just
like the land. The focus for much of this long-distance trade, when it
was not the army, was the city of Rome itself. It was in many cases the
state's imperatives which dictated the patterns of trade, although
the actual operations might be left in the hands of private merchants.

The city of Rome and its surrounding area in the time of Augustus seems to have had a population of at least one million, and
possibly more. The sustaining of that number of people in one area
outstripped all local resources. It demanded the import of massive
amounts of grain, oil and wine from wherever there might be a
significant surplus, often in the southern Mediterranean. The First
Punic War had by 241 BC put Sicily, one of the traditional granaries
of the Mediterranean throughout history, into Roman hands; the

Second Punic War had by 200 BC added southern and eastern Spain, an area which if pacified could yield great agricultural surpluses, particularly olive oil; the Third Punic War in 146 BC yielded up Africa, the homeland of Carthage, well farmed by the Carthaginians (who had a complete technical literature on agronomy, later translated into Latin), with rich potential in grain and oil; then with Cleopatra's death in 30 BC Egypt, which even from biblical times had been associated with grain surpluses, became part almost of the patrimony of the emperors of Rome.

By the late Republic, as we know from Cicero's speeches against Verres, the governor of Sicily in the first century BC, the Romans had been regularly taking grain tithes from Sicily, based on a system there developed by Hieron, the Greek ruler of Syracuse. Similarly, the Romans seem to have been quick to take control of the grain system in Egypt. Dominated by the river Nile and its annual flood, Egypt had always been highly centralized, particularly under the Ptolemies. It was easy for Rome to take over the system of flood control, harvest, transport downriver to Alexandria, and storage in granaries in the Neapolis and Mercurium districts of that city. Grain was then released, through the harbours, with their famous lighthouse, the Pharos, on to the sea, with the proviso now that Rome was the premier, if not the sole, destination for the grain ships.

In fact the ships made not for Rome itself in the first instance, but for Puteoli (Pozzuoli), the great natural harbour on the Bay of Naples which had always been the usual destination in Italy for traffic from the eastern Mediterranean. The Greek states in this area of southern Italy had for centuries developed maritime facilities while Rome itself lacked a proper harbour. Seneca in the mid-first century AD tells in a letter of the excitement generated in Puteoli by the first sight of the forerunners of the grain fleet from Alexandria, and how people gathered to watch the great cargo ships arrive from Egypt. Clearly state officials and some state organization were involved in the Alexandrian grain fleet. But as the discovery of a group of wax tablets at Murecine (near Pompeii and Puteoli) has shown, ordinary businessmen and merchants at Puteoli dealt in part at least in this grain, raised loans on it and speculated with it. There was a mixture of public and private involvement.

By the second century AD the territories in North Africa and the hinterland of Carthage achieved greater and greater development, so much so that the ports of what is today Tunisia sent increasing amounts of grain to Rome. The Emperor Commodus at the end of the century organized an African corn fleet in imitation of the one from Alexandria. By the fourth century AD, as we know from one of the great law codes of the Late Empire, the *Codex Theodosianus*, the collection and transport of grain from Africa was elaborately organized to bring it, and other produce such as olive oil, regularly on the shorter journey from the African harbours to Rome. But the main flow of oil came from southern Spain, as seen in the great tumulus of smashed, round-bellied, oil amphorae in Rome, the Monte Testaccio. The valley of the river Guadalquivir from Cádiz up through Seville and beyond in what was the Roman province of Baetica was an immensely rich source of agricultural produce of all kinds – oil, grain and wine. With good communications by river and road throughout the region, and wealthy shippers and merchants long established at Gades (Cádiz) ready to exploit their opportunities, the traffic from southern and eastern Spain, and southern Gaul, was vigorous.

The types of ships used for this traffic could in some cases be very specialized. We know, for example, of wine carriers, which instead of simply stacking wine amphorae in the hold as was normal, were virtual 'tankers', with a dozen or more *dolia*, giant jars, for *vin ordinaire*, also built into them. There were also specialist 'stone carriers', *naves lapidariae,* strongly built and much needed. Large amounts of building materials, including stone columns, granites and marbles, were transported from quarries in the Aegean, Turkey, Egypt and Africa to decorate the great building schemes of the emperors in Rome.

But the majority of ships were probably rather different in kind, most quite small, able to carry 60–70 tons of very mixed cargo. In one shipwreck, for example, mill stones, as well as metal ingots, amphorae, fine kitchenware and crockery have all been found. A number of ships were larger, with a carrying capacity of 300–400 tons. One of the most exemplary of underwater excavations, off the south of France (Madrague de Giens), revealed a ship of this size, carrying a mass of wine amphorae, stacked with almost scientific precision in interlocking rows. How much bigger even than this Roman cargo ships might have been is an object of controversy. There are literary references to 'monsters' carrying 1,000 tons and more. In terms of ship technology in antiquity there was no reason why ships of such size might not be built, though there might be economic reasons for not going to the limits of what technology allowed. However, it has been argued that the grain freighters from Alexandria to Italy were just such giant ships, not least because bulk carriage of such a commodity on such a route made good economic sense. This must remain uncertain until further evidence accrues. Unfortunately, grain is the most perishable of cargoes and it is the cargo which helps to preserve the remains of the actual hull of a ship on the sea bed, giving some indication of its size.

Whatever their size, the shape and construction of cargo ships remained much the same. They were rounded in shape, with a broad beam, a high after-deck from which the steersman, guiding the two steering oars on either side of the stern, could see ahead, and a broad, square mainsail, which could be quickly reefed by a series of brails, like the working of a Venetian blind. Often there was also a forward small sail at the bow, an *artemon*, a sort of spritsail to help with manoeuvring, or sailing closer to the wind. The hulls were built 'shell first', with shaped and fitted planking held tightly together by tenon and mortice joints (like fine pieces of furniture), with internal ribs only inserted later. The strength of the boat lay not in the ribbed skeleton but in the hull. This was sometimes sheathed with a thin layer of lead, to repel wood-boring marine creatures, placed over a covering of fabric, impregnated with pitch or resin, on the hull itself. Ships constructed so carefully, by such methods, were expensive to build, and when filled with cargo were ruinously costly to lose.

Unlike warships, these cargo ships were the workhorses of the Mediterranean, and were used for transporting passengers as well as cargo. The Acts of the Apostles tells the famous story of Paul's journey to Rome on a grain freighter which ended by being wrecked on Malta. The Emperor Gaius (Caligula) urged his friend the Jewish prince Herod Agrippa to take one of the freighters to Alexandria when he needed to return to Palestine, since their captains 'drive them like racehorses' on their journey. Such passengers would bring bedding, food and one or more servants, to look after them on deck, since there was rarely anything in the way of passenger accommodation below deck.

Given all these considerations and the climatic conditions, it is hardly surprising that winter was regarded as a closed season for moving about the Mediterranean, *Mare Clausum*. Navigation was customary from May to September, or at the outside from April to October. Even so the weather could vary, storms could blow up, local winds cause difficulties in rounding headlands and the direction of the prevailing winds even in summer make a considerable difference to a round trip. The clearest example is given by the run between Puteoli and Alexandria: going to Egypt with the northwest wind behind the ship might take only a week; coming back into the teeth of the wind could take a month or more. The conditions also affected the route taken. The main northerly route from Egypt was by way of Cyprus, southern Asia Minor, either Rhodes or Cnidos, south of the island of Crete, on to Malta and Messina, then up the west coast of Italy. The southerly was along the Africa coast, trying to take advantage of the alternating land and sea breezes as far as Cyrene. Both routes were slow. Returning to Egypt the ship could stand out to sea from southern Italy and expect to be blown to the Nile mouth.

The real motors and stimuli to this and other trade over long distances were clearly the state's needs. It was these needs which helped to create an entire structure of harbours, quayside arrangements, credit facilities and ship sailings, which, once they existed, could be used for a whole range of other trade as well. Once the state rhythms were established, and with them the infrastructure of roads and ports, individual merchants, or groups of merchants could pursue profitable motives of their own. Hence the phenomenon of so-called 'piggy-back' trade in the Roman Empire, where minor cargoes of pottery and other artefacts, which in themselves might not be worth carrying for long distances, sometimes achieve astonishingly widespread distribution. African 'red slip' pottery, a type of tableware, was just such a product. It seems to have achieved its popularity and distribution not least as a result of the vigour of other trade from Africa under the Empire, particularly the agricultural produce, grain and oil, and was carried originally on its back. The disadvantage of this was that if the state grain shipments faltered, or failed for a significant period, so too might the success of this form of decorated tableware, and other 'piggy-back' trade.

Much, therefore, depended on the political will of the emperors to make sure that what they saw as their interests and the interests of the state were properly served. Perhaps the most obvious and famous expression of this will in the ancient Mediterranean was the creation of a huge artificial double harbour near the mouth of the Tiber. It was the work of the emperors Claudius and Trajan in the first and early second century AD, and took decades to complete in each case, from AD 42 to, possibly, AD 64, and from AD 100 to AD 112.

Rome had long made use of the great natural harbour further south at Puteoli in Campania. This was an integral part of Rome's port complex in the late Republic and seems to have had its role enhanced in the early Empire. It was probably Augustus who built the famous arcaded mole there, which was a functional utility, a wonder of hydraulic engineering and a tourist attraction. A whole series of docks and warehouses stretched northwards along the shoreline, the *ripa hortensiana*, and it was these that made Puteoli the great port it was. They may have reached and included the facilities now drowned by the sea but still visible underwater near Portus Iulius and the Lucrine Lake. The interest of all the early emperors in this area is quite clear. Claudius himself sent an urban cohort to Puteoli, as well as to Ostia at the Tiber mouth, to act as a fire service.

The emperors' concern was also for the dangers of the route through the Mediterranean to Puteoli, and from there up to the Tiber mouth. The Jewish historian Josephus in the late first century AD praises the Emperor Gaius for beginning the enlargement of the harbour at Rhegium (Reggio di Calabria) on the toe of Italy, a notoriously dangerous point on the journey through the Strait of Messina, specifically for the benefit of the Alexandrian grain fleet. Similarly the great warehouses, *horrea*, built by Hadrian in southern Asia Minor at Patara and Myra were precisely at the point where Alexandrian grain ships could call, as we know from the story of St Paul. Hadrian, according to Dio the third-century AD historian, was also generous in providing and improving harbours generally.

The sea route north from Puteoli up the west coast of Italy to Ostia at the Tiber mouth, open to storms from the northwest and poorly provided with natural harbours, was equally in need of attention. Julius Caesar, who contemplated the building of a proper harbour at Ostia, to replace or supplement its river wharves, also had it in mind to construct an inland canal from at least Terracina to Rome. Nero revived the idea, and made a determined effort to link the area of Puteoli with the Tiber, by means of canals and inland waterways, using the natural lagoons which lay behind the coast, all the way from Lake Avernus (south of Cumae), to Ostia, and again from Ostia to Rome. Here the river itself followed a most circuitous course, which made the dragging of the barges upriver both tortuous and slow. The project failed, though traces of it still exist near Circeii. The fact that it was started in AD 64, which the commemorative coinage suggests was the date of completion of Claudius' great circular harbour north of Ostia, suggests that it was all meant to be part of a coherent strategy, involving both Campania and the Tiber, for dealing with the problem of Rome's ports. Tacitus and Suetonius represent Nero's actions as pure folly, but similar schemes of canals in the area of the Po valley associated with Ravenna were successful. All over the Empire the Romans exploited and adapted inland waterways, as at the mouth of the Rhône with the famous canals of Marius, the *fossae Marianae*, in the first century BC to ease the burden of their transport problems. It was almost a policy of 'fluvialization', certainly in northern and western Europe.

Claudius' great new harbour at Portus, some 3 km (2 miles) north of Ostia and the mouth of the Tiber, should therefore be seen as no more than a complement to the arrangements in Campania which were expected to continue. Built with immense effort in a lagoonal bay near a bend in the river, to which it was connected by canals, it was an enormous, roughly circular harbour, some 4–5 m (13–16 ft) deep, with an area of 80 hectares (197 acres). It had the limited purpose of making an area near the Tiber mouth safer for a greater amount of shipping. With its lighthouse, whose location has recently been rediscovered by archaeologists from the British School at Rome, it also began to provide a more dignified maritime approach to Rome, though not yet rivalling the splendour of Alexandria. As we know from Tacitus, the expanse of water between the moles was too great to guarantee safety; 200 ships were wrecked in the harbour in a storm in AD 62.

Trajan's project, although it appears simply to be creating a safer inner basin for the Claudian harbour, marked a change. It was a serious attempt to centralize the commerce of the capital, particularly its grain supply, on Ostia and the harbours at Portus. The hexagonal inner basin of about 32 hectares (79 acres), and about 5 m (16 ft) deep, excavated in the land previously crossed by the canals linking the Claudian basin to the Tiber, and now linked itself by one canal, the *fossa Traiana*, to the river, massively increased the mooring for shipping, and the granaries and storehouses near the Tiber mouth. The whole ensemble of basins and canals covered some 1,300,000 square metres (14,000,000 square feet), by far the single biggest port complex known to us from antiquity. At the same time, under Trajan and Hadrian, in Rome the embankments, mooring facilities and warehouses in the Emporium district below the Aventine Hill and in the Forum Boarium, the old 'Cattle Market' in the very centre of the city, were all systematically improved. It seems that, with Nero's attempt at an inland canal now definitely abandoned, Rome was not to be permitted to be so dependent on the distant Campanian harbours. This was reinforced by Trajan's construction of two further harbours nearby, one to the north of the Tiber at Centumcellae (Civitavecchia), the other to the south at Terracina, each with an area of 100,000 square metres (108,000 square feet). In a remarkable grouping these were to act as satellites for the great now double harbour at Portus, and, significantly, they were also connected to Rome by good roads.

Although the scale was smaller elsewhere, this placing of harbours in clusters, which were interlinked, in support of major urban sites, seems typical of the Roman world. Narbonne on the river Aude in southern Gaul had outports at St Lucie, St Martin, Mandirac and La Nautique; Aquileia on the river Natiso was connected to the sea by at least four major channels besides that to Grado, and the canals to Ravenna further down the coast; Antioch on the Orontes had links with Laodicea on the coast as well as with its port at Seleucia-in-Pieria; Hispalis (Seville) on the Guadalquivir funnelled produce through river ports and Gades (Cádiz); Carthage had not only its own internal double harbour, the outer rectangular, the inner circular, but many other mooring places both on the sea and on the Lake of Tunis; and Alexandria, the greatest and most elegant port in the Eastern Mediterranean, had not only its two main harbours on the Mediterranean, divided by a causeway, the *heptastadion*, but port facilities also on other mouths of the Nile, and on Lake Mareotis behind the city facing back towards the Nile. It is striking how the greatest concentrations of population in the Roman Empire are either on the Mediterranean Sea itself, or closely linked to it. The reasons for their foundation may have been political or administrative; but their ability to grow and be sustained in that growth was based on seaborne traffic.

The social and economic structures by which the vigorous seaborne trade was carried on in the Roman world has been the subject of some dispute. There is a tension between the fact that inscriptions recording traders and merchants seem to reveal people of rather low status and of only local significance, and the belief, derived not least from the fineness in the quality of the shipbuilding (and comparative costs of such work from other historical periods), that great wealth was needed in order to indulge in sea trading on any scale. Yet we also know that the wealthy senatorial upper class in Rome had in the second century BC been forbidden to own ships above a certain size, and senatorial literature in both Republic and Empire is permeated with a snobbish and patronizing attitude to trading and sea ventures generally.

The resolution of the puzzle seems to lie in recognizing that although trading 'companies' as such, and as known in other periods of history, did not exist in antiquity, individuals of moderate wealth and only local importance could come together, pool their resources, and act in each other's interest in ports and other key locations around the Mediterranean world. The links are hidden under words like *societas*, *familia* or even simply *amici*, friends. What is also true, and even more important, is that senatorial families, and even emperors, the wealthiest of all, could use their slaves, or their freedmen (that is ex-slaves, who still were bound to them in duty), to act commercially on their behalf, while their own participation was concealed. However it was managed, it is clear that when it came to funding some trading ventures by sea, great sums of money were certainly available when needed.

This is perhaps most obvious in the trade from the Roman world with the East – with East Africa, Arabia, India and, indirectly, China. Although there were famous caravan routes overland through Asia entering Roman territory at cities like Palmyra, or up from the Arabian subcontinent to Petra, the main routes for this trade were by sea, and they added to the unique significance of Alexandria as a port on the Mediterranean.

An unusual source, the *Periplous of the Erythraean Sea*, a traders' handbook, written by an anonymous Greek merchant in the mid-first century AD, gives us considerable detail about this trade, for the Red Sea, for the coast of East Africa as far as Zanzibar, for the coast of Arabia, and for the west coast of India. Not only are places listed (and points of navigation noted), but the goods that could be traded there are itemized. They included ivory, precious stones, perfumes such as myrrh and incense, silk and muslin and above all spices and peppers, for which we know there were great warehouses, the *horrea Piperataria,* at Rome.

From ports on the Egyptian coast of the Red Sea, like Myos Hormos, 'Mussel Harbour' and Berenice, ships set sail either for the East African coast or for India. The East Africa trade was a coasting voyage in ships which did not have to be in prime condition, but it was slow and took some two years to complete the cycle back to the Red Sea. The India trade, on the other hand, was an ocean voyage which had to be made before squally monsoon winds, in the strongest of ships, but the whole cycle back to Egypt took only one year. This was because ships, once they had sailed the length of the Red Sea, could catch the southwest monsoon to India in July, and the northeast monsoon back to Egypt in December. The knowledge of these winds, associated by the ancients with the name of Hippalos, may go back to the second century BC, but it was only from the early Empire that their regular use for commercial purposes really accelerated.

It was a trade which demanded skill, daring and considerable resources in order to finance it. Did the emperors officially encourage the trade or have some sort of state policy in regard to it? It seems unlikely, although they and others enjoyed the fruits of it to the full. It was a luxury trade, quite unlike the movement of essential staples which concerned them within the Empire. A papyrus from Vienna makes clear that it was wealthy private families in Egypt who maintained their own agents in the Red Sea ports for handling their family interests in this overseas trade with India. This did not stop Roman writers like Pliny the Elder in the late first century AD moralizing about it, and claiming that the trade drained the Empire of precious metal. Certainly Roman gold and silver coins have been found in some quantity, particularly at Muziris in southwest India, but after their purity was progressively debased from the time of Nero, and their intrinsic value as precious metal declined, their frequency drops off quite sharply.

The goods were carried across the desert from the ports on the Red Sea to Coptos on the river Nile (where they could be floated with the current downriver to Alexandria). This part of the route did involve considerable organization by the state: provision of wells, resting places and guards. But there were important quarries in the area, for example at Mons Claudianus, which provided materials for major building projects in Rome and elsewhere. The trade from the ports may simply have taken advantage of what was already provided. Certainly, both the trade with the East and the quarries in Upper Egypt added significantly to the variety and exotic nature of the goods being funnelled through Alexandria into the Mediterranean.

It is hardly surprising that a sea which the Romans, and the polyglot populations under their control, had so thoroughly made their own, *Mare Nostrum*, 'Our Sea', should witness not just the circulation of goods, but also of people. With them moved different ideas and in particular different religions. Ports, harbours, refuges and landing places of all kinds were after all points of arrival and departure for journeys on a potentially dangerous element – the sea. They were therefore naturally places of tension before setting out, and thanksgiving on safe landing. Attempts to appease divine powers by ceremonies, and arrangements to sacrifice or pray are to be expected. Ports such as Puteoli or Ostia reveal in their inscriptions and archaeological remains evidence for wide horizons in religious practice, particularly by the second century AD.

Traditional religion in the form of cults to the gods of Olympus, particularly Hermes, the god of traders, existed beside more exotic cults from the east such as Serapis or Isis, often with an epithet like *euploia*, 'fair voyage', attached. Foreign sailors from all over the East brought their deities with them, not least the Jews; a synagogue is among the recent finds at Ostia. What this all meant was that just as the common languages of this Mediterranean world, Greek and Latin, aided the wider dissemination of the Christian religion more than if it had been confined to its original Aramaic, so the flourishing Mediterranean network of communications aided the change from a pagan to a Christian world. The wanderings of St Paul in the first century AD made the point clearly, and it was to be reinforced dramatically by those great engines of Christianization and Christian life in later periods, namely, pilgrimage and crusade. Much of our evidence for the continuity of movement and connection in the Mediterranean into the medieval and later periods comes from the evidence of saints' lives, and the wanderings of their relics. The seaboard of the ancient pagan world, dotted with temples, sanctuaries and holy sites became re-sacralized and ritualized within the new religion. Dedications and shrines on headlands, such as Mount Athos, sprang up in a new Christian, or, as it turned out, Christian and Muslim world.

How precisely that world emerged is not the province of this chapter, and is a matter of controversy anyway. But something must be said here of the disintegration of the Roman Empire, and the effect of that on the unity of the Mediterranean Sea. It seems clear from archaeological evidence that we should not exaggerate the effect of the barbarian invasions from the north on the Mediterranean and its trade. Despite the spectacular success of these invasions, particularly in the Western Empire, excavations in Carthage, Rome and elsewhere demonstrate the persistence of commercial life, although on a diminishing scale, within the Mediterranean until the sixth century AD and beyond. Alaric the Goth's brief capture of Rome in AD 410, and the deposition of the child Romulus Augustulus, the last Roman emperor in the West, at Ravenna in AD 476 by the German chieftain Odoacer were no more than incidents, albeit eye-catching ones, in a complex process of change. Even the establishment of a Vandal kingdom at Carthage from AD 438, with its fleets of raiders, seems not abruptly to have shattered maritime continuity. That kingdom was anyway itself to be destroyed by Justinian's reconquest of the West from Byzantium in the mid-sixth century AD.

But the signs of weakening, and loss of central control, were all there. It was at Ravenna on the Adriatic, sheltering behind its protective marshes, to which the imperial court had retreated from Milan, that Romulus Augustulus was deposed. Power had long since departed from Rome itself. What seems to have happened was a progressive inward collapse of imperial will, certainly in the western Mediterranean. It was that imperial will after all that had created and sustained Rome as the greatest and most populous city the Western world had known, or was to know, until London in 1800. The population of the city fell rapidly from more than a million at its peak to perhaps 300,000 by AD 450, then to some 100,000 by AD 500. What that meant was that even if Vandal Africa was happy to go on sending, or selling, grain shipments to the city, a diminished and enfeebled Rome no longer needed, or could afford, so much. When that happened, the infrastructure, on which so much other trade from Africa, including its pottery, started to disappear, with dire consequences for long-distance trade in general.

Trade continued in the West, but it was more in the nature of small-scale *cabotage* – coasting trade. The high seas were left increasingly empty once more. In the East, the new capital Constantinople, established in AD 313, continued to draw supplies of wheat from Egypt, and mercantile prosperity, with this as its backbone, outlasted that in the West by a good century. But even under Justinian, the Byzantine empire ruled from Constantinople was overstretched financially in trying to fit out fleets also to control the West. Byzantium was therefore no longer capable of taking advantage of the opportunities the western Mediterranean offered; and the barbarian kingdoms of the West were in too rudimentary a state of political and economic development to initiate grand-scale commercial activity without Byzantine stimulus.

A new situation was emerging in the Mediterranean by AD 500 not because the sea was actually divided off at any point but because, as it happened, the changed world was no longer a cohesive unit. The Mediterranean Sea and all the lands surrounding it were no more the monopoly of a single power, ready and able to make the effort of political and administrative will, to impose that interconnection between different countries and continents, on which Polybius had already remarked in the second century BC.

This was a fact of immense importance in the history of Europe, Africa and the Near East. The Roman Empire, which has been described by an acute modern observer as being 'built on water', was gone. The Mediterranean Sea was no longer a Roman lake. No one in future, whatever their claims, would ever again be able to talk of the Mediterranean as 'Our Sea' in quite the absolute way that the Romans had.

The relationship between the different shores of the Mediterranean has been expressed not merely through political and economic contacts, but also through the spread of religion and ideas. The late antique world saw the religious transformation of the Mediterranean, as the monotheistic Abrahamic religions of Judaism, Christianity and Islam gained influence, and paganism contracted, so that the official cults of the late Roman Empire gave way, after Constantine the Great's time, to an increasing emphasis on the Christian identity of the Roman Empire. This did not mean that paganism vanished, for local cults remained a potent force in rural areas of Spain even as late as the Islamic conquest in 711. But philosophical academies based on non-Christian teaching, such as the famous Athens Academy, were closed down, in this case by Justinian in the sixth century. Pagan themes were adapted and adopted in early Christianity as well, so that the cult of the saints smoothly took over from that of local gods, and Parthenos Athene was displaced in many shrines by the Virgin Mary, for example on the Acropolis of Athens.

This readiness of the Church to make compromises in order to win new members gave it a decided advantage in competition with Judaism (still a proselytizing religion as late as the seventh century), and it was a theme that would be repeated in later centuries on other continents – in sixteenth-century Mexico or seventeenth-century Japan. On the other hand, early Christianity showed a startling ability to fragment: the Council of Nicaea in 325, chaired by the as yet unconverted Constantine, set out a complex theology of the Trinity which failed to unite all Christians, and Byzantium thereafter struggled with dissident Christian groups, such as the Monophysites, persecuted in the sixth century, but formidably strong in Egypt in the form of the Coptic Church. Most of the barbarian peoples invading western Europe adopted Arian Christianity, though the Franks became Catholic under their king Clovis in around 500; at this period the Churches of Rome and Constantinople had yet to break decisively with one another, though there were tensions between the Roman patriarchs (the popes) and the court in Constantinople, and the use of Latin in the West set the Roman obedience apart from the largely Greek-speaking churches of the East.

The late antique Mediterranean was a battleground between the Abrahamic faiths. Judaism had acquired large numbers of devotees in areas such as southern Italy and North Africa, and in Asia Minor some city-dwellers adopted a highly ecumenical routine that has been described as 'synagogue on Saturday, church on Sunday'. By 400 the élite in Minorca consisted of the Jewish families of Magona, the moden Maó, and two and a half centuries later Jewish Berbers apparently lorded over swathes of North Africa that had not been tamed by the Byzantine Empire; many of these Berbers were clearly of pagan descent. This success for Judaism occurred despite increasingly severe imperial legislation that sought to deprive Jews of positions of command over Christians, and to deny the right to build new synagogues, an attitude that was underlined in the writings of the fifth-century North African theologian, Augustine of Hippo; he emphasized that Jews had the right to live in a Christian society, but in a depressed condition, as the carriers of the original text of the books of the Old Testament which they failed to understand as evidence of Christian truth. The Visigothic kings of Spain, who had become Catholic Christians only in 589 (having been Arians since 341), initiated a bitter persecution of the Jews, who were seen, along with pagans, as exceptions to the Catholic norm. But this itself was an exception, and Jews were often able to live peacefully and successfully as farmers, artisans or traders.

The third religion to transform the Inner Sea was Islam, which emerged not far from the Red Sea during the early seventh century, and which continued for centuries to look east to Persia as well as west to the Mediterranean. Its original appeal was directed towards the Jews and pagans of the Arabian peninsula;

and its original members and the leaders of its early conquests were Arabians, who considered that Allah had given the Arab Muslims the mission of ruling the world (though not necessarily of converting the world, at least for the moment). But Islam shared many attitudes and preoccupations with Judaism and Christianity; its emphasis on the absolute Oneness of God was also the central feature of Judaism, and like Judaism it provided its followers with a code of laws that controlled every act of daily life, including the choice of what may be eaten. At the same time, Islam accorded Jesus and Mary great honour, and treated Jews and Christians as misguided worshippers of the same God, Allah, rather than as hopeless deviants. This greatly increased its appeal to disaffected Christians when Arab armies swept through Syria and Egypt, drawing to Islam many Monophysites and others, although in lands such as Egypt and Spain large Christian communities persisted.

'Islam' means 'submission', and this submission took two forms: the political submission of those who accepted the authority of the caliphs to rule over them, and the religious submission of those who accepted the religion preached by Muhammad. Islam did not find it as easy to come to terms with the new, non-Arab, Muslims, known as *mawali* or 'clients', as it did with Jews and Christians who accepted the conquerors as political masters and no more. But the coming of Islam deprived the late Roman Empire of its fertile granary in Egypt and of rich towns in Syria and North Africa. These losses in turn intensified the Greek Orthodox character of what we can now call the Byzantine Empire.

FIVE

The Mediterranean breaks up: 500 – 1000

JOHN PRYOR

In the early fifth century Germanic tribes forced their way into the Mediterranean, breaking its Romanized homogeneity for the first time. Spain was occupied by Visigoths and Italy by Ostrogoths. Among the most striking examples of this mass migration is that of the Vandals, who moved through Spain to North Africa.

The Germanic assault and imperial recovery: *c.* 400–560

In 429 a confederation of Vandals and Alans invaded the provinces of the two Mauritanias and Numidia by sea. By 435 the Western emperor Valentinian III was forced to cede all this territory, retaining only Carthage, but even that was captured by the Vandals under Gaiseric four years later and it became his capital. An expedition sent against him reached Sicily in 441 but was recalled because of attacks by Attila the Hun in Thrace. A peace treaty ceded large stretches of Roman North Africa to the Vandals in 442 while returning the far west to the Empire, at least in theory.

Using ships captured in Carthage and then building others, from Africa the Vandals immediately launched raids on Sicily. Under Gaiseric a fleet sailed to Ostia in 455 and systematically pillaged Rome for fourteen days. The Vandals raided Campania in the next few years, and occupied the Balearics, Corsica and Sardinia, the last permanently from 482/3. They raided Sicily and Italy annually, occupying Sicily some time after 468, and sacked the western coasts of Greece as well. The Western emperors did their best to dislodge them but failed. Successive Eastern emperors were equally unsuccessful, and a negotiated peace was concluded in 474.

With the death of Gaiseric, however, Vandal power began to decline, and in 533 a massive sea-borne invasion of Africa from Constantinople under Justinian I's general Belisarios eventually restored the Mauritanias, Sardinia, Corsica, the Balearics and Sicily to Roman (i.e. Byzantine) rule. By 546 North Africa had been pacified.

The Vandal occupation, however, is important; it was not merely a corsair kingdom, but an established régime based on grain production, and integrated into the Mediterranean maritime commercial network. The Vandals were Christian, but adherents of the Arian heresy which taught that God the Son was not co-eternal with the Father, but rather was created by Him from nothing. Although condemned at the Council of Nicaea in 325, Arianism had spread widely among Germanic peoples converted to Christianity: the Vandals and also the Ostrogoths and Visigoths. They and the Ostrogoths remained Arian, and only the Visigoths eventually converted to Catholicism in 589.

In 476 the Roman Empire in the West came to an end and after that the Eastern emperor could maintain only limited naval forces in the Adriatic. In 508 Anastasios I sent 100 galleys of a new kind known as *dromons* to ravage the coasts of Italy; and the Ostrogothic king Theodoric appears to have been unable to mount resistance by sea. Only late in his reign did he begin to consider naval forces for use against either the Byzantines or the Vandals. However, his plans came to nothing because of his death, and a decade later the Ostrogoths appear to have had few naval forces with which to oppose the imperial invasion of Italy under Justinian. The Gothic War opened in 535 with a two-pronged amphibious assault on Ostrogothic outposts. Belisarios was sent with a fleet and army to occupy Sicily and in the following year crossed to Calabria. The first phase of the war resolved itself into a Gothic defence of the heartlands of their kingdom, while every year Justinian sent new forces to Italy by sea. By the spring of 538 Belisarios's command of the sea had forced the Ostrogoths to raise the siege of Rome and retire to their capital at Ravenna. In the spring of 539, Belisarios moved towards Osimo, guarding the approaches to Ravenna. Rimini had been occupied by one of his lieutenants and was under siege. Belisarios left 1,000 men encamped outside Osimo, sent a fleet with an army to Rimini while another advanced up the coast, and he himself swept to the west. The sudden appearance of the fleet over the horizon precipitated a Gothic flight back to Ravenna. Late in the year his command of both the Po and the Adriatic enabled him to starve Ravenna into submission. He entered Ravenna unopposed in 540 and a grain fleet entered its port, Classe, to supply the city.

In 541 a new Ostrogothic king, Totila, realized the need for naval forces to counter those which had been thrown against Italy. In 542 he defeated the Byzantine forces in the north and broke through to southern Italy to besiege Naples. Justinian responded by sending a fleet under the Praetorian prefect Maximinos which was then destroyed by Totila in an encounter for which we have the first clear mention of Gothic use of *dromons*. Maximinos went to Syracuse, stayed there throughout the summer, and then in the autumn sent his fleet to Naples. Caught by a storm, it was driven ashore and mostly destroyed. Totila's command of the sea forced Naples to surrender in the spring of 543. In 545 Belisarios sent to Justinian for a new army, money, arms and horses. Totila moved on Rome, which he cut off by sea.

The siege of Rome by Totila lasted for seven years, from 545 to 552, and its fate depended crucially on command of the sea. Various attempts were made by Justinian's army to bring supplies into the city. Many were defeated but enough got through to keep Rome from surrender. The task was made more difficult because Totila still controlled most of the peninsula, with the Byzantines holding only isolated coastal towns – Rome, Ravenna, Otranto, Crotone and Ancona. When Justinian sent reinforcements of cavalry and horses they had to disembark in southern Italy and be transported round the coast, not overland. The battles that determined the outcome of the struggle were fought at sea, notably the Roman victory off Senigallia in 551.

The tide eventually turned when Belisarios was replaced by Narses in 550 and Totila died in 552. Still without sufficient ships to convey all the troops, the imperial army marched round the head of the Adriatic. In 561 the last Gothic garrisons in Verona and Brescia capitulated, and the Empire again controlled the Italian peninsula and all the islands as well as the entire Mediterranean coastline, except for the strip in the west held by the Visigoths in Spain and the Franks in Languedoc and Provence. But neither of these powers was bellicose at sea, and the unity of the Mediterranean was restored again. Peace, however, was to be short-lived. Within less than a decade a new threat had appeared: the Lombards.

The Muslim assault and imperial recovery: *c.* 560–750

The Lombard invasion of Italy under Alboin in 568 was precipitated by pressure on their Danubian homeland from the Avars in the mid-sixth century. In northeast Italy, the populace of Aquileia fled before the Lombard invasion to the islands of the lagoons, thus founding Venice. The northern inland cities fell quickly, leaving in imperial hands only coastal strongholds which could be supplied from the sea. Pavia fell after three years. In 571 the Lombards swept into southern Italy, establishing a duchy centred on Benevento, and within seven years most of Italy had been occupied. An imperial presence became confined to a newly created exarchate of Ravenna and a belt of territory running southwest to Rome, together with most of Apulia and Calabria. Over the next two centuries it waned progressively, Rome being lost to the popes during the first half of the eighth century. Ravenna fell in 751, and by the opening of the ninth century imperial control was confined to southern Apulia and Calabria. However, the Lombards did not attempt to gain control of the Italian coasts. Although they certainly disrupted Italy, they never assumed a Mediterranean presence like that of the Vandals; and they had little impact on the sea as a whole. Its maritime integrity remained in imperial hands.

Friction with the Empire, however, continued, and in 626, in an unprecedented alliance, the Avars and Persians combined in an unsuccessful siege of Constantinople. But in the following year, the Emperor Heraclius led the Byzantine armies into Persia and won a decisive victory near Nineveh, effectively ending the Sassanid Persian Empire. In Constantinople it appeared that the world had been restored to rights. The East was secure, the Empire again controlled the sea, and the Visigoths, Franks and Lombards were mostly confined to hinterlands and no threat. The emperor might look forward to a long and peaceful reign. However, it was not to be so, for a bare nine years later forces of the newly emergent Muslim religion annihilated the imperial army in Transjordan at the battle of the Yarmuk in 636. The Muslims occupied Syria and Palestine and in 640–42 Egypt also fell. The religious unity of the Mediterranean world was broken. The assault of the Arian Vandals, Visigoths and Ostrogoths had been as nothing compared to that which the Muslims would unleash.

While the Byzantines still had mastery at sea and could attack at will, as in 645–46 when they reoccupied Alexandria and raised a revolt in Egypt, watchtowers and a signalling system were established along the coasts. However, the governors of Syria and Egypt began to create naval forces, at first crewed by native Christians. Construction began on Rawdah island in the Nile opposite Fustat and the fleet first went into action against Cyprus in 649, subjecting the island to a covenant status under which the Cypriots were to remain neutral between Empire and caliphate. Crete, Rhodes and Sicily were raided between 652 and 654, and the fleet also returned to Cyprus in 653. In 655 the first hammer blow to the maritime integrity of the Mediterranean fell. A Muslim fleet engaged the main Byzantine fleet commanded by Constans II off Lycia. The Byzantines were annihilated and the Emperor lucky to escape with his life. This 'Battle of the Masts' opened the central Mediterranean to Muslim attack and the Byzantine fleet of the *Karabisianoi* based on Samos was probably created as a front line of defence shortly thereafter.

Rhodes was occupied in 673 for seven years. In preparation for the great assault on Constantinople, Cyprus was probably reoccupied around 670. The assault began in 671–72 when two fleets entered the Aegean and wintered at Smyrna and in Cilicia and Lycia. In 672 they began the siege, which lasted for seven years although it was not maintained as a close blockade. Muslim squadrons variously retired to Kyzikos, Crete and Rhodes to winter, returning each spring. In the end a new incendiary, 'Greek Fire', shot from weapons mounted on the prows of *dromons*, annihilated the Muslim fleets and forced the lifting of the siege. The remnants of the Muslim armada were destroyed by storms during the retreat. They had to conclude a thirty-year truce and evacuate Cyprus and Rhodes.

Until the end of the century the focus moved to North Africa. As early as 665 an expedition had been sent to Ifriqiya, the Roman province of Africa, without significant results except for the defeat of a Byzantine amphibious force. In 669 the Muslims returned, establishing an advance base at Qayrawan and raiding into the interior against Berber tribes. However, in 681 they overreached themselves with a long-range expedition which reportedly reached the Atlantic. Byzantine naval forces cut their lines of communication and their leader was defeated and killed near Tahuda in Algeria by a coalition of Berber tribes and Byzantine forces. The Berbers and Byzantines then took Qayrawan, forcing the Muslims back to the Egyptian frontier. In 693 a huge army under Hasan ibn al-Nuʻman al-Ghassani finally captured Carthage. A Berber uprising led by a mysterious queen known as al-Kahina, possibly a Jewish Berber, was accompanied by a Byzantine amphibious assault on Carthage. However, al-Kahina was defeated and the Byzantines were forced to evacuate. The days of Byzantine North Africa were over. Since Carthage's harbour had proved too vulnerable to attack from the sea, a new Muslim capital and fortress arsenal was built at Tunis by connecting an inland lake to the sea by a canal through the coastal strip. The governor of Egypt sent 1,000 Coptic shipwrights to populate the new city and to construct a fleet of 100 warships which, under a new governor, Musa ibn Nusayr, from 704 began to open the way to the conquest of the Maghrib by denying the Byzantines access to remaining outposts, and also to raid across the western Mediterranean to Sicily, Sardinia and the Balearics.

Musa was also associated with the invasion of Spain. The circumstances leading to the Muslim invasion of Spain are obscure. For some reason Tariq ibn Ziyad, the governor of Tangier, is reported to have sent an exploratory force across the Strait in 710 on four ships provided for reasons of his own by the Christian governor of Ceuta, a certain Count Julian. The success of the probe persuaded Tariq to lead a full-scale follow-up himself in the following year, again in ships apparently provided by Julian, landing near what was to become known as Tariq's Mount, Jabal Tariq, Gibraltar, probably in April 711. The Visigothic king, Roderick, was away in the northeast putting down rebels; but he marched south, rallying all available Visigothic forces, and the armies met somewhere around the Guadalete river. Roderick disappeared in the battle and the Visigothic kingdom disintegrated. In June or July 712 Musa ibn Nusayr himself landed at Algeciras with a new army. Tariq met his master outside Toledo and the two proceeded to pacify the peninsula. Although Muslim rule remained shaky for some time and the Caliph reportedly considered abandoning the conquest in 718, the Muslims eventually consolidated their rule, except in part of the Asturian mountains in the north, where a Visigothic noble named Pelagius or Pelayo revolted. Tradition records that he won a victory near the rock of Covadonga over forces sent by the Muslim governor, and was later besieged there.

He defied the Muslims until they abandoned the siege, with only thirty men and ten women of the Christians reportedly surviving. Thus was born a small Christian enclave in the Asturias, though how far these Christian warriors saw themselves as the leaders of a national resistance is very doubtful.

On the one hand, the Muslim conquest was in many ways relatively peaceful. Vastly outnumbered, the Muslims simply had to accommodate the Visigothic nobility, as is clear from an agreement of 713 preserved between 'Abd-al-'Aziz ibn Musa and Duke Theodemir. In return for submission he, his lords and the inhabitants of his seven towns were confirmed in their possessions and their right to practise Christianity subject to payment of an annual tribute: the *jizyah*. On the other hand, this was not always the case. At Narbonne, the turning of the town into a Muslim military encampment was preceded by wholesale slaughter of the men and enslavement of the women and children. Successive governors both pressed against Christian resistance in the northern mountains and also crossed the Pyrenees, invading France in 716, 721 and 726, when they reached Nîmes, Autun and Sens.

The most famous of all the governors, 'Abd-ar-Rahman al-Ghafiqi, brought back vast booty but his final expedition ended in his defeat and death at the hands of the Frankish Mayor of the Palace, Charles Martel, at the battle of Tours in 732. But campaigns across the Pyrenees resumed in 737. Gothic Septimania became a Muslim march centred on Narbonne, the Muslim presence being welcomed by some of the indigenous aristocracy as a counter-balance to the Franks. Their assault petered out eventually only because of over-extended resources and a Maghribi Berber revolt in 739 which spilled over into al-Andalus, the Arabic name for Spain.

The second assault on Constantinople by the Muslims caught the Empire at a nadir in its fortunes. Al-Walid's preparations led Anastasios II to prepare the fleet, repair the walls and mount siege engines on them, collect provisions and order those who could not lay up sufficient for three years to leave the city. A pre-emptive naval expedition sent to destroy the Muslims' fleet and timber supplies in Lycia broke up in disarray at Rhodes. When the Muslim assault gathered momentum in 717, the throne was seized by the *strategos* of Anatolikon, who became emperor as Leo III. Under the brother of the Caliph, an army and fleet advanced on Constantinople. For the first time in history, the entrance to the Golden Horn was closed by an iron chain. With many ships attacked and burned by Greek Fire, starving and freezing through a harsh winter, with Christian Egyptian reinforcements deserting, and with forces around the city attacked by the Bulgar Khan Tervel (with whom Leo III had made an alliance), the Muslims abandoned the siege in August 718.

In 725 Leo ordered the removal of an icon of Christ from the Chalke vestibule of the Great Palace in Constantinople, thus pre-cipitating the iconoclastic dispute concerning the adoration of images which wracked and weakened the Empire. In 727 the fleets of Hellas and the Cyclades revolted but were scattered by the impe-rial fleet using Greek Fire. When imperial officials attempted to enforce iconoclasm in Italy revolts flared and the Lombard King Liutprand seized Luni and perhaps Corsica. A naval expedition sent to restore order was wrecked in the Adriatic in 730. In 735 Pope Gregory III and the Lombards drove the Byzantine exarch from Ravenna; but the papacy soon fell out with the Lombards, and in 742 Venice and Pope Zachary returned Ravenna to the Empire. Disorder continued until 787 when iconoclasm was condemned at the Second Council of Nicaea. Although it resurfaced in the ninth century between 813 and 843, the second period lacked intensity and was not as destructive.

Cyprus was recovered and garrisoned by the Muslims in 693, only to be lost to the Byzantines the following year and recovered again in 695. In violation of their covenant, the islanders clearly assisted the Empire continually, and the Muslims had to enforce their suzerainty repeatedly. Crete was also raided, probably in 713. In 703 an Egyptian fleet attacked Sicily at the request of the governor of Ifriqiya, Musa ibn Nusayr; the island became subject to virtually incessant Muslim raids for the next fifty years. Sardinia was also attacked in 708 and 711, and the Balearics were raided in 708. In reverse, the Byzantines attacked Egypt and captured its fleet commander in 709, beginning a series of raids on Syrian and Egyptian coastal towns which were matched by interminable raids and counter-raids by land. The Muslim assault petered out around 750 as a result of Byzantine resurgence and internal problems within the Muslim world. For the next half-century the Empire would have virtually the only naval forces in the Mediterranean. However, during the preceding half-century the struggle had turned the entire Mediterranean into something of a no-man's land.

Equilibrium of chaos: c. 750–875

Until now the Muslim empire had been ruled by the Umayyad caliphs, with their capital at Damascus, but in 750 the last Umayyad caliph was deposed and eventually killed by the forces of the 'Abbasid Abu 'Abbas as-Saffah. His party, the *Shi'a*, believed that the caliphate should have descended through the line of Muhammad's cousin 'Ali ibn Abi Talib, but they had been persecuted and their imams forced underground by Umayyad secret police. Following the 'Abbasid victory, almost all of the Umayyad family were hunted down and killed; however, one, 'Abd-ar-Rahman ibn Mu'awiya, managed to flee through North Africa to Spain, where he seized power in 756. The establishment of the Umayyad emirate in Spain was the first rupture in the unity of the Muslim polity, although merely the beginning. Then, reflecting a shift in the centre of gravity, the second 'Abbasid caliph, al-Mansur, ignored Damascus and founded a new capital at Baghdad in 762. Here Persian cultural influences became prominent; henceforth the caliphate would focus towards the east and south rather than towards the Mediterranean, adopting *Sunni* Islam and throwing off its *Shi'a* connections

The 'Abbasids quickly rose to great power, reaching their zenith during the reign of Harun ar-Rashid. However, upon his death in 809 civil war broke out, leading to the loss of the great Persian province of Khurasan from 821. An attempt to create a new capital at Samarra backfired. There the guards imprisoned the caliphs within their own city, Khurasan remained lost and southern Iraq was thrown into turmoil by a dangerous revolt of black slaves, the Zanj, from 869 to 883.

Disruption and weakness in the heartlands led to disintegration in the West. In the Maghrib (North Africa) governors were fully occupied trying to maintain authority over fractious Arab settlers and Berber tribes and could not exercise any authority west of Ifriqiya. Those Berber tribes who had been converted had been heavily influenced by the *Khariji*, the 'Seceders', who hearkened back nostalgically to a supposed Muslim purity of the age of Caliph 'Umar ibn al-Kattab and who believed that succession to the caliphate should be decided by Allah alone; that is, by the community rather than by heredity. An offshoot of this movement was the state centred on Tahart founded by 'Abdallah ibn Rustam, a leader of the *Ibadi* sect of the Zanata Berbers, who became imam of all the *Ibadiyya* in 777. Eventually the Rustamids were confronted by the *Shi'a* Idrisids to the west and the *Sunni* Aghlabids to the east and forged an alliance with the Umayyads of al-Andalus. Andalusi seamen from Almería/Pechina established a colony near Tenes on the coast north of Tahart in 875–76, bringing the Rustamid state and Umayyad al-Andalus into economic relations.

The *Shi'a* in the Maghrib were represented by the Idrisids, who were descended from a great-great-grandson of 'Ali ibn Abi-Talib, the founder of a new capital at Fez in 793. He and his descendants were proclaimed as caliphs. However, their caliphate began to fragment around 830 as the towns were parcelled out among the family; and in the tenth century it was forced to recognize the suzerainty of the Shi'ite Fatimids, who occupied Fez in 921. From a Christian perspective, the most important Maghribi splinter state was that of the Aghlabids. Ibrahim ibn al-Aghlab was appointed governor of Ifriqiya in 800 by Harun ar-Rashid, but in practice became independent of Baghdad. The Aghlabids took to the sea with ferocity and determination, their fleets harrying southern Italy, Corsica, Sardinia, Sicily and even the Maritime Alps.

The period from the 'Abbasid revolution to the accession of the Byzantine Emperor Basil I in 867 witnessed the peak of Muslim eminence. 'The Muslims', wrote Ibn Khaldun much later, 'gained control over the whole Mediterranean. Their power and domination over it was vast. The Christian nations could do nothing against the Muslim fleets, anywhere in the Mediterranean. All the time the Muslims rode its waves for conquest.' Even if this was something of an exaggeration, conquest of the islands and the presence of fleets across the sea did nevertheless give Muslim powers an ascendancy. However, they did not have it all their own way, and the period was characterized more by inchoate thrust and counter-thrust. Moreover, the Muslim states became at odds with each other and with the caliphate in Bagdhad, while the Byzantines had to reckon with the First Bulgarian Empire, and the Italian peninsula was wracked by strife between Lombards and Franks.

By land, the 'Abbasids maintained the interminable raids and counter-raids across the Taurus frontiers begun by the Umayyads. Muslims built numerous frontier fortress-monasteries known as *ribats*, from which *mujahidun* 'strove for Allah' in *jihad*, both by war and in spiritual exercises. Their Byzantine counterparts were the border lords, the *akritai*, of whom the most famous was the fictional Digenes Akritas. Encounters across the borders were reflected in the epic of *Dhat al-Himmah* and in many tales in later versions of the *Thousand and One Nights*. By sea the first assault came in 790 when a Muslim fleet encountered that of the *Kibyrrhaiotai* in the Gulf of Attaleia and the Byzantine *strategos* was defeated, captured and later killed. In 806 Harun ar-Rashid deported many Cypriots from Cyprus under suspicion of not remaining neutral. Crete and Rhodes were also assaulted during his caliphate.

In al-Andalus, 'Abd-ar-Rahman I was fully occupied consolidating his own rule, though he also repulsed Charlemagne's expedition to Saragossa in 778, which ended in the famous disaster for the Franks in the Pyrenean pass of Roncesvalles at the hands of Basques, rather than of the Muslims as later tradition had it. His successors carried the attack to the Christians, not only to the kingdom of the Asturias, the Basque lands and incipient Christian states in Aragon and the Frankish March of Barcelona, but also across the Pyrenees. In 793 Hisham I's forces destroyed Girona and pushed on to Narbonne and Frankish territory. In 801–3 Louis of Aquitaine captured Barcelona, but in 808 and 809 Umayyad columns threw back his troops from Tortosa, and in 813 or 815 they defeated the Franks outside Barcelona. 'Abd-ar-Rahman II sent an army to Barcelona in 828 which engaged Frankish forces and devastated the lands north to Girona. Barcelona was retaken in 852.

In Italy the old order was changing. Rome and the papacy became isolated from Constantinople, the last emperor to visit Rome being Constans II in 663 and the last pope to visit Constantinople was Constantine in 711. In an imperial vacuum the papacy turned to the Frankish kingdom under its Mayor of the Palace, Charles Martel, and then his son Pepin III. In 751, in response to a set-up question from Pepin as to who should bear the title of 'king', he who held real power or the titular Merovingian incumbent, Pope Stephen I gave him the answer he wanted and Pepin was crowned king. A fateful alliance was forged between the papacy and the Frankish kingdom which eventually led to the coronation of Pepin's son Charlemagne as emperor in 800.

The papal concern was the Lombards, whose king Aistulf demanded in 752 tribute from Rome and control of the fortresses in papal territories. Summoned by Stephen II, Pepin invaded Italy and defeated Aistulf. When the Lombard King Desiderius attacked

Papal territories in 772–73, Hadrian I appealed to Charlemagne who invaded, defeated the Lombard army, besieged and took Pavia and crowned himself in 774. His conquest left Italy with a Frankish kingdom in the north and papal territories in the centre. The south, under Duke Arichis of Benevento, became technically subject to Charlemagne, but no more. In 787 Arichis died and in return for the release of his heir, a hostage at Charlemagne's court, his widow accepted Carolingian suzerainty. However, it remained ephemeral and by the ninth century the Lombards, now with a second capital at Salerno, were dominant in the south.

Al-Hakam I attempted to extend his rule as far as Corsica and possibly Sardinia. An Andalusi fleet had raided the Balearics as early as 798. In 806 Charlemagne's son Pepin, King of Italy, sent a fleet from Italy to Corsica against Andalusi Moors who had pillaged the island; and in the following year, since they had come to frequent the island, Charlemagne sent a fleet to Corsica which gained a victory over them. In 810 the Muslims again sent a large fleet to Sardinia and Corsica and gained almost entire control of the latter. In 813 the Count of Ampurias intercepted them returning from Corsica off Majorca and captured eight ships. In revenge they ravaged Civitavecchia and Nice and attacked Sardinia. Muslim corsairs raided Marseille in 838 and Arles in 842 and 850, and established a permanent base in the Camargue some time before 869. Three hundred ships subjugated the Balearics in 849 and reduced them to the same covenantal status vis-à-vis Muslim Spain as Cyprus had to the 'Abbasid caliphate. However, they were not actually conquered until 902–3.

In the ninth century the Mediterranean also began to experience incursions by Vikings, which stimulated the development of naval forces in al-Andalus. A Viking fleet entered the Tagus in 844 and assaulted Lisbon. Beaten off, they sailed south and sacked Seville. Mauled by Muslim cavalry, they then re-embarked, attacked Asilah in Morocco, and retired to winter in Aquitaine. In 859–60 Viking ships again anchored off the Guadalquivir river. Deterred by Muslim forces, they went on to sack Algeciras and part of the fleet assaulted Nukur in Morocco while the remainder ravaged the Balearics. A detachment raided up the Ebro to Pamplona, and they then sacked Arles, Nîmes and Valence in Provence and Luni in Liguria before retiring.

In the north of Italy, internal strife among the Venetian communities of the lagoons eventually led to Venice's submission to Charlemagne in 805. After the defeat of a Byzantine expedition sent to bring her back to Greek allegiance in 809–10, Pepin attempted in 810 to incorporate her into his own domains, but was forced to withdraw by the Venetians' defence of the lagoons, having won only payment of an annual tribute. Venice began the rise to power that would make her mistress of the Adriatic. The weakness of the 'Abbasid governors of Ifriqiya in the second half of the eighth century gave the Mediterranean islands a respite; but after Ibrahim ibn al-Aghlab seized power his squadrons began to raid across the central Mediterranean again. In 805 they assaulted the Peloponnese, in 812 and 813 Corsica and Sardinia, Lampedusa, Ponza and Ischia. In 820 corsairs captured eight merchant ships returning to Italy from Sardinia. In the following year squadrons raided Sardinia, but were thrown back. Ziyadat-Allah I began the conquest of Sicily in 827. However, Carolingian forces did attempt to return the Aghlabid compliments in kind. In 828 ships from Pisa and Luni raided Bône in Algeria and the governor of Corsica sailed to Africa and raided between Utica and Carthage.

The first half of the ninth century was disastrous for the Byzantine Empire. Relations between the Byzantines and the Bulgars, a Turkic people that had established itself in wide swathes of territory across the Danubian lands, had been reasonably amicable under previous khans; but in 807 a new khan, Krum, opened hostilities. Trapping a Byzantine army in a defile in 811, he killed Emperor Nikephoros I and reportedly made his skull into a drinking cup. In 813 he routed another and advanced on Constantinople; however, the capital was fortuitously spared by his death, and his son Omurtag concluded a thirty-year peace treaty in 816. No sooner was this threat neutralized than the Empire was rocked by the revolt in 820 of Thomas the Slav, who succeeded in winning over most Asiatic themes, including the *Kibyrrhaiotai*. Thomas's appeal has been attributed variously to anti-Greek discontent among ethnic communities, reaction against iconoclasm and inchoate social discontent. But, although able to besiege Constantinople in 821–23, his forces were eventually scattered by imperial squadrons using Greek Fire and the army of Omurtag, who came to the rescue in fulfilment of his treaty.

Weakening of naval defences by the *Kibyrrhaiotai* defection may well have been what made it possible for Andalusi corsairs to land in Crete between 824 and 827. The loss of Crete fundamentally altered the strategic makeup of the eastern Mediterranean. From a fortress port at Chandax (modern Heraklion) the Muslims raided the Aegean for slaves and booty and exercised some control over the southern Aegean, occupying some islands periodically and forcing others to pay tribute. They almost certainly exercised influence over Rhodes and Cyprus also, although they never attempted to occupy them. Around 839 they inflicted a major defeat on a Byzantine fleet off Thasos, and around 860 they raided the Cyclades and penetrated into the Sea of Marmara. Probably as a response, the Empire made the northern islands into a province or 'theme' named 'The Aegean Sea' (*Aigaion Pelagos*) and the southern ones into that of Samos. How effective these measures were is debatable, although the Byzantines did have some successes. Around 840–42 a Cretan force which had landed to ravage the mainland was destroyed. Then in 853, having realized that Egypt was the power behind Crete, a Byzantine fleet attacked Damietta, sacking it, seizing weapons destined for Crete and destroying naval supplies.

The Muslim conquest of Sicily, which began in 827 when the Byzantine naval commander in Sicily revolted and offered Ziyadat-Allah I suzerainty in return for recognition of himself as governor, was even more damaging than that of Crete. Landing at Mazara the

Aghlabid expedition encountered stiff resistance and an assault on Syracuse failed; however, a Venetian relief expedition also failed and Palermo fell in 831, by which time the Muslims controlled most of the west of the island. By 843 they had captured Messina and controlled its crucial Strait. From Messina southern Italy lay exposed to Muslim incursions, which in fact had begun even before the fall of the city. Brindisi and Taranto were seized in 838 and 839, and a Venetian fleet sent by imperial request to relieve Taranto was defeated in 840. In 841 Bari was captured. From there Muslim squadrons raided north, sacking Ancona and inflicting another major defeat on the Venetians in the Gulf of Quarnero in 842. Turning their attentions to Calabria and the west coast they went on to attack Rome itself and to pillage St Peter's in 846. Although driven out by forces of the Frankish Emperor Lothar I, Charlemagne's grandson, who had inherited Italy, and eventually dispersed by the Neapolitan fleet at Gaeta, during these years various Muslim bands managed to establish themselves in strongholds all around the coasts. Bari became the capital of an emirate which survived for thirty years.

In response to Muslim raids Lothar sent his son Louis II against Apulia in 848–49 and he supposedly had some success, although a second expedition and siege of Bari in 852 failed. Subsequent Muslim raids as far as Benevento and into Campania induced Louis to intervene again in 866. In the following year an Aghlabid assault on Ragusa-Dubrovnik induced Basil I to send a fleet to relieve the city and Venice sent a fleet which defeated the Muslims off Taranto. An alliance was then concluded between Louis II and the Empire; however, an allied siege of Bari in 869 failed, and not till 871 did Louis' forces, now assisted by a Croatian fleet, finally take the city. An attempt by the Muslims of Taranto to reverse the setback failed. Subsequently Louis' behaviour alienated the Beneventans, who imprisoned him and then sent him back north under promise never to return. When he died in 875, the Byzantines occupied Bari, which became the capital of Byzantine Italy for the next 200 years.

Christian ascendancy: *c.* 875–1025

Basil I's seizure of the Byzantine throne in 867 marked the turn of the tide against the Muslims, even if it might not have seemed so at the time. Muslim incursions continued in the east against the Empire, in the central Mediterranean against remaining Byzantine possessions in Sicily and into Lombard territories, and in the west into Provence. Nevertheless, in retrospect the Muslim offensive was running out of vigour. The following century saw the Mediterranean frontiers pushed back south everywhere, except in the Iberian peninsula.

Political fragmentation of the Muslim polity continued apace. In Egypt a Turkish soldier of fortune, Ahmad ibn Tulun, acquired the governorship in 868 and extended his authority into Palestine and Syria. Theoretically subordinate to the ‘Abbasids, in practice the Tulunids were independent. A powerful fleet, the first Muslim fleet about which more than skeletal details are known, projected their influence throughout the Levant. Muslim Cilicia came under their control from 878 to 882 and again from 892 to 897. The ‘Abbasids sent an army to Egypt which ended Tulunid rule in 905, but re-establishment of direct ‘Abbasid authority was short-lived. Egypt fell into the hands of another Turkish soldier of fortune, Muhammad ibn Tughj al-Ikhshid, and his sons from 935 until 966.

At this point the Fatimids, who were descended ultimately from ‘Ali ibn Abi-Talib and his wife, Muhammad's daughter Fatimah, entered the stage of Egyptian history. Overthrowing the Aghlabids and Rustamids and gaining authority over the Idrisids, the Fatimid Ubaydallah had established a new capital and naval base at al-Mahdiyyah on the east coast of Tunisia. In 969 the Fatimid general Jawhar conquered Egypt and paved the way for the Caliph al-Mu‘izz to move there in 973. He constructed a new capital, al-Qahira or Cairo, meaning ‘the Victorious’, and from Egypt the Fatimids extended their authority over Palestine, Syria and the Hijaz.

The Byzantines had problems of their own. The threat from Bulgaria had been neutralized temporarily, although it would recur under Khan Symeon. But a new northern threat had emerged. Scandinavians settled along the Dnieper, who became known as the Rhos (hence the names Rus, Russia) launched the first of several attacks on Constantinople in 860. Although beaten off, the attack presaged a new and powerful force which would affect the Empire for centuries, especially up to the conversion to Christianity of Prince Vladimir of Kiev in 988 and the defeat of the last Rhos attack on Constantinople in 1043.

Meanwhile, on the Taurus frontier the virtually independent frontier emirs of the 'Abbasids continued the interminable warfare of annual raids. The river Lamos in Cilicia west of Tarsos marked the border, and from 805 to 946 its banks witnessed a depressing series of prisoner exchanges and redemptions. At sea the Cretans continued their corsair war, raiding Dalmatia in 872, although more normally they confined themselves to the Aegean. However, imperial squadrons began to get the better of them from the 870s. Admiral Niketas Ooryphas destroyed twenty of their ships off Kardia around 873 and in 879 in the Gulf of Corinth he destroyed a squadron which had been raiding the Ionian.

The 'Abbasids also began to rebuild naval forces and by 860 squadrons based at Tarsos were sufficiently powerful to attack Attaleia. From this date until the late tenth century there was constant naval warfare between Byzantines and Muslims, with fluctuating fortunes on both sides. A large Byzantine army sent against Tarsos in 883 was annihilated by its emir, Yazaman al-Khadim, who became renowned for his naval raids. Shortly afterwards he led thirty ships against Euripos. Beaten off by Greek Fire, he continued hostilities until his death in 891. In 898 a Tarsiote squadron encountered a Byzantine fleet, probably that of the *Kibyrrhaiotai*, and defeated it, capturing numerous ships and beheading 3,000 seamen. The victory exposed the Aegean to the depredations of Leo of Tripoli, a former Byzantine seaman from the *Kibyrrhaiotai* who had converted to Islam. In 904 he led a devastating raid into the Aegean and sacked Abydos and

Thessalonika before retiring to Tripoli laden with booty and prisoners. According to al-Tabari, Leo killed 5,000 people in Thessalonika, delivered to freedom 4,000 Muslim captives, captured 60 ships and took thousands of prisoners. Each man on the expedition received 1,000 gold dinars from the proceeds.

In an attempt to end such depredations, Leo VI sent a large fleet to the Levant in 910 under the *patrikios* Himerios. In response, the emir of Tarsos, Damianos, another convert to Islam, ravaged Cyprus for four months, probably because the inhabitants had assisted Himerios. Himerios probably then assaulted Crete unsuccessfully and his fleet was annihilated north of Chios in October 912 by Leo of Tripoli and Damianos. A three-year effort to reduce Muslim capabilities in the Levant and at the entrance to the Aegean had begun successfully but ended disastrously. Not until the third decade did the tide really begin to run out. Leo of Tripoli was defeated off Lemnos in 923 and disappeared from history, and Damianos died besieging the *Kibyrrhaiotai* fortress at Strobilos in the following year.

In Sicily the fall of Enna in 858 confined the Byzantines to the coastal strip from Taormina to Syracuse. All the islands around Sicily fell, Malta in 870. In 871–72 Salerno was besieged for over a year and in 875 the Muslims penetrated the Adriatic as far as Trieste and Grado, razing Comacchio not far south of Venice during their retreat. At the same time they were raiding Calabria and Campania as far north as Rome. The inchoate political structures of the Lombard principalities and the quasi-independent duchies of Gaeta, Naples and Amalfi provided opportunities. In 880 Athanasius II of Naples allowed a Muslim band to settle below Mount Vesuvius. Later another band settled at Cetara on the Gulf of Salerno. Naples and Salerno combined between 881 and 883 to drive out these nests, but the Muslims moved north and joined others on the Garigliano river. In 884 the ancient abbey of Montecassino was sacked. In Sicily Syracuse itself finally fell in 878. The remaining Greeks held out around Taormina until that itself fell in 902.

In 880 an Aghlabid fleet raiding the Ionian Sea was destroyed by the Byzantine admiral Nasar using the bold tactics of a night attack. Continuing west, he landed near Palermo, ravaged its district, captured many Muslim ships and won another victory over an Aghlabid squadron off Punta Stilo while returning to Italy. The fleet returned to Constantinople in triumph and in Italy the Byzantines finally recaptured Taranto. Basil I followed up by sending to Italy in 885 Nikephoros Phokas, who rapidly reduced many towns and fortresses with conduct so exemplary that when Leo VI produced his famous military handbook, the *Taktika*, he devoted a section to it.

In 915 a Byzantine fleet closed the mouth of the Garigliano north of Naples and forces of a papal alliance finally eliminated its corsair nest. However, even if the threat of Muslim conquest had passed, Sicilian corsairs continued to harass the coasts for another fifty years and were joined by squadrons of the new Fatimid caliphate.

In the early decades of the tenth century the Empire was occupied by new threats from the north. Although educated in Constantinople, Symeon of Bulgaria proved an implacable and formidable enemy. In 896 he annihilated one Byzantine army, after which he agreed to a truce. Hostilities were nevertheless renewed and Symeon crushed Byzantine armies again in 914 and 917. Bulgar columns raided as far south as the Gulf of Corinth, creating conditions in which Romanos Lekapenos was able to seize the throne. His attempts to neutralize the Bulgars had only limited success; and in 922 Symeon invaded again and won a victory at Pegai on the Sea of Marmara. Adrianople was lost temporarily. The Bulgar threat was removed only by a defeat at the hands of Prince Tomislav of Croatia in 926 and by Symeon's death in 927.

It was during the reign of Tomislav (*c.* 910–28) that an effective Croatian political entity came into existence among those Croatian Slavs who had entered the Balkans in the seventh century. South of Croatia and along the coast in the province of Duklja lived other Slavs who became known as *Serboi* or Serbs. North of those around the mouth of the Naretva river and as far north as the Cetina and in offshore islands lived tribes of the Neretljani, known to the Venetians as the Narentan pirates, who seriously menaced Venetian shipping from the ninth century. Doge Pietro Tradonico sailed against them as early as 839 and Doge Pietro Candiano I led another expedition in 887 which ended in his defeat and death in battle. Pietro Candiano III returned to the attack in 948. But their menace could not be eliminated and Venice continued to pay protection money for safe passage along the Dalmatian coast. Not until 1000 did Pietro Orseolo II finally subdue them and consolidate Venetian hegemony in the Adriatic, taking the additional title of Duke of Dalmatia.

The Spanish Umayyads reached the zenith of their power during the long reign of 'Abd-ar-Rahman III, who adopted the title of caliph in 929. When he perceived the danger posed by the new Fatimid fleet, he built his own; and this enabled him to take Melilla in 927 and Ceuta in 931. The most important Umayyad naval base was Pechina and its port of Almería, inhabited by an admixture of sailors of Arab and Spanish origin. Prior to 884 they formed a self-governing community, and in the mid-tenth century they moved down to Almería, which also became home to many Jewish merchants. Under 'Abd-ar-Rahman III their fleet was the main Umayyad fleet operating against the Fatimids in the Maghrib and, if we can believe Ibn Khaldun, during his reign the Umayyad and Fatimid fleets both grew to a formidable 200 ships each. Around 890 a band of Andalusi corsairs landed at St-Tropez and fortified themselves on a hilltop at Fraxinetum, La Garde Freinet. From there they raided as far west as Marseille, north to Vienne, east to Asti, and northeast to the abbey of St Gall in Switzerland. Attempts to expel them in 931 and 942 failed, and not until 972 did the counts of Provence and Turin succeed in doing so. Wrecks of tenth-century Muslim ships found off the coast of Provence suggest that the enclave enjoyed lively maritime communications with the main Muslim world.

By the 920s Italy was divided between a Byzantine theme called Longobardia, the Lombard principalities of Capua-Benevento and Salerno, Papal territories to the west of the Apennines, and the kingdom of Italy from Abruzzi to Tuscany, ruled by descendants of Charlemagne. However, although there continued to be kings, real control of much of the north lay with the margraves of Tuscany, Ivrea and Friuli, and the dukes of Spoleto. From 922 the whole of the peninsula was seriously disrupted by Magyar raids which reached Apulia and Salerno and into the Balkans, reaching Constantinople in 934. Their assaults were halted only by their defeat by the German King Otto I at the battle of the Lech in 955.

In Sicily the Fatimids replaced the Aghlabids as overlords from 910. In 925 a squadron sent to Apulia sacked Bruzzano and Oria, taking many Jewish prisoners back to Ifriqiya. Then, in 927, a fleet of 44 ships sailed from al-Mahdiyyah against Taranto and sacked it. In 935 they even sacked Genoa.

The last half of the tenth century was a period of continuous warfare on all fronts. The forces of Islam were divided, with Umayyad ships attacking Fatimid possessions and vice-versa throughout the Mediterranean. The Byzantines were at odds with both factions as well as with the Bulgars and the *Rhos* in the north. But the Empire was slowly gathering strength. In 941 a third *Rhos* attack on Constantinople had been scattered and in the following year the Emperor Romanos Lekapenos responded to a request for assistance against the Muslims of Fraxinetum by sending a squadron to Italy which destroyed the Muslim ships with Greek Fire.

In 956 the strategos of the *Kibyrrhaiotai* won a famous victory over the Tarsiote fleet off Lycia, freeing the way for a new assault on Crete. Romanos II gave command to Nikephoras Phokas, who successfully completed the task between July 960 and March 961. And, after he had become emperor himself, Nikephoros Phokas pushed into Cilicia in 963. An attempt to reconstitute the Egyptian fleet to relieve Tarsos failed when the squadron of 36 ships was mauled in a storm and the remnants were defeated off Cyprus in 965. Both Tarsos and Cyprus were recovered. Nikephoros followed up with a push into Syria in 969 which regained Antioch and northern Syria west of Aleppo and north of Tripoli. He was assassinated by John Tzimiskes, who became emperor in his place and continued the same policy, capturing Beirut in 975 and forcing Damascus to pay tribute, although a siege of Tripoli failed.

Svjatoslav of Kiev had invaded Bulgaria in 969 and deposed Khan Boris II, intending to transfer his own capital from Kiev to Preslav. However, John Tzimiskes' army relieved Preslav and forced Svjatoslav to retire to Silistra. Under John's successor Basil II, *Boulgaroktonos*, the 'Bulgar slayer', the Empire reached the peak of its medieval power. A Byzantine fleet mounted the Danube and destroyed Svjatoslav's ships, forcing him to surrender. He was intercepted and killed while withdrawing. Bulgaria was annexed to the Empire and its Khan, Boris II, taken to Constantinople. After further campaigns Basil finally triumphed at the battle of Kleidion in 1014. The sight of 14,000 Bulgarian captives sent home blinded was said to have led to their khan's death within two days. Although resistance continued, by 1018 Bulgaria was pacified and incorporated into the Empire.

In February 962 the German ruler, Otto I, by now titled Roman emperor, had come to Rome to be crowned. Among his other interests, that in southern Italy was aroused by claims to imperial suzerainty over Capua-Benevento and Salerno. He visited Benevento in 967 and next year returned to both Benevento and Capua, turning his army against Byzantine Bari. Finding it impregnable he sent an embassy to Constantinople which Nikephoros Phokas dismissed contemptuously, giving rise to an impassioned narrative of it by Otto's emissary, Bishop Liutprand of Cremona. The struggle was resumed in 969 but Nikephoros's successor John Tzimiskes ended it by proposing a marriage between his niece Theophano and Otto's son Otto (II). The wedding took place in St Peter's on 14 April 972 and Otto I withdrew from the south.

From 965 southern Italian waters were left to local Byzantine forces, to those of the growing cities of Naples, Gaeta and Amalfi, and of the princes of Salerno, and above all to those of the Kalbite emirs of Sicily. Their raids from 975 contributed to inducing Otto II to intervene. In 981 he marched into Apulia and Calabria, provoking the emir, Abu-l-Qasim, to cross the Strait. At Punta Stilo the armies met in a disastrous defeat for Otto II, who, in a famous story narrated by Thietmar of Merseburg, escaped only by swimming his horse out through the waves to take refuge on a Byzantine *chelandion*. Eventually he made his way back north, his policies in ruins, leaving southern Italy to its own devices. Despite his fascination with Byzantine culture and claims to imperial Roman authority, his son Otto III would trouble only the Lombard principalities of Capua and Benevento, but not the Byzantine and other territories to the south.

After moving to Egypt the Fatimids had taken no action against the Byzantine Empire for some time. Hostilities intensified only in the 990s with a series of encounters, including a Byzantine raid on Alexandria in 993. Probably as a response, in 996 al-'Aziz began to construct a large new fleet at Cairo. A fire which destroyed some ships provoked suspicion of merchants from Amalfi, and the mob killed 100 of them and looted local Christian churches. The fleet was reconstructed and 24 ships were despatched to Tripoli but were wrecked on the Syrian coast. Nevertheless, 20 ships could still be sent in 998 to put down a rebellion in Tyre and they were capable of defeating a Byzantine squadron assisting the rebels.

In Spain the impressive naval forces which 'Abd-ar-Rahman III had created were maintained by his successors. When the Vikings returned to Lisbon in 966, they were defeated off Silves by the fleet of Seville. Nevertheless Al-Hakam II ordered a fleet to be built in the Norse style in order to be able to close with the Vikings. Another assault in 971 was countered by bringing the Almería squadrons around to Seville; and in the following year the fleet was sent to Ceuta and then to Tangier, which it captured from the last Idrisids.

Al-Hakam died in 976, but during his reign had enjoyed diplomatic relations with Constantinople, of which the permanent reminder is the prayer niche in the Great Mosque at Córdoba, which was ornamented by Byzantine craftsmen and those they had trained. He was succeeded by his young son Hisham II, but real power passed to the *hajib*, or chief minister, al-Mansur, 'the Victorious', known to the Christians as Almanzor. He assembled the fleet at Alcacer do Sal for his famous campaign against Santiago de Compostela in 997, which brought the bells of the cathedral back to Córdoba. Having made the caliphate the terror of the Christian states to the north, he died on campaign in 1002. However, ironically, the very policies by which he had done so, reliance on Slavic slave Mamluks and Berber and Christian mercenaries rather than the Muslim *jund* of the Arabic aristocracy of al-Andalus, led to disintegration after his death. His son died in mysterious circumstances in 1008, after which the caliphate began to collapse.

In the Iberian peninsula, and indeed for the most part across the Mediterranean, the eleventh century would belong to the Christians. The extinction of the Umayyad caliphate in 1031 led to the era of the *taifa* or 'party' kings, *muluk at-tawa'if*, emirs ruling over localized city states, who became no match for the growing strength of the kings of Castile and Aragon. Toledo fell in 1085, an event of epoch-making cultural significance. In the east, by 945 the 'Abbasid caliphs had fallen under the control of the *Shi'a* Daylami clan of the Buyids, who would hold the real power until their own overthrow by the Seljuq Turks in 1055. Egypt would remain Fatimid but slide into anarchy and civil war during the caliphate of al-Mustansir from 1036. Until the death of Basil II in 1025 the Empire held the ascendancy in the East, and her own slide into anarchy did not become apparent for another three decades. But it was in the central Mediterranean that the really important developments would take place. Venice was already a Mediterranean power by 1000. To a lesser extent so also was Amalfi. But in the eleventh century Amalfi would be overshadowed, and Venice rivalled, by Pisa and Genoa. The maritime cities of Italy, soon followed by those of Provence, Languedoc and Catalonia would begin to flex their muscles. Together with the strengthening of the economy, society and religious confidence of Western Europe this would lead to perhaps the most monumental event of the Middle Ages: the First Crusade (1095–59).

The assaults of the Seljuqs on the Empire from around 1070 and that of the Almoravids, al-*Murabitun*, in the Maghrib from about 1060 and across into al-Andalus from 1086 were formidable but ultimately futile. Although it would be resuscitated vigorously by the dynasty of the Komnenoi (1081–1185), even the Byzantine Empire was already losing ground to the dynamic growth of the Latin West and would eventually be overwhelmed by it.

The substantial political changes described in the previous chapter were matched by highly significant economic changes. A great debate among twentieth-century historians of the Mediterranean world concerned the evidence for an economic break in relations between East and West in the early Middle Ages. Assuming such a break occurred, was it the result of the barbarian invasions, which isolated Spain, France, the Rhineland and northern Italy from the flourishing economy of the Byzantine East, which then included Egypt and what are now Israel, Lebanon, Syria and Turkey as well as large swathes of southeastern Europe? Or was the key moment the rise of Islam, which brought Egypt, Syria, North Africa and eventually Spain under the rule of a new religion, between the early seventh and the early eighth century? Or was it the coming to power in the West of a new, Western emperor, Charlemagne, who assertively extended his rule over areas such as central Italy which had previously been part of the Byzantine sphere of influence?

The great Belgian historian Henri Pirenne drew attention to the decline in the trade in gold, spices and papyrus, for long an essential medium for writing, and more recent archaeological evidence, though equivocal, has tended to support the view that the economy of East and West diverged significantly around 750, with a small trickle of eastern imports arriving in ports such as Naples and Marseille, scattered survivors of an earlier era in which large-scale commerce had criss-crossed the Mediterranean (as can be seen in the chapter on the Roman *Mare Nostrum*). In Pirenne's scenario, the long-distance merchant of the early medieval West was often a Jew or a Syrian Christian, so much so that Judeus became synonymous with 'merchant'. Ibn Khuradadbih, a Muslim writer, described how the caravans of the Jewish long-distance merchants known as the 'Rhadanites' crossed Europe and North Africa, bringing slaves from the pagan East of Europe to Muslim Spain, where rulers valued the military skills of many of these 'Saqaliba', or Slavs.

The reality was, rather, that the economies of the eastern and western Mediterranean had long possessed distinct characters, partly imposed by the wetter climate of the western Mediterranean lands, which were suited to the cultivation of a wide range of agricultural goods, while the eastern lands, though often rich in grain (as the case of Egypt proves) were drier, supporting large urban populations that made up for their shortfall in essential goods by means of short- and medium-distance trade. Thus it was possible for a massive city such as Cairo to subsist though it stands on the very edge of the desert. The East was more urbanized, particularly the Islamic lands, though Byzantium had a megalopolis in Constantinople that traded across the Black Sea and the eastern Mediterranean to feed its swollen population.

By the tenth century merchants within the Islamic lands were linking Spain, Sicily, Tunisia, Egypt and Yemen with India; active in this trade were the Jews based in Old Cairo, or Fustat, who have left many merchant letters from the period 950 to 1150 in the deposit called the Cairo Genizah, now largely preserved in Cambridge University Library. Despite the existence of political boundaries between competing Muslim caliphates, these merchants knew their way across the Mediterranean, trading in silk and cotton and spices. But the Mediterranean they sailed was that Islamic Common Market which had been created as a result of the conquests of Islam; they penetrated rarely into Latin Christendom. Indeed, out of Latin Christendom would come the new masters of the Mediterranean, the Venetians, Genoese and Pisans, self-confident Christian traders with more than an element of crusading fervour.

One town known to the Genizah Jews was Amalfi, which, with Gaeta and Salerno, and with the towns of Apulia (Bari, Trani, and so on) continued to maintain business ties with Byzantium; Amalfi and Gaeta also sent merchants to Muslim Sicily, the Maghrib and Egypt. Amalfi had not been a Roman settlement, but was one of a series of towns that emerged as a refuge for those escaping from the barbarian invasions; others were Dubrovnik (Ragusa) in Dalmatia and, most famously, Venice. Amalfi lived from the sea, with no real hinterland, but it was the one Latin port Muslim merchants had really heard of, if we are to believe geographers such as ibn Hawqal in the tenth century. Its leading merchant families had ties to the court in Constantinople; and the Amalfitans were also accused of making deals with the Saracen pirates who infested the Tyrrhenian Sea, in order to protect themselves from raids which reached Rome and beyond. However, Amalfi acted as business agent of the great mother monastery of the West at Montecassino, and supplied the courts of popes and southern Italian princes with silks and spices. Amalfi remains, however, a place of mystery: half the town collapsed into the sea in the fourteenth century, by which time it was no longer in any sense a competitor of Genoa or Venice, but merely a regional centre of trade in such goods as salt pork and rough cloths.

Its decline has been attributed to the Norman conquest of southern Italy, which brought it under outside rule, to a Pisan raid in the twelfth century, to its loss of favour in Constantinople. It did not take part in the crusades, which, as the next chapter shows, enriched other Italian cities greatly. Above all, it did not have the capacity to penetrate with its goods into areas such as northern Italy, southern France, the Rhineland and Flanders, which were among the trading partners of Venice and Genoa. It was left behind, a relic of the time when trans-Mediterranean commerce through Italy was small in scale, and did not penetrate far beyond Rome and Naples.

The Amalfitans were Christian merchants venturing into a Mediterranean dominated by Muslim navies and by Muslim and Jewish merchants. After 1100 the Mediterranean was effectively to turn into a Christian sea.

SIX

A Christian Mediterranean: 1000 – 1500

MICHEL BALARD

During the last five centuries of the Middle Ages, the Mediterranean underwent many significant changes. The first was the changing sequence of powers that exercised political authority over its shores: the expansion of the Western powers was balanced by the decline of Muslim power in the Arab countries, but also by the rise of Turkish power in the areas conquered by the Ottomans, culminating in the fall of Constantinople to the Turks in 1453. The second major change was the so-called 'medieval nautical revolution' (a term used by both Frederick Lane and by Roberto Lopez, two of the major historians of Venice and Genoa, respectively). This period saw an unprecedented expansion in trade, and provided the means for technical progress which would not be surpassed until the nineteenth century. Regularly used maritime routes criss-crossed the Mediterranean, though they were also the object of ferocious rivalries, first of all between Christians and Muslims and later on between one Christian power and another. In addition, the political transformations taking place in the regions bordering the Mediterranean greatly influenced the question of who exercised mastery over the sea, though dominion over land did not necessarily imply dominion at sea.

Around 1000, the Mediterranean was still virtually a closed sea. Beyond the Strait of Gibraltar there extended the terrifying open spaces of the 'Ocean of Shadows'; on the other hand, the Strait also functioned as a link between the Muslim lands of al-Andalus

(Muslim Spain) and the Maghrib (North Africa). Regular seasonal trade along the coasts enabled the exchange of Spanish produce for the goods of the Sahara and of the plains of Atlantic Morocco. All this had little effect elsewhere, apart from a limited amount of direct trade between Seville and Alexandria. In the north, the Swedish Varangians in their longboats made their way up and down the rivers of Russia; coasting along the shores of the Black Sea, they established periodic maritime links to Constantinople, bringing to Byzantium honey, wax and furs. This traffic was conducted subject to agreements between the Byzantine court and the Russian princes, and did not extend beyond Constantinople itself. However, in the southeastern zone of the Mediterranean, most of the trade coming from the Indian Ocean was deflected from the Persian Gulf to the Red Sea, as a result of the crisis in the Abbasid caliphate described in the previous chapter. The new Fatimid dynasty that ruled Egypt from the mid-tenth century onwards redirected Indian Ocean traffic towards the port of Aydhab on the western shore of the Red Sea, and from there to Qûs and the Nile; this guaranteed a prosperous future to the Fatimid cities of Cairo and Alexandria.

At the start of the eleventh century, there is a striking contrast between the power of the Byzantine Empire and of the Muslim world, by contrast with the weakness of Latin Europe. Under Basil II, Byzantium acquired control of virtually all the Balkan peninsula, recovered Asia Minor right up to Armenia, and controlled the Italian boot, not to mention Cyprus and Crete. In other words, a great part of the Mediterranean sea coast came under the domination of Byzantium, in the form of maritime 'themes' or provinces, whose function was to ensure the effective defence of the coasts. Around this time, by contrast, the Muslim world seems to fragment into pieces; but, while the Abbasid caliphate lost its glitter, the Buyids assured control of Baghdad and the Fatimids, originally from central North Africa, came to power in Fustat (Old Cairo). In the western Islamic lands, Muslim Spain saw the last glories of the Umayyad caliphate, under the day-to-day government of the Amirid viziers: Madînat al-Zahra and Córdoba are the jewels in the crown of a state that was beginning to disintegrate.

As for the Christian lands, they were just beginning to emerge from a long period of stagnation. Although Venice, Pisa and Genoa began their reconquest of the Mediterranean Sea, Sicily experienced profound Arabization and Islamization under its Kalbite rulers, while the Christian kingdoms in Spain were still often subject to the authority of al-Andalus and were more preoccupied with their own survival than with maritime expansion. The sea itself was still largely under the control of Islam.

Sea routes in the eleventh century

We know rather little about maritime technology in the eleventh century; the terms used to describe ships, and the different types of ship, are still little understood. Underwater archaeology provides evidence, combined with that of the Arabic ceramic plates or *bacini* inserted in the walls of the church of S. Michele in Pisa, revealing that three-masted sailing vessels were in use: the *shâm* (galley) or *kharrâq* (ship suited to the open sea), with curved prow and swelling poop. The masts carried a yard parallel to the deck and used a lateen (triangular) sail. Wrecks found off Provence reveal that the vessels were of skeleton construction; the planking was nailed together and assembled freeboard (i.e. with a predetermined space between the upper line of planking and the line of flotation), which implies meticulous caulking. At this period there was little distinction between war ships and trading vessels, apart from what was placed on board: arms, war *matériel* and the so-called Greek Fire.

Although suitable wood was in short supply on long stretches of the southern shores of the Mediterranean, arsenals were established in Egypt at Alexandria, Damietta, Tinnis and Fustat, making use of wood from northern Syria and the Maghrib or that carried off during raids on Anatolia. Similarly there were arsenals in Muslim Spain at Seville, Denia, Valencia and especially Almería; meanwhile in the

Christian ports of northeastern Spain and of Italy fishing vessels were transformed gradually into trading ships suited to the open seas. Hard by the well-forested mountains of the interior, Barcelona, Genoa and Venice easily found the resources they needed to make possible an expansion of naval construction. As early as 1104, Venice set up an arsenal, which was eventually to become the largest industrial plant in the medieval West.

Sea trading needs substantial amounts of capital, to organize the financing of ventures and the sharing of risks. The reconquest of the Tyrrhenian Sea from the Muslims had given the Pisans and Genoese booty which they reinvested in naval construction. The *parias* or tribute payments sent by the Muslims to the Christian rulers of northern Spain helped the Catalans to build their fleets. But this in itself was not enough. It was essential to borrow or to dispose of shares in an enterprise in order to build a ship, equip it and fill it with cargo. We have to wait until the twelfth century for documents that show the process by which a ship was notionally divided into parts, but even before 1000 companies of merchants had begun.

Among the Muslims we find two types of contract: the *shirka* or *sharika*, a sharing of assets between two or more people who invest capital and labour, and above all the *qirâd*, a contract under the terms of which an investor passes a sum of money to an agent, to be used to make profit on his behalf, on the basis of an agreement made before the venture commences. The borrower exchanges the money for merchandise which he intends to sell at a higher price. These formulae, which were in use by the eighth century, are often believed to have influenced the commercial contracts in use in Italy. The 'sea-loan', whose origins can be traced back to the money loans of antiquity, furnished the merchant with the capital he needed, repayable on the safe arrival of the ship; the lender would receive a fixed percentage of the profits in exchange for bearing the risks. More flexible still were the *commenda* and *societas maris* ('sea company'): one partner provided the capital, the other the labour, sometimes complemented by a contribution to the capital. How one chose the exact type of contract depended on the financial resources of the contracting party. From the last quarter of the tenth century, it was the *commenda* of the Mediterranean world that became the most commonly used type of contract: its flexibility made it an instrument of progress not just in business affairs but also progress up the social ladder.

Three communities of investors and merchants divided up Mediterranean trade among themselves at the start of the eleventh century: the Muslims, the Jews and the Christians. Since Islamic jurists condemned Muslim trade in non-Muslim lands – the 'abode of war' or *dâr al-harb*, that is, infidel territory – few Muslim merchants can be found in Christian Europe. Indeed, the commercial sphere of each of these groups of traders was quite distinct, and they followed different trade routes, along which they carried different commodities. The Cairo Genizah documents, retrieved from an ancient synagogue in Old Cairo, reveal that Jewish merchants were present in every corner of the Mediterranean; up to 1150, they dominated major areas of the trade of Muslim Spain; they created an extensive network of communications linking Spain to Egypt and linking North Africa with Syria, though the hinterland of the Near East was less familiar to them. Their Mediterranean trade itself fed into trade routes that extended as far as Yemen and India, from which they brought spices and jewels.

As for Christian merchants, it was the initiative of the Italian merchant republics that brought the Western lands out of their long-standing commercial lethargy. The Venetians were in theory still 'subjects' of Constantinople, and enjoyed commercial privileges in the Byzantine Empire: in 992, they were granted a reduction in the taxes payable at the narrows of Abydos in the Dardanelles, before acquiring total tax exemption in 1082 as a reward for naval aid against the Normans in Albania. In addition, the little town of Amalfi played a significant role: its merchants had a colony in Constantinople from the tenth century, and their commercial network rested solidly on the triangular trade linking southern Italy, Tunisia, Egypt (where the Fatimids welcomed them) and the Byzantine Empire. On the Tyrrhenian shores of Italy, Pisa and Genoa launched a maritime conquest of the western Mediterranean, clearing the islands of Corsica and Sardinia of Saracen pirates and attacking al-Mahdiyyah, the main port of Tunisia, in 1087. The booty from the raids and conquests, added to profits from agricultural surpluses, provided capital for the commercial expansion of both these Tyrrhenian ports.

Mediterranean traffic in the eleventh century was still fairly simple in character, without strong signs of specialization. It was concerned with everyday consumer goods, with raw materials, with luxury items and with human merchandise as well – the slave trade. From the eastern Mediterranean there arrived Egyptian linen, dyestuffs, spices, drugs, perfumes, precious stones and pearls, while Constantinople sent westwards silk cloth, liturgical implements and works of art, like the bronze doors that ornament churches at Amalfi, Salerno and Canosa. The western Mediterranean provided olive oil and soap, wax and honey, skins and leather, coral and saffron, but above all wood and base metals which were lacking in the Islamic lands and without which Muslim armies and fleets could not have been adequately equipped.

The Slav population of the eastern shores of the Adriatic provided, until the tenth century, the human merchandise of the slave trade, to which were later added sub-Saharan Africans, until the time when the Christian conquests in Spain offered a source of Muslim slaves. The ports of North Africa, which were the terminal points of the trans-Sahara caravan traffic, were centres for the exchange of salt and cloth against wool and skins, as well as for the purchase of the gold of 'Sudan', the lands south of the Sahara. Only in the twelfth century did the textiles of western Europe begin to invade these markets.

From the First Crusade to the arrival of the Mamluks
(*c.* 1100–1250)

The end of the eleventh century saw dramatic changes in the Mediterranean political landscape. In the Iberian peninsula Christian conquest went ahead, despite the resistance of the Almoravids, Berbers who had been called in to rescue the fragmented 'party kingdoms' of Muslim Spain. The so-called Barbastro crusade of 1064 sent shock waves throughout Muslim Spain, while the capture of Toledo by Alfonso VI of Castile in 1085 and the occupation of Valencia by El Cid in 1094 also had profound effects. In 1147, a new wave of Berber invaders from Morocco, the Almohads, briefly halted Castilian and Aragonese expansion, but a coalition of Christian kings in the Iberian peninsula routed the Almohad armies at Las Navas de Tolosa (1212). After this, the route to the south lay open to the Christians: after the capture of Seville in 1248, al-Andalus was reduced to little more than the small Nasrid kingdom of Granada, which survived until 1492.

The Christian conquests were, naturally enough, accompanied by major population movements: those Muslim populations that were not expelled, known henceforth as the *mudéjares*, consisted of a small minority among the overall population of Iberia, although there did remain some areas, such as Valencia, where the Muslims long constituted a majority even under Christian rule. North of the Pyrenees, the Capetian kingdom demonstrated a new interest in the shores of the Mediterranean. The Albigensian crusade (from 1209), waged against dualist heretics, brought the northern French down to Languedoc, which was incorporated into the royal domain twenty years later, following the intervention in the south of King Louis VIII. For the first time French royal authority touched the Mediterranean. In these new lands Louis IX built the town of Aigues-Mortes, to give his kingdom a Mediterranean port and to provide facilities for his crusading enterprises. Meanwhile, in northern and central Italy, the end of the eleventh and beginning of the twelfth centuries saw the emergence of the Communes, city-states that were governed by consuls drawn from the local élite; with the help of the papacy, these cities resisted the pretensions of Emperor Frederick Barbarossa and then of his grandson Frederick II, who was also king of Sicily (d. 1250). Developments in the south of Italy took on a different character, with the creation of the Norman kingdom of Sicily (including also southern Italy) in 1130; this became the base for a lively policy of Mediterranean expansion and, under Frederick II, for intervention in the politics of northern and central Italy as well.

The growing strength of the Western powers can be contrasted with the increasing debility of the Eastern Mediterranean states. Under the Komnenos dynasty, the Byzantine Empire did its best to resist the Turkish advance, suffering defeat twice, at Manzikert in 1071 and then a century later at Myriokephalon in 1176. Byzantium's Mediterranean dominion had been eroded with the loss of southern Italy to the Normans and of much of Anatolia to the Seljuk Turks. The final blow, however, was committed by the armies of the Fourth Crusade: in 1204 Constantinople was seized and pillaged, and its lands were divided among the victors (Venice acquired a claim to Crete, which was to become one of its most important Mediterranean possessions). Even the eventual reconquest of Constantinople from the Latins by Michael VIII Palaiologos (1261) did not lead to the recreation of the old universal empire, but to the creation of a Greek national state, which proved incapable of resisting the growing pressures of the Italian merchant republics on the one hand, and of the Turks on the other. In the Muslim world, the attempts at unification under the Zengids in order to make a common front against the Crusaders failed. This aim was taken up again by Saladin, who made himself master of Egypt in 1171 and then of Syria; but with the death of the champion of the *jihad* against the Latins in 1193 the common cause was again abandoned. His own lands were divided between his Ayyubid successors, who preferred to argue among themselves and even to make deals with the Crusaders, rather than to conduct a holy war.

The Crusades mark an important moment in Western expansion, the beginning of the process of reversal of forces in the Mediterranean, to the advantage of the Latin West. In the history of the Inner Sea, the Crusades brought a major expansion of sea traffic and began the Western colonization of Islamic lands. For a long time scholars believed that the Crusades coincided with the beginning of the Levant trade: the maritime republics were supposed to have become involved in the crusading expeditions in the hope of forcing open new markets. This over-simplified view is not sustained by the evidence. In fact, Genoa, Pisa, Venice and Amalfi already had commercial ties to Egypt, Syria and the Byzantine Empire 150 years before the First Crusade; they even had their own trading stations in some of those places, as had Venice and Amalfi at Constantinople. For this reason, these cities did not show immediate enthusiasm for the Crusade following the appeal for aid made by Pope Urban II in 1095: three years and more were needed before their fleets reached the eastern Mediterranean. The fact remains, however, that their aid was indispensable in the conquest of the coastal towns of Syria and Palestine, and in establishing regular links between the Frankish states newly created in the Levant and Western Europe; for it was thence that came the money, arms, horses and finished goods that were essential for the survival of the Latins in the East.

In exchange for naval aid the crusading leaders offered quarters in the conquered towns, as well as commercial and legal privileges; these enabled the Italian merchant communities to escape from the ordinary jurisdiction of the Latin states in the East. Genoa was asked to help convey eastwards the troops of Philip Augustus and of St Louis, while Venice launched 200 ships to transport the armies of the Fourth Crusade on their journey in 1202. The direct consequence of these efforts was the almost total disappearance of Arab fleets, of which few traces can be found after the capture of Ascalon by the Franks in 1153. The Mediterranean had become a Latin sea. And within the Mediterranean Latin merchants took the place of the Jews and Muslims in the traffic carrying luxury goods of Far Eastern origin westwards.

The beginnings of European colonization were another consequence of the Crusades. In each port of Syria and Palestine which had been conquered with their help, the maritime republics obtained from the kings of Jerusalem, the princes of Antioch or the counts of Tripoli very advantageous concessions of rights. Entire quarters passed into the hands of the Italian communes, offering them everything they needed for daily life: a church, a warehouse or *fonduk*, a palace (to serve as the office block), an oven, a mill, a bathhouse, a slaughterhouse and some arable land outside the town which could help with supplies. Acre, Tyre, Beirut, Tripoli, Laodicea and Antioch were divided in this way among the Italian merchants. At the head of each community, a consul, *bailo* or viscount exercised four principal functions. They maintained the rights of the mother-city over its overseas possessions; they presided over courts of justice which protected their fellow citizens against the possible depredations of local lords; they administered the goods and the revenues of the commune; and they intervened in favour of merchants, keeping an eye on contracts, wills and the apportionment of the goods of those who died intestate.

In other words, in the ports of the Latin East each privileged commune possessed all the structures necessary to conduct the social and economic life of a stable community that sought to escape from all outside interference. Other concessions included exemption from customs dues and taxes on commercial deals, generally known as *comerchium*, which in some cases was a total exemption, in others just a reduction; and jurisdictional privileges, permitting the members of the Italian communes to be judged solely by their own officials. The Italian (and Provençal) quarters were thus real colonies within the Latin states of Syria and Palestine.

Elsewhere, in Constantinople as in Egypt, the Italians possessed no more than trading stations still subject to the authority of the ruling power. In the Byzantine metropolis, the Italian republics obtained rights to quarters hard by the Golden Horn under the Komnenian emperors (1081–1185). The Venetians, Pisans and Genoese became absorbed in fierce rivalries which culminated in skirmishes between the communities, and in a rise in xenophobia among the native Greek population. The Venetians were expelled from the Byzantine Empire in 1171, and their goods were seized, while the Genoese and the Pisans were the victims of an anti-Latin riot in 1182. Under the Angelos dynasty (1185–1203), one or another of these Italian powers, profiting from the weakness of the Byzantine Empire, managed to obtain compensation for the attacks and further trading concessions. The Fourth Crusade enabled the Venetians to make themselves effective masters of Constantinople, and to take under their wing the feeble new Latin Empire that took its place.

Meanwhile, in Egypt, the activities of the Western merchants did not really give rise to the creation of a colony; the Fatimids and the Ayyubids preserved control of the *fonduks* which they had granted to the Italian communes, to Pisa and Venice in the twelfth century and to Genoa around 1200. They imposed restrictive measures, limiting the freedom of movement of these merchants in their lands, intervening in Latin trade and concentrating the commerce of the Western merchants in a closely delineated space, the better to watch over them. The Egyptian rulers retained their authority over the quarters conceded to the European merchants.

Benefiting from these privileges, the Italian maritime republics had no other aim than the establishment of their dominion over the sea. This dominion could be exercised thanks to the simultaneous use of two types of vessel which characterized the fleets of the great maritime centres of the Mediterranean: long ships equipped with oars, but also with one or two masts carrying lateen sails; and rounder vessels, propelled solely by the wind. These two types, which Frederick Lane saw as inheritors of traditions going back to the Phoenicians, evolved a great deal during the Middle Ages.

According to the contracts made between the commune of Genoa and St Louis, the thirteenth-century galley was 40 m (131 ft) in length, 5.5 m (18 ft) in breadth. It was graced by two masts with lateen sails, and was reinforced by a castle-like structure around the midden mast. It was propelled by two oarsmen at each oar and not by superimposed oarsmen as in the ancient world. By using oars, these vessels could manoeuvre well when entering and leaving ports, and oars were valuable when trying to make progress in a flat calm, while the lateen sail enabled effective use to be made of the winds. These ships moved easily between duty as warships and pirate ships, and duty as merchant vessels carrying precious goods; they rarely carried more than 20 to 30 tons of merchandise, with a crew of 140 men. This generated high transport costs. The galley family also included several similar types of ship: the galeass, which was shorter; the *galiote*, a small bireme galley, and the *saetta*.

In the category of bulky round ships, there existed a great variety of types. The most common was that simply known, from the Latin word *navis*, as the nef. Descriptions of Venetian nefs, such as the famous *Roccaforte* (38.19 m/125 ft long, 14.22 m/46 ft broad, 9.35 m/30 ft high at the middle), and the very precise measurements which can be found in the orders sent by St Louis to the Genoese shipyards, reveal the existence of sizeable round ships with two or three covered areas or bridges, raised at the ends to form towers fore and aft, themselves crowned with platforms on which stood the staterooms of the most eminent passengers and by crenellated and bratticed castles. These vessels, with their lateen sails fixed to long oblique cross-yards, required a crew of more than a hundred men, kept busy with the ceaseless raising and lowering of the sails, and this meant that the costs of running such a ship were onerous indeed. The thirteenth-century nef could carry in its hold up to 500 metric tons of goods; in other words, the productivity was 5 tons per crew member. Such heavy ships were complemented by middling and small vessels whose increasing activity is a sign of the great growth in commercial exchanges in this period: for example, the *lignum* ('wood', in Catalan *leny*), the *tarida* and the *bucius*.

How were these two main types of ship equipped and used? The high cost of cordage, anchors, sails and ironmongery meant that from the twelfth century construction costs tended to be shared. Depending on the importance of the ship, the capital that was to be invested in its construction was divided into sixteen, twenty-four or thirty-two parts: 'carats' in Genoa or Venice, *setzenes* (sixteenths) at Barcelona. These parts or shares were themselves divisible, and they could be sold or passed on to others, in such a way that risks were spread, but shipping also attracted investments that otherwise would never have been directed out to sea. Contracts for the hire of ships, drawn up by notaries, make plain the costs of transport for both passengers and merchandise.

As far as passengers are concerned, we see a slight fall in costs between the fares demanded of the troops of King Philip Augustus at the end of the twelfth century, and those asked of St Louis' emissaries in the mid-thirteenth. Pilgrims and Crusaders had to make do with a narrow space on the mid-deck, while the merchants took advantage of rather preferable conditions. They had the advantage of free transport to the East for themselves, their servants and part of their cargo. In Genoa, for example, freight costs could be measured by weight – *ad cantaratam* – or else the group of investors might hire rights to the whole vessel for an agreed sum, *ad scarsum*. According to the former system, those investing could demand that the goods be weighed at departure and that freight costs be paid in Genoese money. If, in addition, the merchants promised to return from overseas on the same ship, and also promised to load a similar quantity of goods to that which they had brought from Genoa, they would benefit from a discount on the return fare, but would have to pay it in the besants that circulated in Acre, rather than in Western currency. This rather complex system met the credit requirements of the merchants, which were less critical in Syria than back home, since they had sold their merchandise in Syria, whereas on leaving Genoa they found that all their capital was tied up in the cost of acquiring the cargo.

It was on this basis that there came into existence during the thirteenth century a fairly regular rhythm of maritime movement between the great sea ports of the West and the coast of the Levant. Departures for the Holy Land, Constantinople or Egypt normally took place at two periods each year: in the spring, they set out between 15 March and 1 May, though sometimes earlier. The second sailing normally occurred between 15 August and 30 September, but could in special circumstances happen as late as 15 October. Return journeys were also divided into two seasons, the summer and the months of November to December. A winter pause in the East, often limited to only a few weeks, broke the rhythm of navigation. It is worth asking whether convoys to protect the Levant sailings were also provided, which would then imply that the public authorities were taking an interest in the movement of trade. In Venice, the convoys of state galleys, the *mude*, only appear at the very end of the thirteenth century. In Genoa, the gathering together of investments for the Levant during a period of a few weeks, accompanied by the require-ment that shipowners must observe the city statutes, suggests that the nefs set out together, at least for part of the trajectory; this was less a journey conducted under a single command than one where the shipowners aimed to help each other. And indeed the resurgence of piracy in the fourteenth century made it a requirement to travel in convoy from 1334.

The Italian notarial contracts show how massively trade expanded between 1150 and 1250. Maritime routes multiplied and criss-crossed one another; direct links were established between the East and the Iberian peninsula, and eventually (1277) with England and Flanders. The Italians regularly visited the ports of the Maghrib, and they expanded their activities at Alexandria, apart from the times when a Crusade was under way. The Venetians took charge of the trade of

Latin Constantinople, and tried to make their way into the Black Sea, though without great success. Commerce expanded: the transport of Crusaders and pilgrims, including sometimes Muslim pilgrims on the *hajj*, was added to the carriage of an ever more diverse range of cargoes. Nor was it simply a question of trade between East and West: the Italian fleets were much engaged as well in trade between different eastern countries. A record of the lading of the Marseille nef the *Saint-Esprit*, which is based on 150 contracts drawn up between 14 and 31 May 1248, on behalf of the clients of the shipowner, illustrates marvellously well the variety of Western exports towards the East. There was a large quantity of cloth from Champagne, Languedoc, Flanders, England, Basel and Avignon, gold wire from Genoa and Lucca, fustians made of linen and cotton, linen of Paris and Germany, alongside saffron, tin, coral, mercury, fox pelts. For the export of Western cloths eastwards had taken on the character of a bulk trade by the end of the twelfth century. Wood and iron, which were in principle forbidden to be exported to Muslim lands because of their possible use in armaments, are well attested in the sales made by Italian merchants. The Iberian peninsula could add to these goods olive oil, wool, fruits, cloths of its own and quite a lot of human merchandise, as the Christian conquest of Muslim Spain made further headway: each stage of the *Reconquista* threw on to the market large numbers of slaves, for which Barcelona and Genoa were the major points of sale.

From the East came the traditional spices, perfumes and dye-stuffs, vying with sugar, linen, raw cotton, raw silk and the fixative alum (from the 1260s, when Phocaea fell into the hands of the Zac-caria of Genoa), as well as some textiles made of silk and cotton, *camelots* and brocades. What was new was the prominent place occupied among Oriental exports by agricultural goods and by raw materials. The great Italian cities, as well as Barcelona and Marseille, were experiencing strong population growth, but lacked the local food supplies to sustain this, which made them dependent on the grain surpluses of Sardinia, Sicily and further east, particularly in times of bad harvest at home. In 1156 the Genoese entered into a treaty with the king of Sicily in order to gain easy access to Sicilian grain and cotton; and they and the Pisans battled hard for control of the wheat lands of Sardinia, which also offered leather, cheese and other basic raw materials. Non-ferrous metals, which were in poor supply at home, were actively sought out by the Western merchants in the East. Although the balance of payments between East and West was very much in the East's favour around 1000, this began to change gradually, as the Western textile exports increased and began to smother the Eastern cloth industries, leading to industrial decline in the Near East. The West had the advantage of easier access to silver supplies than the Eastern lands, and much silver was used to make payments in the East, in effect to 'balance the books'; Catalan, Pisan and Genoese merchants also eyed the gold dust which reached the ports of the Maghrib across the Sahara; enough gold had been accumulated in Western trading cities by the mid-thirteenth century for Florence to begin minting gold coinage of its own in 1252.

The Mediterranean in the twelfth and thirteenth centuries also experienced important human migrations. Merchants have already been mentioned, even though their movements generally were only seasonal ones. But there were also those who established themselves permanently in the Holy Land or the trading centres of the Levant. The Latins in the Crusader states constituted 15 to 20 per cent of the population, perhaps 100,000 to 140,000 people. Pilgrims and Crusaders chose to take up residence in the kingdom of Jerusalem or on the coast of Syria, without planning to return to the West. They settled in towns, to be sure, but also, as recent research shows, in the countryside, in areas which had a significant eastern Christian population, while they tended to avoid the areas that had long been Islamized. Italian settlers took up residence in the trading centres set up by their city of origin; this was a migration with something of a national character, and it was a further example of a process of *inurbamento* by which the Italian city-states were drawing in population from the surrounding countryside, or *contado*. Venice systematically organized the Latin settlement of Crete, which was divided into sixths or *sestieri* just like the mother-city herself. In all, nearly 3,500 Venetians came to settle the island, a rather small figure by comparison with the subject Greek majority. Migration also affected the western Mediterranean lands: in Sicily, the old Muslim population declined, and large-scale immigration from northern Italy began to Latinize the island during the twelfth and early thirteenth centuries; in Spain, areas conquered from the Muslims, such as Majorca (1229) and Seville (1248), were resettled with Christians and Jews from the north of Spain.

Thus Western colonization of Eastern Mediterranean lands had few cultural effects, despite its demographic and economic significance. The main areas in which the transmission of the classical and Arab intellectual inheritance took place were the Italian south and the Iberian peninsula, especially Toledo. Elsewhere, it makes more sense to speak of coexistence rather than of acculturation. Christians and Muslims lived in separate worlds, even though spatially they were very close to one another. Each was the other's infidel.

From 1250 to the Black Death (1348–50)

The hundred years between the arrival of the Mamluks and the Black Death saw profound political changes in the areas bordering the Sea. In the West, the Spanish *Reconquista* reached its peak with the reign of King James I of Aragon (1213–76), conqueror of Majorca and Valencia, leaving Islam only the small Nasrid kingdom of Granada. These victories led to the Christian colonization of conquered lands, and the sale in the slave markets of many Muslim prisoners. While Majorca emerged as a significant centre of trade linking Europe to North Africa, Barcelona and Seville were confirmed in their role as maritime centres of the first rank, with the Catalans seeking to establish themselves in Sardinia and in Sicily following the revolt of the

Sicilian Vespers (1282), and even in the duchy of Athens. Meanwhile Seville acquired a key role on the routes leading to the Atlantic. In France, the Capetians strengthened their position in the south: after the creation of seneschalsies in Carcassonne and Beaucaire, which brought the royal domain right up to the Mediterranean, Louis IX gave his support to the construction of a port at Aigues-Mortes, and did not stand in the way of his brother Charles of Anjou when he accepted a papal proposal to take charge of the kingdom of Naples and Sicily, from which the last Hohenstaufen claimants were elimi-nated. Rivalry between him and the Catalans resulted in a division of his kingdom, with Sicily going to the Catalans and southern Italy to Charles and his Angevin successors. In the Maghrib, the disintegra-tion of the Almohad Empire brought the new dynasties to power in Morocco, around Tlemcen in modern Algeria and in Tunisia; and all of them favoured commercial ties with the Christians.

In the East, the Mamluks, slave soldiers who had become masters of Egypt, delivered the final blows to the Frankish states in Syria, which disappeared when the armies of al-Ashraf took control of Acre in 1291. The West could not accept the loss of the Holy Land; the papacy tried to impose trade boycotts against the Muslims, but found limited co-operation among the maritime republics. From the 1340s, the papacy began to issue trade licences, the profits from which would in principle help fund new Crusades. Theorists, lay and ecclesiastical, drew up many schemes for the recovery of the Holy Land, which assumed the co-operation of the Italian fleets and emphasized the role of Cyprus, the Latin Christian advance post in the Levant. None of these schemes was realized, in view of the reluctance of Western rulers who were more anxious to strengthen their own states than to fight for Jerusalem.

In Anatolia, the Seljuks were forced to accept Mongol over-lordship; the two Mongol khanates, that of the Golden Horde and the Persian Il-khans, established peaceful relations with Western merchants. These merchants took advantage of this to penetrate as far as Central Asia and even China, in the wake of Marco Polo: for more than three-quarters of a century, Mediterranean trade reached as far as Cathay. In the area of the Bosphorus, the restoration of the Greeks in Constantinople (1261) opened the Black Sea to their allies, the Genoese, and soon to the Venetians as well, even though the latter had supported the Latin Empire of Constantinople to the bitter end. Genoese and Venetian trading bases were established on the shores of the Black Sea: at Caffa on the Crimean coast, at Tana close by the Don estuary, in Trebizond, capital of the empire of the Grand Komnenoi. The Black Sea became a key link in international trade, bringing together Mediterranean trade and the Asian steppes.

The failure of the Crusades after 1270 induced a crisis in the cost of maritime transport which made the Western maritime cities think hard about the productivity of sea trade. The result was the 'Nautical Revolution of the Middle Ages', expressed in important technological changes which were only rendered obsolete in the nineteenth century, with the arrival of the steamship. At the start of the fourteenth century in both Genoa and Venice we begin to see the introduction of light galleys, *sottile*, which took full advantage of the qualities of a long, oared vessel; in addition to their use in piracy and war, they were well suited to the transport of light, high-value goods. Alongside these there were the great galleys, *galee grosse*, whose builders sought to combine the advantages of the galley with those of the round ship – a larger loading capacity – in order to increase the productivity of maritime trade. In Venice, the Romania galleys, bound for Greece and beyond, had a length of 40 m (131 ft), were 5 m (16½ ft) wide and could carry about 130 tons. But those bound for Flanders were even longer; they could be 50 m (164 ft) long, 9 m (29 ft) wide and could carry as much as 250 tons.

During the fourteenth century the use of a single rudder and two mainmasts was standard practice; the mainmast would have three lateen sails and one square sail, while the foremast would carry storm sails. These were the 'galleys of the market', fitted out by the state and auctioned to bidders by the Venetian Senate, for the profit of the merchants. The transformations in round ships were even more important: nefs with lateen sails were replaced by cogs, square-sailed and with a sternpost rudder, of which the first appearance in Genoa can be dated to 1286, and in Venice to 1312. But in Genoa the nef became an enormous round ship, with one to three *coperte* and a length to width ratio of about 3.6; its carrying capacity was 1,000 *botti* and it served the trade in bulk goods, especially the alum of Phocaea. However, in Venice the cog was merely the smallest of the larger ships; and in Barcelona it was a small ship with a superstructure, for Catalonia remained faithful to the *nau*, carrying a single rudder at the rear, with one or two covered areas and a carrying capacity of 300 to 700 *botti*. Navigation itself became safer thanks to the use of portolan charts and other maps: Pietro Doria used such a chart to explain the position of the ship *Paradiso* to St Louis while they were sailing on crusade to Tunis. The 'Nautical Revolution of the Middle Ages' increased the productivity of maritime transport, reduced costs and rendered easier the carriage of bulky goods. Thus a new élan stimulated the great Mediterranean trade routes.

All the same, the increased rivalries and the rise in piracy placed limits on naval activity. Maritime laws and regulations proliferated in all the major ports: the statutes of Zeno in Venice, the *Liber Gazarie* in Genoa, the *Llibre del Consolat del Mar* in Barcelona. It was necessary to organize trade in such a way as to avoid the perils of the sea and of pirates. Voyage by convoy (*in conserva*) became the practice in Genoa, while around 1300 the Venetian Senate put into operation the *muda* system, consisting of convoys of galleys armed by the state, which hired them out to the highest bidder. Thus in the first decades of the fourteenth century there came into being regular maritime routes towards Flanders, Romania, Cyprus, Little Armenia, and also towards Alexandria, despite the rigour of the papal prohibitions against trade with the Muslims. The arrival of the *mude* in Venice provided a rhythm to trade, stimulating the rise and fall of prices and the re-export of Oriental products. Notwithstanding these precautions, piracy became a scourge, fostered by the rivalries between the maritime republics. Reprisals and attempts to control pirates achieved nothing. The Mediterranean became an unsafe sea, well before the appearance of Turkish ships in the second half of the fourteenth century.

The opening of the routes to Central Asia and the Far East, rendered possible by the Pax Mongolica, was counter-balanced by the opening of routes towards the Atlantic, a major event of the end of the thirteenth century. In 1277, for the first time as far as surviving records reveal, a Genoese ship entered the Strait of Gibraltar to reach northwest Europe. The maritime link, which became regular after 1298, between the two economic poles of Christendom, Italy and Flanders, increased the importation into the Mediterranean of English wool, and Flemish and French cloths; it contributed to the decline of the Champagne fairs and the land routes along the Rhône and through the Alps by which products of the textile industry had previously reached the south and eastern produce had reached the north. While Venice insisted on the use of its own ships and on an obligatory halt in Venice herself, Genoa accepted the need to create a direct liaison between the East and Flanders or England. Indeed, two of its citizens, the brothers Ugolino and Vadino Vivaldi, even tried in 1291 to reach the Spice Islands by circumnavigating Africa. These precursors of Vasco da Gama or Christopher Columbus disappeared into the Dark Ocean, leaving behind the memory of an enterprise which the Portuguese were to take up again methodically in the fifteenth century. The Mediterranean became the heart of an international trade network, the true home of the discoveries and of the project for exploring the world that lay beyond.

This enlargement of horizons was in fact accompanied by an unexpected contraction of trade in the Mediterranean world. In Genoa, the value of the tax farm for the customs house, the *denarii maris*, stood at £3.6 million in 1293, more than double its value in

Genoese pounds in 1347, on the eve of the Black Death. However, the former figure does show that the loss of trading stations in Latin Syria was to a high degree compensated by the rise in business in Constantinople, the Black Sea, even Egypt, and above all in the western Mediterranean. The end of the thirteenth and the start of the fourteenth century saw the organization of the Venetian system of *mude* or convoys, mentioned earlier, whereby the Senate auctioned the services of the armed galleys carrying the most precious cargoes to and from Greece, the Black Sea, Cyprus, Little Armenia, Alexandria and Flanders. The Senate fixed who would command the ships, where and for how long the ships would halt, and what the freight charges would be. The auction price is a precious indication of the economic and political mood, for its expresses the hopes or fears of the merchants about the likely profit to be drawn from maritime trade. In less systematic ways, Genoa and Barcelona also intervened to regulate traffic and to protect their subjects from the danger of piracy.

The 'good thirteenth century' in the Mediterranean, stretching half a century beyond 1300, ended with a real catastrophe which upset the demographic balance: the Black Death. Starting most likely from the trading post at Caffa in the Crimea, the great pandemic spread like wildfire throughout the Mediterranean: Constantinople was afflicted during 1347, Messina and Marseille by December of that year, the great Italian cities and then those of Catalonia and Aragon by June 1348. The mortality varied between regions, but perhaps a third of the population died, while the recurrence of the epidemic in subsequent decades acted as a brake on the growth of the great Mediterranean cities, which needed at least half a century to climb back to the position they had held before 1348. At the same time, war in the Aegean and the Black Sea (1348–55), setting Genoa against Venice, Byzantium and the Catalans, disrupted trade and weakened the West in the face of the rising power of the Ottoman Turks.

Expanding horizons (1350–1500)

In the course of this century and a half, the Mediterranean political landscape underwent profound transformations. In the West, Aragonese-Catalan expansion continued in Sardinia and above all southern Italy, from which Alfonso the Magnanimous expelled the Angevins and became, after the capture of Naples in 1442, the master of both shores of the western Mediterranean. After long years of civil war in Castile and Aragon, the marriage of Ferdinand of Aragon to Isabella of Castile, and the success of this pair against the armies of Portugal, initiated the era of the Catholic Monarchs, who brought Christian rule to all Spain by their victory over the Muslim kingdom of Granada in 1492; the same year, thanks to their support, the Genoese Christopher Columbus first set foot in the New World, and the Jews were expelled from their many realms. Six years later, the Portuguese Vasco da Gama succeeded in circumnavigating Africa, reaching India, a discovery which threatened to undermine Italian supremacy in the Mediterranean spice trade.

Italy was in the grip of severe political crises. In the kingdom of Naples, the Angevins were in confusion, offering Alfonso of Aragon the chance to overthrow King René, his rival as heir of Queen Joanna II. The Great Schism, when two, or even three popes, claimed to rule simultaneously, brought chaos to the Papal States, while in northern Italy communal liberties faded away, leaving in their place the power of princes such as the Visconti of Milan, who extended their conquests throughout Lombardy and even for a time gained power in Genoa, where struggles among the noble clans consumed the city. Venice still pursued its vendetta against Genoa, especially during the War of Chioggia (1377–81), and then launched itself into the conquest of the mainland or *Terraferma* to ensure the security of the Venetian lagoon. Florence became a maritime power by annexing first Pisa (1406) and then Livorno (1421), before passing under the control of the Medici, who managed both the family bank and, to all intents, the Florentine state. Despite intervention by the French kings, who sought to realize their rights in Genoa and supported Angevin claims to Naples, the Italian powers came together in 1454 to sign the Peace of Lodi, which laid out for several centuries the basic political geography of the peninsula: several small principalities which, at the end of the fifteenth century, became embroiled with the king of France, who had been summoned by Milan to intervene militarily in Italian affairs.

In the eastern Mediterranean, the major political change was the advance of the Ottoman Turks. Entering the Balkans for the first time in 1354, the Turks were brought to a halt at the start of the fifteenth century by their defeat at the hands of Timurlane (Ankara, 1402); but from 1421 they began to sweep up the remnants of the Byzantine Empire once again. The ineffectiveness of the union of the Greek and Latin Churches agreed at the Council of Florence in 1439, and of the Varna Crusade of 1444, a disastrous attempt to provide Western aid to the dying Byzantine Empire, were confirmed by the fall of Constantinople on 29 May 1453. Next, the Ottomans took over the scattered possessions of the Greeks and Latins in the Balkans, attempting to cross into Italy. They were pushed back at Otranto (1480–81), but henceforth they constituted a great danger for Christian Europe, which had to await the victory over the Turkish fleet at Lepanto in 1571 for comfort.

It is, however, in the fifteenth century that we see the Levant trade attain its greatest prosperity. It benefited from many technical innovations. Notarial contracts, often drawn up for a single voyage, gave way to longer-lasting societies or companies, which extended their network of factors and representatives across the entire Mediterranean: that of the famous 'Merchant of Prato', Francesco di Marco Datini, and, in the fifteenth century, that of the Medici, who gained the concession of the Tolfa alum mines near Rome. They put into operation a well-developed information network, handled letters of exchange and other sophisticated banking techniques, and used maritime insurance to protect themselves against the dangers of sea transport.

Ships continued to improve: alongside the galleys, used by the Venetian Senate, cogs (*coche*) invaded the sea, heavy round ships with square rigging, and they became the standard merchant vessel, to the point where the word *cocha* disappeared in favour of the generic term *navis*. At the end of the fifteenth century, they evolved into the heavy carracks. Catalonia remained faithful to the *nau* with one or two *coperte* and a capacity of 300 to 700 *botti*. The move to larger tonnages favoured Genoa, which was more interested than Venice in the trade in heavy articles (alum, metals), in cereals and in raw materials. Various ships of middling and lesser tonnage (*ligna* in Genoa, *marano* in Venice, *leny* in Barcelona) offered the means for coastal navigation, redistributing goods that had arrived at the great ports.

These great ports to all intents controlled large-scale, long-distance Mediterranean trade, which had become increasingly complex. Papal prohibitions on trade with the Muslims were progressively lifted, in response to the closure of the Mongol spice and silk routes in the second half of the fourteenth century. Papal licences, originally conceded to specific merchants for a single year, became general by 1400: Venice obtained one for twenty-five years in 1399, taking the lead among the western nations present in Syria and Egypt. The *mude* (convoys) of Alexandria and Beirut became regular annual events, and were sometimes complemented by convoys of cogs in order to load Syrian cotton. In the last decades of the fifteenth century Venice sent an average of seven galleys each year to Alexandria and Beirut, and invested more than half a million ducats in spice purchases, as well as more than 150,000 ducats in cotton. Other nations had a lesser role in the Levant trade. The Genoese, while they did not neglect Alexandria, interested themselves more in Chios, with its trade in alum and mastic. They had a massive presence in the western Mediterranean, at Seville and Cádiz, which were really points on the route to Flanders and England. The hostility of the Catalans towards the Mamluk sultans damaged their Levant trade, for which two or three ships a year sufficed. As for the other Western merchants (the French, sent by Jacques Cœur, the Provençaux, the Montpelliérains, the Florentines, the Neapolitans, the Sicilians, the Anconitans, the Ragusans, the English), they remained very modest in scale and appeared only intermittently. The conquest of Constantinople by the Ottomans reduced to a trickle the trade with Greece and the Black Sea, which the Genoese mainly managed until the capture of Caffa and the other Crimean colonies in 1475.

To these direct exchanges between East and West, we must add the north–south traffic, which was also vital: wool and grain from northwest Africa, salt from Ibiza, Sardinia and the Adriatic, fruit and oil from southern Spain, wine from Calabria, wheat from Sicily, gold from Black Africa, all of which reached the shores of the Inner Sea. Raw materials and food products were exchanged for manufactured goods with a high added value. This was 'unequal exchange', which for some economic historians stands at the root of the underdevelopment of many a Muslim land, and of several southern European territories such as Sicily. To assure themselves of the benefits of trade, the Western merchant powers entered into treaties with the Hafsids of Tunis, the Marinids of Morocco or the Aragonese kings of Sicily. They created little merchant colonies throughout the western Mediterranean. Venice set up new *mude*, the *Trafego* bound for northwest Africa or Aigues-Mortes, while the Genoese made Seville into the headquarters of their operations in the western Mediterranean, as well as the jumping-off point for the colonization of the Atlantic islands.

Trade was not the only reason for the displacement of people. Even before the seizure of Constantinople by the Turks, many Greek scholars found refuge in the West, often carrying with them manuscripts; this stimulated a revival in the study of Greek in Italy, which played a significant part in the rise of humanist studies and in the transmission to the West of part of the classical inheritance. Other refugees from the Turks included Albanians and Slavs, who set up settlements in southern Italy. In the Iberian peninsula, the completion of the *Reconquista*, with the capture of Granada by Ferdinand and Isabella in 1492, was followed by the expulsion of the Spanish Jews (required to convert or leave) and ten years later of the Muslims under Castilian rule. Thus new diasporas upset the ethnic balance within the Mediterranean world.

By 1500 two great blocs divided the Inner Sea between themselves: the Christian West, divided, feeling threatened by the inexorable advance of the Turks; the Ottoman Empire, which would soon overwhelm Mamluk Egypt and which was assuming the entire political inheritance of the Muslim world. Byzantium had disappeared, and with it the idea of Christian universalism, which the nascent Russian principality began to claim in its stead. Although threatened, the great ports of the Christian Mediterranean still retained clear economic supremacy: Venice dominated the great Levant trade, though the arrival of the Portuguese in India was about to challenge this. Genoa, which would participate in the great transatlantic discoveries, was emerging as Spain's banker, while Catalonia was losing ground to Charles V's Castile. The Mediterranean was no longer the centre of the world, as it had been in 1000; it remained nevertheless the crucible in which the modern state would be forged.

The previous chapter described changes, particularly in the eastern Mediterranean, that brought the Italians effective dominion over the waters of the Inner Sea. Links were created to the Black Sea, too, which provided the forest products of the Asian steppes as well as grain from Crimea and Ukraine, and hazelnuts from Trebizond. Another significant change at the opposite end of the Mediterranean occurred in 1277 with the opening of the Atlantic exit to shipping bound for Flanders and England, where vessels were loaded with cloth and raw wool aimed at Mediterranean producers and consumers (for the fourteenth century was the golden age of the Florentine cloth industry).

As in the waters of the eastern Mediterranean, the western extremities of the Mediterranean were a battleground between Christians and Muslims, for until 1492 an Islamic state still controlled Granada, with its two flourishing ports of Málaga and Almería; and until its lasting capture by the Christians in 1462 Gibraltar generally lay in the hands of the rulers either of Morocco (the Berber Marinids) or those of Granada (the Nasrids). The great Muslim port of Ceuta opposite Gibraltar was also the object of intense competition, changing hands time and again. For in the Strait of Gibraltar, no fewer than six powers competed for influence: the Moroccans sought a toehold in southern Spain; the Granadans with great agility played them off against the Castilians, in order to preserve their own delicately balanced independence; the Catalan navies of the king of Aragon intervened, chopping and changing between allies, Christian or Muslim, but anxious to preserve free access through the Strait; the Genoese acted likewise; and the Portuguese arrived out of the blue in 1415, seizing the great Muslim port of Ceuta, which underwent immediate economic collapse and depopulation, leaving them with an expensive command post and none of the trade in gold and silk of which they had no doubt been dreaming.

This event, the fall of Ceuta (which ever since has remained in Iberian hands, being transferred to Spain in 1668), is often seen as the first moment in the expansion of Portugal and the creation of the great trading network and empire which would link Lisbon, and beyond that Antwerp, to the Indies without passing through the Mediterranean. Yet there can be no doubt that the Portuguese court, and in particular the enthusiastic Prince Henry 'the Navigator', saw the capture of Ceuta as a sign that their remote Iberian kingdom had re-entered the Mediterranean war against Islam, from which it had been cut off by the lack of a frontier with any Muslim states since the mid-thirteenth century. Portugal hoped to seize a share in Morocco and Granada, even though in these areas Castile was generally agreed to have a prior claim (while Aragon-Catalonia had reserved to itself the conquest of Algeria at some time in the future); and in 1497 the Castilians asserted their claims in Morocco with the capture of Melilla, a Spanish town to this day.

While it is easy to think of the divide between Muslim Granada and Morocco and Christian Castile, Portugal and Aragon as one between a Christian and a Muslim world, the economy of Granada was increasingly dominated by Genoese, Florentine and Catalan merchants, without whom, indeed, the revenues of the Granadan state would have been significantly less, and the Alhambra palace might never have been built. Málaga and Almería offered Western merchants silk, dried fruits and leather goods. Another product in high demand in northern Europe was the pottery of Granada, and similar Hispano-Moresque ceramics produced in the Moorish style in Valencia. In the fifteenth century, whole dinner sets emblazoned with coats of arms were regularly sent through the Strait to royal and noble purchasers in England and Flanders.

A similar economic role was played by Valencia and its *horta* or countryside; though a Christian kingdom, under Aragonese rule, since the 1230s, Valencia had a large population of Moorish artisans and farmers, who produced rice, fruits and ceramics for consumers as far away as England. In the fifteenth century, Valencia boomed; it became a halt for long-distance shipping bound for the Atlantic, and enjoyed massive levels of foreign investment by Genoese, Milanese, Flemings and Germans who were keen to buy its sugar, ceramics, dried fruits and rice, for export to northern European consumers; we even have German bankers from Ravensburg buying their own sugar plantations in far-off Valencia, to be worked by Moors in their service. Meanwhile, an intensive short-distance traffic around the coasts of Spain brought massive quantities of Biscay fish to Barcelona and Valencia, especially in Lent; and there was a constant traffic bringing wood from the Costa Brava to the shipyards of Barcelona, or grain from southern France. By 1450 regional specialization in the production of foodstuffs, raw materials and finished goods stimulated a commercial revival, founded on short-distance exchanges, and historians are increasingly sceptical of the view that territories such as Catalonia and Sicily had entered into steep economic decline.

One very significant development was the growth of interest in Granada and certain other sources of sugar and dried fruits that lay in the western Mediterranean and the eastern Atlantic, at a time when access to markets in the eastern Mediterranean which traditionally supplied these goods was rendered difficult by the Turkish invasions. So Granada, Valencia and Sicily all flourished as sources of good sugar in place of suppliers in Syria, while the supply of currants and raisins from Greece dried up, with Granada and Valencia offering alternative sources. This was a major change that was taking place in the fifteenth-century Mediterranean, a shift westwards in the sources of supply for luxury goods, so far westwards, indeed, that it passed beyond the Strait of Gibraltar into the newly discovered territories of Madeira, the Azores and the Canary Islands, with their new sugar plantations, and eventually, in the sixteenth century, would shape the future of the Caribbean and Brazil as centres of sugar production.

SEVEN

Resurgent Islam: 1500 – 1700

MOLLY GREENE

In an earlier chapter we have seen how the Roman *Mare Nostrum* was split and would not be reunited again. The cities and towns along the Mediterranean coastline had formed the vital centre of first the Roman Empire and then of the new faith of Christianity. Then, in the seventh century, in a series of lightning-fast conquests, a small group of warriors of uncertain identity thundered out of the Arabian peninsula and took the southern shores away from Roman Christendom, including some of its most historic cities – Jerusalem, Alexandria, Carthage. From that time onwards Muslims and Christians have faced each other across the Mediterranean and for almost as long historians have been debating the consequences of that divide. In modern times the name most associated with these debates is the celebrated Belgian historian Henri Pirenne.

Pirenne, who wrote in the first half of the twentieth century, devoted his life to the study of the transition from antiquity to medieval civilization. Although he was principally concerned with Europe, his argument had implications for historians of Islam in the Mediterranean world that could not be ignored. Pirenne argued that it was the Islamic invasions, not the fall of Rome, that destroyed the unity of the Mediterranean and ended the Roman world. Trade was the focal point of his argument: the Arabs closed the Mediterranean to the commerce of the West and international trade collapsed. Pirenne's ideas were so influential, and so productive of further debate, that they came to be known as the 'Pirenne thesis'. In the decades following his death (1935) a number of prominent medievalists and Arabists took on his arguments about the early Islamic polity and the policies it followed in the Mediterranean world. Although other parts of Pirenne's thesis have withstood the test of time, historians now generally accept that the Arabs neither desired to close or actually did close the Mediterranean to the commerce of the West.

A second Muslim advance

Almost a millennium after the Arab conquest a new Islamic power once again reached the shores of the Mediterranean. And, once again, it conquered a historic Christian city, Constantinople, the city of Constantine, capital of the Eastern Roman Empire or Byzantium. These new victors were part of a vast wave of Turks from the steppes of Central Asia. Their capture of Constantinople was the brilliant culmination of a westward advance that had been under way for at least three centuries. The Turkish warriors who took the Christian capital identified themselves as a dynasty, the Osmanli, or followers of Osman, their founder. In the Western world they are known as the Ottomans and they founded an Empire that endured for 600 years.

Outside a small group of specialists, this second Islamic advance has generated much less scholarly consideration, despite the fact that, to contemporaries, the capture of the great Christian city by infidels was a shocking event. This must be because, by the time European historians reach the fifteenth century, they are already anticipating the shift in the locus of European history far to the north and west and away from the Mediterranean: 'from the world of cloudless skies and blue seas to the dark and rainy climate of northern Europe'. In modern historical consciousness the conquest of the New World, which followed close on the heels of the Ottoman victory in Constantinople, has overshadowed the second Muslim advance in the Mediterranean world. Events in the Mediterranean were simply not believed to be as important for subsequent European history – and hence for Western historiography – which explains why, generally speaking, 1492 is a much better known date than 1453.

This does not mean that opinion is lacking on the Ottomans in the Mediterranean world; simply that it is less carefully considered. Not surprisingly, old ideas resurface, ideas that have been discarded for the Arabs but still cling to the Turks. They cluster around the image of closure and intrusion, whether metaphorical or actual. The appearance of the Ottomans meant the erection of a Muslim 'Iron Curtain' in the Mediterranean, a forbidden zone where Westerners might reasonably fear to tread and beyond which Muslims were loath to go, an Asian outcropping in an essentially Western sea. In 1968 the great medievalist Shlomo Goitein wrote: 'the unity of the Mediterranean world was disrupted only when the Islamic countries were taken over by intruders from the outside, mostly from Central Asia and the Caucasus, who had no share in that tradition'. The Turks, wrote Goitein, 'came from the depths of Asia,' and had 'no feeling for the sea ... they have always been more warriors than sailors'. The Ottomans closed the overland spice route that had once reliably brought spices across the Arabian deserts and into the ports of the Levant; this assertion is particularly galling, given that the Ottomans and the Venetians together tried mightily to prevent the re-routing of the spice trade. In George Kennan's words, their presence in the Balkans 'had the effect of thrusting into the southeastern reaches of the European continent a salient of non-European civilization'.

In fact the Ottomans restored, as much as they broke with, tradition. It is true that their extraordinary advance led to an extended period of warfare with Western powers – most notably Venice and Habsburg Spain – but, after all, warfare was not exactly new to the Mediterranean. What is more notable is that the Ottomans recreated, and even extended, the old imperial unity of the eastern Mediterranean that had been most closely associated with Byzantium and, before that, the Roman Empire.

The Ottoman Mediterranean: war

In the spring of 1451 Sultan Mehmet began work on a new fortress on the European side of the Bosphorus (Bayezit I had already built the fortress on the Asian side, Anadolu Hisarı, in 1393). He selected a spot overlooking the narrowest part of waterway and called it, appropriately, Boghaz-kesen, 'the cutter of the strait' or 'the cutter of the throat'. It is known to us today as Rumeli Hisar. Three great cannons, the largest that had yet been seen, were placed in one of its towers. Now, with a fortress on each side of the Bosphorus, he controlled all traffic between the Black Sea and the Mediterranean. Shortly thereafter, he declared that every ship sailing through the Bosphorus must stop for inspection; those who disobeyed would be sunk. Very soon, Mehmet was given the chance to show that he was serious. In November of that year a Venetian cog tried to sail through without stopping. Cannon balls weighing somewhere between 181 and 272 kg (400 and 600 lb) shot out of the great guns and the ship was sunk. Brought before the sultan, the crew was decapitated and the captain, Antonio Rizzo, impaled. Mehmet's destruction of the Venetian ship was the first impressive demonstration of the importance of artillery in naval combat in the Mediterranean. But, in firing his guns from land at a target sailing close to shore, he was also solidly within the age-old traditions of galley warfare. This co-mingling of new and old was entirely characteristic of the sixteenth century and thus provides an appropriate introduction to the Ottomans as a Mediterranean power.

It was in the sixteenth century that the Ottoman Empire expanded out of the Balkans and the Aegean and became a Mediterranean power. In 1516/1517 Sultan Selim defeated the Mamluks and absorbed the entire Levantine coast. At the same time, pirate-entrepreneurs, the most famous of which was Khaireddin Barbarossa, were entering into alliances with the North African rulers who were threatened by Spain. By the 1530s these informal relationships had evolved into formal incorporation into the Empire. In the same decade Barbarossa, now

Suleiman's naval commander, conquered many of the Aegean islands (most notably Crete and Chios), although important Venetian and Genoese colonies remained. In the course of expansion the Ottomans fought repeated wars with the Venetians and, especially, the Spanish, who were their arch-enemies in the Mediterranean (and elsewhere). Throughout the sixteenth century a number of places in the central and western Mediterranean changed hands several times or were fiercely contested. Philip II of Spain failed to take Jerba in 1560; and five years later the Ottomans gave up their siege of Malta. The Ottomans wrested Algiers away in 1529, but the Spanish managed to hold on to Oran until 1708. Spanish conquests east of Algiers were reversed by the end of the sixteenth century. Then there were the spectacular sea battles, such as Lepanto (1571), where no territory changed hands but naval losses were nevertheless extensive.

What were the Ottomans and the Spaniards after in their extended confrontation in the Mediterranean? Although we are often told that, in the seventeenth century, the Ottomans lost control of the Mediterranean, John Guilmartin's argument of 1974 still stands. Neither the Ottomans nor the Spaniards were ever in a position to control the Mediterranean, so it was not theirs to lose. The strategic thinking behind control of the seas, a concept which developed out of the North Atlantic experience, mandated that an enemy's maritime commerce be destroyed. This was done by, first, destroying his fleet and, second, blockading his ports so as to cut him off from maritime trade. Neither of these aims was possible or indeed meaningful in the sixteenth-century Mediterranean.

Maritime trade routes in the Mediterranean were not vital to the international trade of either power. Spain's primary maritime trade was in the Atlantic while the most important trade routes under Ottoman control were overland. The only exception to this was the Alexandria–Istanbul route, and the Ottomans zealously protected it. Second, for reasons particular to the technology of the galley, 'full-dress' engagements on the high seas between opposing fleets tended to be inconclusive. Finally, even if it were possible to destroy the enemy's navy (an anachronistic term in this instance), it would prove impossible to blockade his ports. Galleys, with their need to take on food and water frequently, simply could not stay at sea for an extended period of time. For these and other reasons, the goal of military strategists in the Mediterranean theatre was not to take on the enemy's fleet but rather to seize and control as many fortified ports as possible. The more ports they controlled, the more able they were to equip, protect and deploy large numbers of galleys. Indeed, Guilmartin argues that power at sea was heavily determined by power on land. Fortified ports were also important as bases for the incessant raiding, the *guerre de course*, that was such an important part of Ottoman–Spanish hostilities. The Ottoman siege of Malta, for example, was an attempt to secure a raiding base within striking distance of Spanish possessions in the western Mediterranean. Most naval conflicts, then, were fought in close vicinity to a fortified port – if not actually in the port itself – and were clashes between a fleet of galleys and the defenders of the port. Mehmet's actions in 1451 were squarely within that tradition (although of course in this case the ship was trying to get away).

The use of cannon, though, was new; and the critical story of the sixteenth century is how gunpowder weapons changed warfare at sea. It is ironic that the Spanish and the Ottomans were quick to place artillery on their galleys, for in the end it was the proliferation of artillery that rendered the galleys ineffective. Throughout the sixteenth century, both sides found themselves reluctantly caught in a costly upward spiral which only worsened with the appearance of well-armed northern ships later on. As they loaded more and more guns on their galleys they found that the galleys themselves had to be bigger and stronger. Thus they had to carry more men, both fighters and oarsmen, and this meant more provisions at a time when prices were rising and guns were taking up more and more room. Galley warfare became horribly expensive. The ever-increasing logistical requirements of deploying even one galley, let alone a fleet, also further reduced the already limited range of operation. By the mid-sixteenth century the Ottomans could not venture any further west than Tunis and expect to have time to settle into a protracted siege before the onset of winter storms.

Fernand Braudel reminds us that, although the Mediterranean has always charmed northerners with its sun, its colours and its warmth, it is fundamentally a poor region with few resources. The ever increasing scale of war in the sixteenth century ran up against this environmental constraint. The Ottomans and the Spaniards found that they could no longer summon up the requisite materials – both human and otherwise – to feed their war machines. Seen in this light, the battle of Lepanto in 1571, which was classic galley warfare, was not so much a turning point as the last spasm of a system that was slowly grinding to a halt, collapsing under its own weight. Although Spain (in alliance with other Western powers) did defeat the Ottomans, she was no more prepared to pursue her advantage by sending galleys into the eastern Mediterranean than the Ottomans were to try and land in Andalusia. The unwillingness, rather than the inability, of the Ottomans to engage in large-scale galley warfare with Spain is shown by the fact that, one year after Lepanto, the Ottomans had rebuilt their fleet. After Lepanto both the Ottomans and the Spaniards retreated into their separate corners of the Mediterranean, unwilling to pay an escalating price for continually shrinking gains. Thus the age of 'great wars' drew to a close. The seventeenth century would see a very different type of conflict at sea, more diffuse, more anonymous, and so harder to trace.

The Ottoman Mediterranean: trade

In trade, as in so many other areas, the Ottomans sought to restore an imperial unity and order that had been lost in the eastern Mediterranean with the proliferation of small states and the decline of large ones. The Ottoman sultans had no desire to prevent Western merchants, or any other merchants for that matter, from trading in the Ottoman lands; nor did they seek to impose a barrier between themselves and the world of international commerce. It would have made no sense for them to do so; the customs revenue from trade was a vital source of revenue and of course the goods themselves were important as well. They were determined, however, to assert their sovereignty and thereby avoid the extreme dependency that had characterized Byzantine–Latin relations in the late medieval period. Kate Fleet has made the fascinating observation that the Ottomans seem to have been more determined economic managers than the other Turkish emirates. Why this should be so is not clear. By contrast, Spain and the papacy actually forbade trade on ideological grounds. Under the Muslims, attitudes to trade in the Iberian peninsula had to some extent been laissez-faire; Christian Iberia would be much less so. The Latins, principally the Genoese and the Venetians, would no longer be able to enjoy full exemption from tariffs nor unlimited access to markets. This change has come down to us as Ottoman obstruction of Western traders. Steven Runciman, for instance, blames the demise of the Genoese trading colonies in the Black Sea in part on the fact that 'fewer and fewer merchants were prepared to pay the tolls demanded by the Sultan's officials there'. The notion that Mehmet the Conqueror raised tolls on trade after 1453 is now disputed; the extant archival material shows no complaints about tolls by Genoese merchants. It is again Kate Fleet who demonstrates the continuity of Ottoman policy before and after 1453. This suggests, as she points out, that the Genoese withdrawal from the eastern Mediterranean most likely had little to do with Ottoman policy.

Once they had captured Istanbul in 1453, the Ottomans attempted to reconstitute in full the trading links that had allowed Byzantine Constantinople to flourish, even to the point of utilizing the same Byzantine buildings to promote commerce, and keeping the same business centres. They were determined that the imperial city would once again be a grand capital; and any discussion of the eastern Mediterranean under the Ottomans must understand first and foremost the enormous pull of Istanbul. By the sixteenth century it was the most populous city in Europe. The crucial link was with the Black Sea, which was a vital source of cheap provisions, much more so than the relatively crowded and resource-poor Aegean. Indeed it is not going too far to say that the wheat, meat and salt from the sparsely populated northern coasts of the Black Sea made Istanbul's growth possible, just as they had done for the Byzantines before 1204. Mehmet the Conqueror acknowledged the importance of the Black Sea when he styled himself 'the Sultan of the two lands and the Khakan of the two seas'. The state that controls the Strait has always striven to establish control over the Black Sea as well. In order to ensure Istanbul's provisioning, Mehmet prohibited foreign ships from exporting certain goods from the Black Sea area, among which were grains, cotton, leathers, beeswax, animal fat and slaves. As we have seen, all ships had to stop at the castles on the Bosphorus for inspection. The international trade of the area, already in decline even before 1453, necessarily shrank even further after that date. But its regional trade underwent a huge expansion as ports such as Akkerman, Caffa, Costanta and Burgas shipped massive amounts of wheat, raw materials and slaves to the fast-growing capital.

The Ottomans were not content with conquering the territories of the Byzantine Empire. In 1517 they took Egypt and put an end to Mamluk rule in the Levant. Conquests in North Africa were quick to follow. Egypt is one of the traditional granaries of the Mediterranean (the other being Sicily) and now, for the first time in almost a millennium, Istanbul and Egypt were under the rule of the same master. The grain levy from Egypt to Constantinople that had been abolished by the Arabs in the seventh century resumed and the grain of the Nile valley became another vital source of food supplies to what was now Istanbul. A Spaniard writing home in 1581 marvelled that eight ships had arrived from Alexandria, laden with wheat, and yet this would not supply the city for more than a day.

The unification of the eastern Mediterranean basin under the Ottomans in the sixteenth century was not only a boon for the capital city. It also served to solidify a shift that had been under way since the late Middle Ages. Throughout the medieval period the western Mediterranean had been tightly integrated into the long-distance luxury and spice trade that originated in Asia. Muslim Spain was one place where East and West (or, more properly, north and south) met and exchanged goods. A solid block of Islamic states stretching from Arabia to Iberia linked the two great seas, the Mediterranean and the Indian Ocean, and merchants moved easily across this vast territory; it is this world that is recorded in the documents of the Cairo Genizah studied by Shlomo Goitein. A vital trade route moved south from Spain, along the southern shores of the Mediterranean and then by sea or overland to the Indian Ocean. The northern shores of the Mediterranean were at first incidental to this international economy. As is well known, the Spanish *Reconquista* and the rise of the Italian mercantile republics put an end to this world. Less attention has been paid to what happened after that. The nexus between East and West moved to the eastern Mediterranean where it would stay until the seventeenth century (reports of the death of the spice trade in the sixteenth century turn out to have been premature). Muslim and other merchants who used to come to Iberia to buy goods for transport to the East now relied on other markets to supply the same goods. Already by the late thirteenth century, for example, Egyptian slave dealers looked to Central Asia, not Spain, for supplies.

The eastern drift of the international silk market was particularly critical in the rise of Ottoman power. By the early thirteenth century the Andalusi silk industry, which had provided the preeminent exports of Muslim Spain, was in decline. There were a number of reasons for this; an important one was that both Italian and Muslim merchants now found that they had better access to Byzantine, Chinese and then Iranian raw silk once disorders in the Mongol Empire limited trade with China. The Italians and the Muslims both benefited from the Pax Mongolica, which opened the silk road to China. The Italians also benefited from their increasing control over Byzantine markets. By 1300 most of the raw silk consumed by the Italian silk industry came from the Caspian provinces of Persia (later still, Italy itself became a significant raw silk producer). The new route to the West ran straight through Anatolia. In 1326 the Ottomans established their first capital at Bursa, in western Anatolia, and thus became the masters of this vital new trade route. They then set about making Bursa a world market between East and West, not only for raw silk but for other goods from Asia as well. This effort was a resounding success. 'The city,' Professor Inalcık writes, 'became the great emporium for Asian trade, overshadowing Baghdad and other Near Eastern outlets of world trade.' Later on, with the conquest of Syria and Egypt, the Ottomans benefited from the revenues of the spice route through the Red Sea as well.

The new importance of the eastern Mediterranean ports, which predated the Ottoman advance but which they certainly capitalized on, and the unification of the northern and southern shores under one ruler combined to give the sixteenth-century eastern Mediterranean a dynamism and a unity that it had not known for many centuries. A highly developed regional economy based on the provisioning of Istanbul existed side by side with the great international cities – Bursa, Cairo, Aleppo – which were now the meeting points of East and West.

Imperial Islam

With the defeat of first the Byzantines and then the Mamluks, the Ottomans put an end to a very long period of political fragmentation in the eastern Mediterranean. Secure in their position as leaders of the Islamic world, the sultans of the fifteenth and sixteenth centuries sponsored a brilliant revival of high cultural life, as well as the strengthening of Islamic civilization in the Mediterranean basin. While the medieval Muslim world was perhaps held together by the doctors of the law and the ceaseless travels of international merchants, now a confident imperial Islam radiated outward from Istanbul, reaching deep into the river valleys of the Balkans and across the sea to the ancient cities of the Arab world.

In the Balkans the Ottomans pursued an energetic programme of urbanization. Cities like Sarajevo and Mostar were Ottoman creations; while other places, such as Plovdiv (in today's Bulgaria) and Kavalla (in today's Greece) grew from minor towns to great commercial and cultural centres. The Selimiye mosque of Edirne, built by Sinan in the second half of the sixteenth century, is considered by many to be the crowning achievement of Ottoman architecture. In all these places Ottoman notables, in accordance with the initiative and generosity expected of the sultan's servants, established pious endowments known as *evkaf* (sing. *vakıf*, i.e. *waqf*) to fund the buildings that were indispensable for an Islamic city and an expanding empire. Mosques, schools, baths and khans proliferated, along with covered markets, aqueducts and monumental bridges of great beauty, such as the one made famous in Ivo Andrić's book *The Bridge on the Drina*.

In the Arab world, Suleiman the Magnificent rebuilt the walls of Jerusalem and a steady building project, facilitated, again, by the institution of *vakıf*, expanded the ancient cities of the Arab world. Mamluk Cairo had largely been confined to the old Fatimid town of al-Qahira. Under the Ottomans, the city quickly outgrew these limits. Following the construction of public fountains we can see that settlement of areas further to the south began as early as the sixteenth century. After that new neighbourhoods grew up in the west, beyond the canal which had traditionally marked the western edge of the city. The nineteenth-century historian Ali Pasha Mubarak noted that the city's tanneries were moved to a more remote location in the sixteenth century, and links this explicitly to the growth of the population. The Ottoman governor of Aleppo in the mid-sixteenth century, Husru Pasha, was responsible for beginning the development of the area south of the Citadel. He had built what we might call today a shopping district, including the great khan of Qurt Bey, warehouses and shops. The new building project stretched over 4 hectares (12 acres) and the revenue went to support the mosque in Aleppo that bears his name.

Even in distant North Africa the coming of the Ottomans, who pacified the tribes and confronted the Spanish, led to a revival of urban life. Between 1500 and 1580 the population of Algiers tripled and, again, the élite commissioned the construction of mosque complexes to meet the social and religious requirements of urban life. The congregational mosque of the Ottomans in Algiers, with its dome and its circular minaret, brought the spirit of the East to the cities of North Africa where minarets were traditionally rectilinear and the mosques themselves were covered with green tiles.

These élite projects were part of a much larger trajectory in Ottoman society and politics. After 1453 the sultans had an empire to protect and this meant that groups from the heady days of the frontier principality, principally the *gazi* warriors and the more antinomian Sufi orders, were now seen as threats and were systematically marginalized. Henceforth the servants of the palace were to be the emissaries of Ottoman culture. Paradoxically perhaps, frontier society had been the site of both an Islamic warrior ethos and a complex intermingling of Muslim and Christian society, particularly within the framework of the mystical orders. The revolt of Šeyh Bedreddin, early in the fifteenth century, united Turcomans, *gazis*, Christian peasants and other malcontents in an attempt to dislodge the Ottomans.

It is striking that, at the opposite end of the Mediterranean, the Spanish Habsburgs, too, were putting an end to frontier society and its long history of Christian–Muslim co-existence, although in a much more dramatic and definitive way. If we consider these two projects together, and add to that the stabilization of the military frontier after Lepanto, we must ask whether there was a similar hardening along cultural or religious lines. Andrew Hess has indeed argued this point: 'to state it baldly, I believe that the separation of the Mediterranean world into different, well-defined cultural spheres is the main theme of its sixteenth-century history'. Hess's argument is a convincing one for the western Mediterranean. The Spanish *Reconquista* broke the long-standing ties between the Iberian peninsula and North Africa and the sea now divided the Christian from the Muslim world.

The picture is more complicated in the East, however. In the first place, the Ottomans revived, rather than defeated, the imperial project that had known such longevity in the eastern Mediterranean. It was a source of pride, rather than weakness, for the sultan that he ruled over such a diverse collection of nations and religions. Second, it is often forgotten that the eastern Mediterranean is the point of intersection for not two, but three, enduring civilizations: Islam, Latin Christendom and Eastern Orthodoxy. Here the Ottoman conquest was experienced not only as the advance of Islam at the expense of Christianity, although that was certainly part of the story, but also as a very welcome reversal of the fortunes of Latin Christendom. For the first time in many centuries, the Orthodox Church was backed, even if for reasons of *Realpolitik*, by a strong and expanding military power. The Ottomans continued the policy which Muslim rulers had followed since Saladin's recovery of Jerusalem in the twelfth century: to play the Latin and the Orthodox Churches against each other. This was in order to prevent the formation of a united Christian front which could threaten the Empire. The Ottomans and the Orthodox Church shared an interest in reining in the Latins who had, after all, launched the Crusades and, later on, played such a dominant role in the Byzantine Empire. The revival of the Orthodox Church followed apace.

This process was most significant, naturally, in those areas of the Empire where the Latins had been strongest, namely the coasts and islands of the eastern Mediterranean (particularly in the Aegean) and in Palestine. Further inland, in the Balkans, for instance, the dynamics were rather different. In Jerusalem a monk named Germanos arrived from Istanbul in 1543 to take charge of the patriarchate. Through his reforms he ensured that the hierarchy of the church in the city would be Greek-, rather than Arabic-, speaking. Less than ten years later he added his support to an ultimately successful Muslim campaign to oust the Franciscans from the lower storey of the church of the Cenacle. The Greek hierarchy of the Orthodox Church would score much greater victories against the Latin Christians in the seventeenth century, including winning control over the church of the Nativity and most sites in the church of the Resurrection.

In the Greek-speaking world of the islands, the Ottomans conquered one piece of Catholic territory after another, in a series of wars that lasted from the fifteenth to the early eighteenth century. In all these places an Orthodox, Greek-speaking hierarchy replaced the departing Latins. Throughout their 500-year rule on the island of Crete, the Venetians allowed no Orthodox bishops on the island and would move to arrest anyone who managed to evade the prohibition. Now the roles were reversed. In the 1530s the central Aegean island of Naxos surrendered to the Ottomans and agreed to the appointment by the patriarch of Constantinople of a Greek Orthodox bishop. When a Latin bishop appeared on the island in 1540 without receiving permission from the Ottoman authorities he was arrested.

Ottoman culture itself was not synonymous with orthodox Islam. It was an empire based on an innovative combination of multiple inheritances: Inner Asian, Anatolian, Byzantine, Islamic and European. Certainly, as the empire grew the Sultans were eager to encourage the more conservative aspects of the Islamic tradition. But they had no intention of turning their back on, for instance, Sufism and Sufi practice, as long as it was not allowed to disrupt the stability of society and the state. In the seventeenth century a series of Ottoman sultans defended Sufi practices against a sustained attack by Islamic reformers. The Ottoman sultans themselves continued to have strong personal ties to certain Sufi Orders. Sultan Murad IV, who ruled from 1648 to 1687, is a good example. His mother was a generous patron of the Halveti Order. At his accession ceremony, Murad chose the sheikh of the Celveti Sufi Order to gird him with the dynastic sword. This sheikh had been the beloved *pir* (teacher) of his father, Ahmed I. During his reign, Murad enjoyed the performance of the *sema*, the mystical dance that is part of Mevlevi ritual, at the palace.

Finally, the Ottoman court was an enduring site of cultural innovation across religious boundaries. Towards the end of the sixteenth century, for example, the sultans began to turn away from their exclusive reliance on Persian musicians and repertoire at court. This relationship had come about because of the great prestige that was accorded to a wide variety of Persian art forms. In the seventeenth century a new musical synthesis that drew on Turkish, Armenian and Greek musical traditions would emerge.

The seventeenth century: trade wars

The seventeenth-century Mediterranean sits uneasily between the age of Ottoman expansion which preceded it and the European-led commercial boom of the eighteenth century. A murky time of corsairs, free-wheeling consuls and converts of uncertain identity, it has often been overlooked by historians with their orientation towards the state. Throughout much of the period, no one power was able to dominate the sea. The Italian city-states had lost their position of dominance – the strength of the Venetian merchant marine was cut in half between 1550 and 1590 – but France, due to internal turmoil, was not yet in a position to replace the Italians: in his monumental study of the trade of Marseille, Paul Masson characterized the seventeenth century as one crisis after another and one in which the French were continually threatened with the ruin of their commerce. In fact, French commerce in the ports of the eastern Mediterranean fell from 7 million livres in 1648 to between 2.5 and 3 million livres in 1660. It did not begin to recover until 1685. The Dutch and the

English were maritime powers of the first order, certainly, but their presence, at least east of Italy, was intermittent. Thus late in the 1630s the Venetian bailo observed that there were only two Dutch merchant houses in Constantinople and that Dutch ships were an infrequent sight there: 'the ships which sail to Constantinople from this nation are rare and they have only two merchant houses here' (*rarissimi sono li vascelli che capitano a Costantinopoli di quella natione e due sole le loro case di mercanti*). The Ottomans had to struggle just to maintain a minimal amount of order in certain key sea lanes, such as the route between Cairo and Istanbul.

Because of this, the Mediterranean world was more multinational and fragmented than it had been since the fourteenth century. Underneath the surface, however, a historic change was in the making. It was during this time that certain European leaders, particularly the French monarchs, fought hard and ultimately successfully to impose something like a nation-state grid on what had traditionally been a cosmopolitan world defined more by religion and empire than by nation or state. In the first half of the century, however, Europe was sunk in the miseries of the Thirty Years' War, and the corsairs ruled the seas. Their supremacy was made possible by the decision of both the Ottomans and the Spaniards, after battling each other nearly continuously throughout the sixteenth century, to call a truce. The two empires turned their attention elsewhere, the Ottomans to the East and the Spanish to the New World.

The North African coastline was the centre of Muslim privateering, while the small island of Malta sheltered the most fearsome Christian predators, the Hospitaller Knights of St John, formerly of Rhodes and, prior to that, Jerusalem. Algiers was the most powerful North African city; in the 1620s she had around a hundred armed sailing vessels and something like eight galleys. The Knights of Malta, along with a host of other lesser-known Christian pirates such as the Knights of Santo Stefano in Pisa, concentrated their activities in the eastern Mediterranean. Christian piracy in Ottoman waters had been almost unknown prior to the Ottoman defeat at Lepanto (1571) but after that date they swarmed in and feasted off the rich Ottoman trade for well over a century. The greatest prize of all was the convoy of ships that sailed regularly between Egypt and Istanbul. One particularly spectacular attack happened in 1644. A ship sailing to Egypt from Istanbul with a number of high-ranking Ottoman officials on board was captured near Crete by the Maltese. Many were killed, including the chief of the harem, whose treasure was shared out among the pirates. This outrage, combined with a more favourable international situation, convinced the Ottomans to try to wrest Crete away from Venice, since they believed that the Venetians were in the habit of giving the Knights of Malta safe haven on the island (a charge which the Venetians vigorously denied). The Ottomans did, eventually, conquer Crete; but their victory did little to improve security in the eastern Mediterranean. They must have been discouraged when, in 1669, the very year of their victory, a fleet led by one Gabriel de Témėricourt captured an enormous galleon and some smaller ships sailing to Egypt from Istanbul.

The ships of the North African regencies – Tripoli, Algiers and, to a much lesser extent, Tunis – operated much more in the western Mediterranean and even out into the Atlantic. Their rise to power in the early sixteenth century, after all, was inseparable from the Ottoman confrontation with Spain, and this orientation continued even after the sultans had retired from the fight. The protracted war between England and Spain at the end of the sixteenth century was another great opportunity for them as the English used the African ports as a base from which to attack their enemy. It was during the course of this war that English adventurers flocked to the North African coast, and these cities became even more international. In 1609 the English consul in Algiers recorded the arrival of a great ship, built in Lübeck and manned by a mixed crew of Turkish, English and Dutch sailors. English pirates moved slowly eastward and were very active in the multi-pronged attack on Venetian shipping that did so much to destroy Venice's centuries-old position in the Levant. A Venetian official on the island of Crete in 1604 vented his frustration in a report sent back home: 'these damn bertons which sail in these waters to their heart's content, stealing from and plundering everyone, and not permitting even one caramousal, loaded with grain, to approach, as they used to'.

As the century progressed, the North Africans were presented with another great source of prizes close to home. An increasing number of Dutch and English ships were sailing through the Strait of Gibraltar, to trade first with the Italian cities and then with the Ottoman Empire itself. These great vessels, along with a host of smaller French ships, presented a very tempting target; and the attacks of the 'Barbary pirates' (as they were known in Europe) on European shipping became one of the best-known features of the seventeenth-century Mediterranean world.

Despite the prominence of corsairs who (on both sides) justified their activity in terms of religion, it would be a mistake to assume a clear-cut battle between Christianity and Islam in the way that Spanish–Ottoman rivalry defined the sixteenth century. Christian corsairs were just as likely to attack Christian shipping – the concerted attack on Venice being the most spectacular example – and the sale of safe-conduct passes (to protect the buyer from corsairs!) was brisk across religious lines. The North Africans were known to sell safe-conduct passes even to Maltese merchants; and the French merchant D'Arvieux, in Tunisia in the second half of the seventeenth century, observed with some astonishment: 'the ports of this kingdom are free to all the world.... The Maltese even, although the irreconcilable enemies of the Tunisians and of all the people of Barbary ... come here laden with their own flags displayed.'

In 1647, in response to pressure from Catholic officials in the Holy Land, the Knights of Malta forbade Maltese ships from approaching within ten miles of the Palestinian coast. In 1697 the forbidden zone was increased to fifty miles. In 1679 the French king Louis XIV issued an order prohibiting French subjects from serving in Maltese corsairing ships on cruises in the Levant. More generally, he exerted heavy pressure on the Knights to withdraw their ships from the eastern Mediterranean. Various threats were issued, such as the seizure of all the Order's possessions in France. The combined efforts of the papacy and, more importantly, the French government, were eventually successful in ending Catholic piracy in the eastern Mediterranean, for although it was not until the early 1740s that the Grand Master of the Order formerly declared that no more corsairs should be licensed to cruise in the Levant, activity over the prior twenty years had been minimal. The interesting point is that it was two Christian powers, rather than the Ottoman navy, which reined in the last remnants of the medieval Crusaders in the eastern Mediterranean. What were their motives?

The case of the papacy is quite straightforward. It wanted to protect, and to be seen to protect, Christians in the Near East. It also sought continuously to discipline the Knights of St John who were, after all, a papal Order, but did not always comply with the wishes of Rome. The French monarchs had rather different motivations. By the 1660s peace had returned to France and Jean-Baptiste Colbert, the King's minister, was hard at work expanding French trade in the Mediterranean. This meant, first and foremost, increased dealings with the Ottoman Empire; and in this context the Knights of St John had become an irritant. The Knights, faithful to their crusading ideology, claimed for themselves the right to disrupt and punish commercial relations between Christians and Muslims, even if the Christian ships in question belonged to His Christian Majesty. In an age of French commercial expansion, this was no longer acceptable. Pressure on the Knights of Malta was just one measure among many whereby the French monarchy strove to reshape the contours of Mediterranean commerce in such a way that trade would now serve the state, rather than the disparate goals of individuals of uncertain identity and allegiance. By the last quarter of the century the corsairs of both North Africa and Malta were no longer allowed to stop and inspect French ships, looking for cargo or passengers disallowed by the rules of the *corso*. At the same time, the state tightened its control over French consuls in the Mediterranean, and granted jurisdiction over all French individuals in the Levant to the Marseille Chamber of Commerce.

Across the Mediterranean, Louis XIV sought to break the ties of marriage, property and religion that had developed between Frenchmen and locals. The connection between these policies and nation-building is made clear by the remarks of the King's emissary, Pitton de Tournefort, concerning the French colony on the Aegean island of Sikinos which he visited in 1700:

> there is no harsher punishment for an old sinner than to marry in Greece, ordinarily the women that they marry are without virtue or property; and yet one sees many doing this, despite the vigorous prohibition of the King who, for the honour of the nation, has very wisely ordained that none of his subjects be allowed to marry in the Levant without permission of the King's ambassador or one of his agents.

The state, in other words, did not just defend national trade in the Mediterranean; it was instrumental in its creation and much of that work was done in the seventeenth century. The disciplining of the two great pirate cities – Valletta and Algiers – meant not only a more peaceful sea in the eighteenth century, although that was an important result; it also meant the suppression of two multinational societies organized along religious lines in favour of trading communities defined in national terms.

Livorno and Smyrna

The seventeenth century saw the growth of two great trading emporia that were able to capitalize on the chaotic and violent conditions of the time. Livorno and Smyrna (today's Izmir) symbolized their age, just as surely as Genoa and Venice had earlier stood for the rise of the Italian maritime republics. The port of Livorno (Leghorn), which grew from a small settlement of roughly 500 to a commercial centre of over 12,000 people by the middle of the seventeenth century, was the creation of the Medici of Florence. The Medici, beginning with Ferdinand I (1587–1609), realized success in part because they were innovative in facing the problems of the age. In their prime, Genoa and Venice passed port regulations designed to favour their own merchants and their own shipping to the exclusion of others (thus a Cretan merchant named Costa Michel managed to ship a cargo of pepper to Venice early in the fourteenth century, but when he reached the city the pepper was seized because his name did not appear on a list of Venetian citizens). By the seventeenth century, however, the naval capability and the mercantile vitality of all the Italian port cities was in decline. The key to success lay not in excluding foreigners, but rather in attracting them to one's port rather than the port of one's neighbour. This was difficult for older cities with well-established hierarchies, such as Venice, which offered no special privileges to foreigners in order to protect its own merchants.

Livorno, as a new settlement, was free of such obstacles. The Medici passed a series of privileges, known as the *Livornine*, in 1591 and 1593. These laws invited foreign merchants to come and settle in Livorno and offered them such things as freedom of trade, tax exemptions, good housing, storage facilities and a relative freedom of religion. Special attention was paid to the Jewish refugees from Spain, many of whom were by now settled in the Levant and North Africa. They would be ideal intermediaries between Tuscany and the Ottoman Empire. While multinational port cities were commonplace in the Ottoman Empire, they were still remarkable enough in Christian Europe for Livorno to become known as 'the ideal city and the fatherland of everyone' (*la città ideale e la patria di tutti*). The Medici also skilfully promoted Livorno as a free port (*porto franco*), a place where the transit trade was not taxed and foreign merchants settled in the city paid less duties than elsewhere. The *Livornine* profited by an extended grain crisis in the Mediterranean that hit the Italian peninsula hard. For the first time, shipments of grain from northern Europe – Germany, Poland, England – became widespread and the Grand Duke of Tuscany was at the forefront of the movement. In 1590 he became the first Italian ruler to send agents to Danzig (Venice followed soon after), and over time Livorno became the master of the grain trade. Not surprisingly, northern merchants were also invited to settle in Livorno, and the new port became the favourite of the English, under the slightly bizarre name of 'Leghorn'.

While Livorno drew great profit from the transit trade between East and West, it also benefited from its propinquity to the ports of North Africa. As a city of the seventeenth century, Livorno was deeply implicated in the corsair economy that linked the northern and southern shores of the Mediterranean. A Venetian report from 1624 explained how it worked: 'Livornese, Corsican, Genoese, French, Flemish, English, Jewish, Venetian and other merchants are settled in Algeria and Tunisia. They buy up all the stolen merchandise and send it to the free port of Livorno and from there it is distributed all over Italy.' These ties, although widespread and well known, were not publicized, for obvious reasons. Publicly, the Medici supported the Christian Crusade against the infidel, despite the policy of religious tolerance in Livorno itself. The port was the home base of the Knights of Santo Stefano, founded in 1562 in imitation of their more famous counterparts on the island of Malta. Owing to the Knights' raids, Livorno enjoyed a lucrative trade in captured Muslim slaves, whether Turkish or North African, and Cosimo II (1609–21) made sure that ten galleys were always at the ready for such forays. In 1607, to cite just one example, the Knights burned Bône, the principal commercial port of eastern Algeria, killing 470 people and taking 1,500 captives.

The port of Smyrna (Izmir), on the western coast of Anatolia, was remarkably similar to Livorno in the seventeenth century, although the context was different. Throughout most of the sixteenth century, Smyrna was just one of many small port towns along the Anatolian coast. Whatever modest amount of agricultural surplus might become available was sent along to the imperial capital. Istanbul encouraged this relationship; the Sultan was anxious to ensure the provisioning of the city and did not want the Empire's foodstuffs diverted to Western merchants. Towards the end of the century this quiet situation began to change. There had always been some Western merchants operating in the area, and low-level smuggling, made easier by the jagged coastline with its many inlets, was an enduring fact of life. With the repeated grain crises of the 1590s, the number of Western merchants – first Venetian, then Dutch, English and French – began to grow, as did the amount of smuggling. Smyrna was at the centre of this trade. Grain-hungry Western merchants and their Ottoman collaborators were helped enormously by a series of disorders in western Anatolia known as the *celali* revolts which extended well into the seventeenth century.

Low levels of security made it difficult for the Ottoman government to enforce provisioning of the capital (at state-mandated low prices) as it had in the past and locals quickly took advantage. In a document from 1592 we read about a 'rogue and a robber' named Fırıncı oglu Reis in the vicinity of Smyrna who wandered about and presented himself as the captain of a royal galley, sent down to buy grain for Istanbul. He bought copious amounts of grain in this manner, at the official low price, and then turned around and sold it at an enormous profit to Western merchants. Attracted initially by grain, the Westerners soon discovered that the fertile valleys of western Anatolia produced many other products as well: honey, fruit, nuts, cotton wools and tobacco to name just a few. Later on in the seventeenth century Smyrna became famous as the Mediterranean outlet for silk coming from the East. Fuelled by a combination of Western demand, Anatolian insecurity and local complicity, Smyrna began to grow rapidly. In 1600 fewer than 5,000 souls inhabited the town; by 1650 that number had risen to 30,000 or 40,000. Whereas no European consuls were resident in Smyrna in 1600, the Dutch, the English, the French and the Venetians all had representation by 1620.

Like Livorno, then, Smyrna was a new city which began to surpass older commercial centres such as Aleppo in the seventeenth century. And, as with the Italian port, those who drove the city's growth, those who throve there, were newcomers, particularly from northern Europe. The Dutch and the English favoured Smyrna, in part because its commercial networks were still developing, and thus not already dominated by the older Mediterranean powers such as the Venetians and the merchants of Marseille. Venetian traders were present, of course, in Smyrna but they proved much less able to adapt to the changed conditions of the seventeenth century, whereas the Dutch and the English flourished. The Venetians, through long force of habit and bureaucratic rigidity, complained to Istanbul about bandits and corrupt officials who were hindering their trade. The English and the Dutch paid these same people off and worked steadily to extend their reach into the hinterland.

Part of this effort involved the recruitment of local middlemen – Jews, Greeks and Armenians – and thus seventeenth-century Smyrna also foreshadows the rise of the non-Muslim Ottoman communities, particularly the Christians. This development was specific to the eastern Mediterranean. The Jewish community expanded and experienced a great cultural revival as the result of the immigration of large numbers of Jews of Spanish descent; as well as being home to many Jewish artisans, the city was a centre of Hebrew printing from the mid-seventeenth century, and of Jewish mysticism (it was the birthplace of Shabbetai Zevi who claimed to be the Messiah and attracted a huge following).

Two cities, then, newly sprung, filled with foreign merchants who did not hesitate to trade with pirates and make deals with bandits. There was, however, a vital difference between Livorno and Smyrna.

Livorno's commercial prosperity marked the successful realization of the ambitions of the Grand Duke of Tuscany. Smyrna's rise, while beneficial to a number of Ottoman individuals, was not the result of Ottoman policy and in important ways came into conflict with goals of the political class in Istanbul. This is not to raise up, yet again, the worn-out spectre of Ottoman decline. Recent scholarship has shown that, over time, the Ottomans were able to respond to and to take advantage of increased commercialization in the eastern Mediterranean. This does not change the fact that Istanbul was not making the new rules.

The period discussed in the previous chapter, marked by
the turbulence of piracy and by the confrontation between
Habsburg Spain and Ottoman Turkey, was also one of
displacement of population and demographic crises. One source
of crisis was bubonic plague, which was relatively subdued in
the sixteenth century, but which returned with a vengeance
in the mid-seventeenth; its impact in Milan at this time was
graphically recorded by the Italian novelist Alessandro Manzoni
in his *I Promessi Sposi* published in 1827, for which he diligently
studied the archives of the city, where he believed two-thirds
of the inhabitants had caught the plague. However, even if
there were fewer major outbreaks across the region than in
the fourteenth and fifteenth centuries, plague appears to have
become endemic in areas such as Smyrna, and the merchants
of the town seem to have accepted it as a fact of life, or rather
death. Overall, in fact, the recurrence of plague does not appear
to have checked a gentle but firm rise in population from the
late fifteenth century onwards, which stimulated demand for
grain, and reinvigorated the grain trade of regions such as Sicily;
some Dutch and other northern merchants found it profitable to
bring northern grain into the Mediterranean.

The presence of northern merchants, in significantly larger
numbers, in the early modern Mediterranean also reflected
the relative decline of the traditional mercantile powers in the
Inner Sea. Whether or not the Catalans were a spent force in
international trade by 1450, they clearly were by 1650, all the
more so as political unrest in Catalonia damaged the economy
and accelerated the Castilianization of a once proud culture.
Genoa had shifted its attention towards the servicing of the
transatlantic trade through Seville, and the provision of banking
services to the Habsburgs in Spain, though it remained an
exceptionally powerful economic force in areas such as the
Spanish kingdom of Naples. Venice was diversifying, with the
expansion of its textile and glass industries and an increasing
tendency for the patrician families to invest not in long-distance

trade but in lands on the *Terraferma* that stretched deep into the Lombard plain; the failure to pursue aggressive marriage policies left many Venetian noblemen unmarried and many noblewomen in nunneries, with the result that a number of leading families became extinct by the eighteenth century.

Another major demographic change was the result of the religious conflicts that divided the Inner Sea. The incomplete expulsion of non-Christians from Spain following the fall of Muslim Granada in 1492 had serious consequences in Valencia and Aragon, territories ruled by Ferdinand the Catholic without the official help of his first wife Isabella. There, partly for fiscal reasons, Muslims were allowed to practise their religion until 1525, when the existence of numerous forced converts, baptized during the revolt of the Germanías, led Charles V to decree the suppression of Islam in Aragon and Valencia. Little attention was paid to the Christianization of this Moorish population, henceforth known as the Moriscos, and attempts to enforce the wearing of Christian costume and to suppress 'Moorish' practices such as traditional dances met with little success; indeed, many Christian clerics were afraid to enter Morisco villages where they were supposed to officiate. The result was that Islam was far from extinguished in Spain, though the Inquisition pursued Moriscos when it could not find Marranos (secret Jews), Protestants and witches.

The root of the problem was that no one was very keen to deprive the eastern seaboard of a large, industrious population: the manufacture of distinctive Hispano-Moresque pottery continued; rice and other exotic products were cultivated; Spain did not have the human resources readily to repopulate Morisco areas; it had already been seen with the expulsion of the Jews in 1492 that such an expulsion could have severe economic effects (in the mid-seventeenth century the king's minister Olivares concluded that Spain's interest would be served by re-admitting Jews, though nothing was done); and in any case the Moriscos were officially Christians, which made their expulsion problematic. Against this was the argument that they were seen as potential allies by the Turks, an argument underlined by the constant raids on the Spanish coasts which had, for example, devastated Majorca and had led to the re-foundation of many of the coastal settlements inland. It was only in 1609–14 that an expulsion of the Moriscos took place, most transferring to North Africa where they joined early communities of Andalusis, Muslims of Spanish descent, in such places as Algiers and Bougie. Some, of course, were ready to return favour for favour, raiding the shores of the land from which they had been forced. About a quarter of a million Moriscos can be shown to have been thrown out of Aragon and Valencia.

The Turks adopted a diametrically opposed policy towards religious minorities. They had already welcomed the Spanish Jews, whose artisan skills were well-known. They made Istanbul into a city in which substantial non-Muslim communities flourished, so that there was a large Jewish quarter in Galata, and very substantial Greek and Armenian settlements. By the eighteenth century a semi-official system was in place that accorded honour to the leaders of the religious communities such as the Greek Orthodox patriarch, whose authority still extended over large areas of Greece and Asia Minor, and the Haham Bashi or chief rabbi of the Jews; they allowed them considerable autonomy in managing the affairs of their community so long as they paid the taxes that were due.

It was a system that built on the principle of conditional toleration established in the early Islamic empires, now as then necessitated by the existence of large areas where Islam was a minority religion, though it did gain many new adherents as far west as Bosnia and Albania. The price the Christian communities paid was the levy of young men for the Ottoman army, the famous janissary corps. The Ottoman world combined brutality with a laissez-faire attitude in many areas;

it combined economic revival in Istanbul and Smyrna with economic decline in Albania and Greece, areas caught in the conflict between Spain and Turkey. The question was whether the sources of strength would continue to triumph over the sources of weakness by the eighteenth century.

EIGHT

The Mediterranean as a battleground of the European powers: 1700–1900

JEREMY BLACK

Halfway through the period covered by this chapter, an epic battle took place between two European powers which decisively affected Mediterranean history for a century to come. On 1 August 1798, a British fleet under Admiral Horatio Nelson found its French counterpart anchored in Aboukir Bay on Egypt's Mediterranean coast. At dusk, Nelson unexpectedly attacked, and did so on both sides of the French line: on the shallow inshore side of their line, where the French were not prepared to resist, as well as simultaneously on the other side, a manoeuvre that was not without risks: HMS *Culloden* ran aground and was unable to take part. In a battle fought at night in which the British fired at very close range, the French lost eleven of their thirteen ships of the line present; the other two fled, though both were lost by the end of 1800.

The nature of the French position was such that Nelson had been able to achieve a battle of annihilation, first defeating the ships in the French van and then pressing on to attack those moored behind; the latter had been unable to provide assistance. French gunnery proved inadequate, and the French were not only poorly deployed, but also failed to respond adequately to the British attack. The British navy worked as a well-integrated force. Nelson had ably prepared his captains to act vigorously and in co-operation in all possible eventualities, and had fully explained his tactics to them. British seamanship was superior, and the well-drilled gun crews outshot the French.

This decisive battle changed not only the strategic situation in 1798, wrecking Napoleon's Egyptian campaign, but also the history of the Mediterranean. From 1798 until the post-1945 decline of British naval power, the Mediterranean was, if not a British lake, then at least a sea dominated by their naval strength. This was to be the precondition of British imperial strength in the Mediterranean and on the shores of the sea, both directly – in Malta, the Ionian Islands, Cyprus, Egypt and Palestine – and indirectly. It was also the precondition of British economic power in the region.

How did this situation come about? Why was it that in 1798 British and French forces were competing for control of Egyptian waters? To answer that question we must go back a hundred years and understand how the Mediterranean had come to occupy a quite new position on the international stage. It was no longer the centre of the world. Islam's advance had been stopped, Venice sunk into decay, and the key routes of trade and cultural exchange no longer ran across and around the blue sea. In an age when Captain Cook explored Europe's 'dark side of the Earth', when Robert Clive blazed the trail for Britain's empire in India, when European nations began to dominate the world, so that, for instance, Anglo-French forces would occupy Peking in 1860, it is easy to treat the Mediterranean as an inconsequential backwater. But this too would be a mistake.

Islamic decline, Western revival
The decline of Islamic power in the seventeenth and eighteenth centuries is a complex issue. The Ottoman defeat outside Vienna by Austrian, German and Polish forces in 1683 is often presented as the beginning of an inevitable process of Ottoman decline that also would come to encompass that of the entire Islamic world.

16. In the mid-sixth century the Ostrogoths under King Totila besieged Rome for seven years. According to legend, Totila, wishing to visit St Benedict in his monastery of Montecassino, first sent a soldier dressed as himself. Benedict saw through the impostor, and Totila, impressed, came and knelt before the saint, as depicted by Luca Signorelli in a fresco at Monteoliveto Maggiore, Chiusure.

Καὶ αἰχμάλωσία ἡ Θεσσαλονίκη στόλος Ἀγαρηνῶν

17. Devastating raids menaced Byzantine towns and cities. Thessalonika, in northern Greece, was attacked in 904 by Leo of Tripoli. Thousands were killed and thousands more were carried off as slaves, as shown here in the chronicle of the eleventh-century Byzantine historian John Skylitzes.

18. Different cultural traditions were brilliantly combined in the palace chapel of the Norman rulers of Sicily at Palermo, with work by Byzantine mosaicists, Islamic carpenters and Fatimid painters – here a seated ruler is feasting, attended by servants.

19. A Spanish merchant exchanges his goods for spices in scenes from a manuscript of the Cantigas de Santa Maria by King Alfonso the Wise of Castile, 1252–84.

20. 'La Contarina', a Venetian ship combining oars and sails, took pilgrims to the Holy Land from 1479 to 1494. Passengers complained that they had to share their quarters on the way back with cotton, beans and casks of malmsey wine.

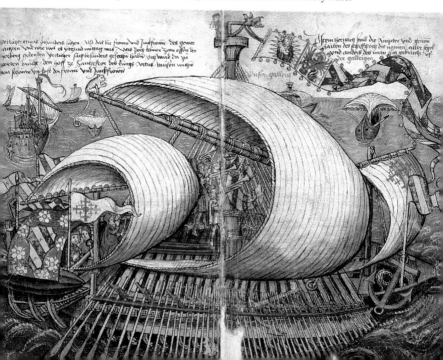

21. Venice in 1486 was the leading maritime and trading power both in the Mediterranean and the whole of Europe. In the centre is the Doge's palace, its waterfront crowded with boats of all types.

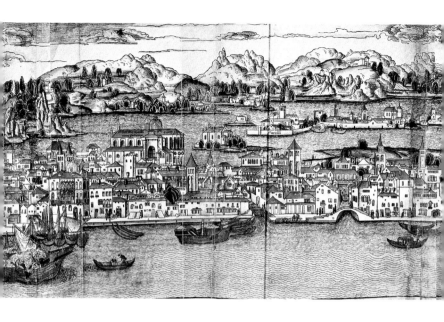

22. In the strategy of the great powers the city of Naples was of crucial importance. By 1791, the date of this painting, its rulers, a branch of the Bourbon family, were turning against the French Revolution and in 1793 joined the coalition at war with France. It then became an important base for Nelson's navy.

23. The Mediterranean lifestyle has been vividly caught by the poets and painters of the North, for whom the warm climate, blue sea and relaxed way of life had a peculiar charm. Martinus Rørbye left his native Denmark in 1834 and travelled to Rome. In 1840 he was in Sicily and made sketches for his large canvas *Morning in the Piazza Marina, Palermo*, one of the masterpieces of the Danish 'Golden Age'.

24, 25. Contrasts of thirty years – the Promenade des Anglais, Nice, at the turn of the twentieth century (above) and Juan-les-Pins in 1930 (below). Sunshine and sunbathing have conquered.

26. Artists of the Impressionist and Post-Impressionist generation (around 1900) 'discovered' the Mediterranean as another Garden of Eden. Henri Edouard Cross made his home at St-Clair near St-Tropez, where this painting is set. His Pointillist technique catches the shimmer of light on the water, and the atmosphere of magical stillness.

27. The Mediterranean as playground was an image already firmly in place in 1910, as it still is today. This colour lithograph by Charles Besson, with its roses and not altogether convincing aeroplane, makes the point with irresistible panache.

In 1717 Belgrade fell to the Austrians, in 1783 the Russians overran the Crimea and in 1827 the Egyptian fleet was smashed off Cape Navarino, ending Ottoman chances of retaining Greece.

Yet there are also important counter-indicators. In 1711, the Ottomans forced the surrounded Peter the Great of Russia to accept humiliating terms at the River Pruth, and in 1715 the Venetians were driven back from the Morea (the Peloponnese in southern Greece) in one of the most decisive campaigns of the century. Although the Venetians held Corfu against Ottoman attack in 1717, the Ottomans held the Morea against a Venetian counter-attack. In 1739, the Austrians were driven back into Belgrade by the Ottomans, and their frightened generals surrendered the fortress. The Ottomans retained both the Morea and Belgrade into the next century.

At sea, Ottoman naval power in the early eighteenth century was not what it had earlier been in the Arabian Sea or off the coast of East Africa, but it remained significant in the Black Sea and the Mediterranean. At the turn of the century, the Ottomans abandoned their traditional dependence on galleys and built a new fleet of sail-powered galleons which carried more cannon. In the first half of the century, the Ottomans were able to hold off Christian naval forces in the eastern basin of the Mediterranean. In 1718, off Cerigo, the Ottoman fleet had the advantage over an opposing Christian fleet, principally consisting of Venetian warships; the Christians lost nearly 2,000 men.

Further west, European powers dispatched expeditions to show the flag and deter the North Africans from privateering – for example the French show of force under Joseph de Bauffremont in 1766 – but these had little lasting effect. Occasionally, privateering bases were attacked, but they generally proved difficult targets. In 1775, a Spanish attack on Algiers was repelled when exposed Spanish troops were subjected to heavy fire and their artillery was delayed by the coastal sand. In 1784, when a large Spanish fleet attacked Algiers, a line of Algerian warships prevented the Spaniards from coming inshore.

Nevertheless, further east, the rise of Russia exposed the Ottoman Empire to a formidable foe that it was unable to counter. In 1739, the Russians successfully invaded Bessarabia and Moldavia, defeating the Ottomans at Stavuchanakh, and capturing Khotin and Iasi. In the war of 1768–74, the Russians were spectacularly successful in the campaigns of 1770 and 1774, breaching the Ottoman fortress system on the Danube. In the war of 1787–92, the Russians were again victorious and again advanced south of the Danube.

They were also successful at sea. For the first time, a Russian fleet entered the Mediterranean, where it overwintered and was resupplied at Livorno. On 5 July 1770, the Ottoman fleet of twenty ships of the line and frigates, and at least thirteen galleys, was outmanoeuvred by a smaller Russian squadron off Chios and almost totally destroyed by fireships. About 11,000 Ottomans were killed. The Russians were then able to blockade the Dardanelles, although their attempts to capture Lemnos, Euboea and Rhodes were unsuccessful. Encouraged by Russian promises of assistance, the Greeks in the Morea rebelled, but the Russians failed to provide their promised support, and it was difficult to co-ordinate Greek action. The Ottomans were able to suppress the revolt. However, Russian naval power had a serious economic effect on the Ottomans. Other Mediterranean powers were forced to consider the possible implications of Russia spreading her power. When her warships at Zante disregarded Venetian quarantine and other regulations in 1773, observers wondered what military, political and commercial consequences might flow from Russian gains from the Ottomans, including a possible base in the eastern Mediterranean.

The projection of Russian naval power into the Mediterranean was to be repeated during the French Revolutionary and Napoleonic Wars, when in 1799 a Russo-Ottoman force captured the Ionian Islands. As the two powers had been bitter enemies, this remarkable co-operation was a testimony to the unexpected consequences of French aggression. It was also a sign that the Mediterranean

Islamic world was now, at least in part, dependent for its security on European assistance. Alliances between the Ottomans and Christian European states were not new, and in the early sixteenth century the Ottomans had co-operated with Francis I of France against Emperor Charles V, but these alliances changed in character in the eighteenth century to become increasingly defensive.

Again, the late eighteenth century was the crucial period. There had been earlier talk of driving the Ottomans from the Balkans, when Austrian or Russian forces had done, or seemed about to do, well, for example in the early 1690s, 1711 and 1770–71, but this became far more insistent from the 1780s. The Russian annexation of the Crimea led to interest by others in equivalent gains. A memorandum of 1787 in the French foreign ministry archives claimed that, if France joined her ally Austria, and Russia, against the Ottoman empire, she herself could hope to acquire Crete and Egypt from the latter. The French occupation of Cyprus and Rhodes was also suggested, and the need to prevent Britain occupying Egypt was emphasized. In 1798, French troops were to land in Egypt and attack the Mamluk beys who wielded most influence there.

There had been a major shift in the pattern of French policy that was to have great consequences for the Mediterranean. Hitherto, France had been the firmest Christian ally of the Ottomans, in the sixteenth and seventeenth centuries, because the French saw them as their ally against the Habsburgs, and in the eighteenth, because they saw Russian power as a threat to their understanding of Europe. By the 1780s, France had achieved a dominant position in the foreign trade of the eastern Mediterranean. For both political and commercial reasons, she was the most influential foreign power in the Ottoman Empire, and also supplied military assistance. The French were also increasingly aware of the strategic importance of Egypt. In 1785, they signed an agreement with the beys opening the Red Sea route to India to trade over the Isthmus of Suez. Marseille merchants sought to exploit the route.

The views of the French were of particular importance because France's position in the Mediterranean had been greatly strengthened earlier in the century. Louis XIV of France's second grandson, Philip, Duke of Anjou, had gained the Spanish throne as Philip V (1700–46) and defeated an Austrian Habsburg candidature in the War of the Spanish Succession (1701–14). The Austrians had been compensated with Milan, Naples and Sardinia, but this was unacceptable to Philip. In 1717 the Spaniards invaded Sardinia, and, in 1718, Sicily. Most Sicilians failed to support their king, Victor Amadeus II, ruler of Savoy-Piedmont, and the island was rapidly conquered. However, the other powers were determined to ensure that changes to the 1713–14 peace settlement took place only with their consent. The British fleet, whose preparation had failed to dissuade the Spaniards from invading, destroyed most of the Spanish fleet off Cape Passaro on 11 August 1718. A poorly supplied Austrian force failed to drive the isolated Spaniards from Sicily, but their position was weakened by British naval mastery, and Spain was successfully invaded by French forces. The War of the Quadruple Alliance ended in 1718 with Sicily going to Austria and the island of Sardinia to Victor Amadeus.

War in Italy resumed in 1733 when France, Spain and Victor Amadeus attacked the Austrians, planning to win Milan for the latter and Naples and Sicily for Don Carlos, the eldest son of Philip V by his second wife, Elizabeth Farnese. French and Sardinian forces easily conquered the Milanese that winter. At Bitonto in 1734, one of the most decisive battles of the century, Spanish forces defeated the Austrian army in southern Italy. This was followed by the Spanish conquest of the rest of the kingdom of Naples and Sicily. Fighting ended in 1735, and, by the Third Treaty of Vienna of 1738, Carlos was left with Naples and Sicily, although the Austrians regained Milan. The great powers dominated the fate of Italian principalities. Italy was required to provide the equivalents and the equalling-out that compensated for gains elsewhere. With the death of John Gaston, the last of the Medici, in 1737, the Emperor's son-in-law, Francis, succeeded to Tuscany as a compensation for his own loss of Lorraine to Louis XV of France's father-in-law. Suggestions that Tuscany remain independent were ignored.

Austrian attempts to challenge the Bourbon position in southern Italy in the War of the Austrian Succession (1740–48) were unsuccessful, and the Austrians also failed to regain conquered Genoa once they had been driven out by a popular revolt in December 1746. However, the war also showed the vulnerability of Italian states. When, in 1742, Don Carlos prepared to attack the Austrians in Italy, he was intimidated by the threat of British naval bombardment. This forced Carlos to declare his neutrality in what can be considered to be one of the most striking displays of naval effectiveness that century.

Keen to expel the Austrians from Italy, the French foreign minister, d'Argenson, had proposed that Charles Emmanuel, ruler of Savoy, Piedmont and Sardinia, become king of Lombardy and leader of an Italian federation. D'Argenson's argument that the Italian rulers sought liberty against the excessive and tyrannical power of Austria, and that the Bourbons should exploit this, was rendered academic by Charles Emmanuel's decision to rejoin the Austrians. The peace left the Bourbons dominant in southern Italy and the Habsburgs in the north, while Charles Emmanuel gained more of the Milanese. The Habsburgs had to yield Parma and Piacenza to Louis XV's son-in-law, Don Philip, thus creating a new Bourbon principality in Italy.

The settlement ended the Italian Question and ensured that Italy was mostly peaceful until the early 1790s. Austria, France and Spain, their Italian interests secured, were able to turn their attention from Italy, Austria to conflict with Prussia and, in the 1780s, renewed conflict with the Ottoman Empire, and France and Spain to oceanic struggles with Britain. Sardinia's expansionist aspirations were effectively muzzled by the new territorial stability of Italy.

France was unwilling to lend support to schemes for gaining territory from the Milanese, and no power would support Sardinia in her plans to acquire sections of the Ligurian littoral from Genoa, the pursuit of which, in the case of Finale in the 1740s, revealed the weakness of the idea that Charles Emmanuel might act as an impartial leader of an Italian league.

The rivals: France and England

In 1768, the French government purchased the island of Corsica from Genoa. Much of the Corsican population had, however, long been rebellious and French occupation was resisted. Initially, Corsican resolve, knowledge of the terrain and fighting qualities, combined with French over-confidence and poor planning, led to Corsican successes, but, in 1769–70, larger French forces, better tactics, and the use of devastation, terror and road construction led to success. Corsica was incorporated into France, making a French subject of Napoleone di Buonaparte, who was born in 1769. The French had also benefited from the absence of foreign support for the Corsicans. The conquest was criticized by, among others, Voltaire and Rousseau, who felt that the government should concentrate on domestic problems rather than foreign adventurism, and romanticized the Corsicans. French administrators, however, produced a blueprint for the social and economic development of the island.

Interest in preserving the Ottoman Empire reflected shifts in the Mediterranean world, and in wider geopolitics. In the latter case, it was, in a new departure, a concern of the British in the late eighteenth century. Anxiety about the possibility of Russian expansion towards the Mediterranean led in 1791 to the Ochakov crisis, in which the British nearly went to war with Russia and, for the first time, considered sending a fleet to the Black Sea. The crisis led to the dispatch of British military observers who argued that there was need for a total reform of the Ottoman system. George Koehler, a German in the British artillery, spent six months in 1791–92 studying the situation. He argued that more than the acquisition of new weaponry was necessary. Instead, 'a complete revolution in their government, finances, national character, mechanical arts, etc. must be accomplished ... this indifference which reigns through every branch of their government both civil and military is perhaps the greatest of all their obstacles to improvement'. George Monro added in 1793: 'It appears to me a perfect impossibility that the Ottomans can keep possession of Turkey in Europe much longer; without the assistance of some of the European powers: or unless they made such an universal change in every department: as would occasion a thorough revolution in the Ottoman constitution.'

Such comments marked the new attitude towards Oriental civilizations, with the fear and awed respect of the sixteenth century replaced by contempt and a sense of superiority that ignored the inherent strengths of other cultures. These comments also looked forward to the great crisis of the Mediterranean world in 1797–99.

In 1797, Venice, a long-lasting fulcrum of Mediterranean culture and trade, and, for much of the previous millennium, power, lost its independence. The French Revolution, which transformed the balance of power in Europe, led to the rise of Napoleon, first as the apparently irresistible general of the Republic, then as First Consul (1799) and finally as Emperor (1804). French policy aimed at exporting the ideology of revolution and (which amounted to the same thing) extending French influence in both northern Europe and the Mediterranean. Napoleon marched on from his triumphs over Sardinian and Austrian forces in northern Italy to within 112 km (70 miles) of Vienna. The Austrians were forced, in the Treaty of Campo Formio (1797), to accept a new settlement of Italy, that left France with the Ionian Islands, Venetian Albania and Mantua, and much of northern Italy under a French client state, the Cisalpine Republic, while Venice and the Veneto were ceded to Austria.

However, this was not to be for long, for Napoleon's victory over Austrian and Russian forces at Austerlitz in 1805 brought Venice, the Veneto and Venetian Dalmatia to his kingdom of Italy: the fate of the Mediterranean was being settled a long way from its shores. Napoleon had become King of Italy in 1805 and had crowned himself with the

Iron Crown of Lombardy. In 1808, the kingdom was expanded with the seizure of Ancona and its surrounding area, while France directly gained Tuscany in 1807, the Papal States in 1809 and Austrian Dalmatia (Trieste, Fiume and Croatia) in 1809.

Napoleon not only seized Venice. He also took antiquities from there to France, part of a process of cultural pillage that was also designed to exalt France. This policy was comprehensively developed by Napoleon in Italy in 1796.

The Napoleonic dream

After conquering northern Italy in 1797, Napoleon planned to invade Britain, but, having decided that such an invasion would fail, he pressed, instead, the case for an invasion of Egypt, in order both to retain his own military position and for France to be better able to challenge the British in India. Mounted in 1798, this invasion was a major independent initiative on the part of Napoleon. It revealed a characteristic absence of the sense of mutual understanding that is crucial to the successful operation of the international system. He assumed that the Ottomans, the imperial overlords of effectively autonomous Egypt, could be intimidated or bribed into accepting French action, which indeed followed a whole series of provocative acts. These assumptions were coupled with a contempt for the Ottoman Empire as a military force.

The last French force sent to Egypt had been a Crusader army, and, as with the Crusades, it is necessary to understand this invasion in psychological as much as 'rational' terms. Napoleon's sense of grandiloquence and his belief that the Orient was there to serve his views emerged from his recollection:

> In Egypt, I found myself freed from the obstacles of an irksome civilization. I was full of dreams ... I saw myself founding a religion, marching into Asia, riding an elephant, a turban on my head and in my hand the new Koran that I would have composed to

suit my needs. In my undertakings I would have combined the experiences of the two worlds, exploiting for my own profit the theatre of all history, attacking the power of England in India and, by means of that conquest, renewing contact with the old Europe. The time spent in Egypt was the most beautiful in my life, because it was the most ideal.

Having first easily overrun vulnerable Malta, Napoleon's army landed in Egypt on 1 July 1798. After capturing Alexandria, he defeated the Mamluks at Shubra Khit (13 July) and Embabeh, the battle of the Pyramids (21 July), victories for defensive firepower over shock tactics. French rifles were described as 'like a boiling pot on a fierce fire'.

Cairo fell, but we have reached the battle of the Nile, with which this chapter began. Nelson's victory stranded the French. In the face of a hostile population, which mounted a brutally suppressed rising in Cairo, Napoleon consolidated his position, sending Desaix up the Nile to control Upper Egypt. Napoleon and most of his army invaded Palestine, then ruled by the Ottomans. El Arish and Jaffa were taken, but Acre successfully resisted, helped by British naval gunners. Napoleon's siege train had been captured by British warships, he had underestimated his opponents, and successive French assaults on Acre all failed.

Napoleon fell back on Egypt, where, on 25 July 1799, he defeated a newly landed Ottoman army at Aboukir, storming the earthworks with a cavalry charge. This was of scant benefit. In the face of British naval power, the French were still isolated. Napoleon fled back to France by sea, and the army left in Egypt was defeated by a British expeditionary force in 1801.

The British had exploited their naval position in the Mediterranean by seizing Minorca in 1798, blockading the Gulf of Naples in 1799, and capturing Malta in 1800. The basin was now a front line between the alliance systems of two clashing empires, as it was to be again with the First World War and, far more clearly and significantly, with the Second World War. Unlike, however, the clash between Rome and Carthage, this was not a struggle controlled by Mediterranean powers. Instead, it was one in which the Mediterranean was understood in terms of geopolitical axes devised by strategists in distant capitals, and its resources were used to support their strategies. This helps to explain the French invasion of Spain in 1808, and the British counter-intervention, as well as the campaigning of both powers in southern Italy and in the Adriatic. A British force landed in Calabria in July 1806 and attacked the French who had invaded the kingdom of Naples after Austerlitz. This was the only British invasion of southern Italy prior to that in the Second World War. To the British troops who defeated the French at Maida in Calabria in 1806 this must have seemed as distant as the Roman legionaries had found Britannia.

Yet it would be misleading to suggest either that all rivalries and issues could be fitted into the Anglo–French struggle, or that the mighty forces of these empires could overawe other powers. The British were given a clear demonstration of this in Egypt in 1807. Six years earlier, a British army, initially under Sir Ralph Abercromby, had defeated the French and forced their capitulation. In 1807, however, the British discovered the dangers of pressing on with inadequate knowledge in the face of hostile local forces. In order to prevent the French from establishing a presence there when Britain began hostilities with the Ottomans, 6,000 men were sent to besiege Alexandria. It fell rapidly, but misleading information about the need to expand the area of control in order to ensure supplies led to an attempt to gain control of Rosetta, a crucial point for trade on the Nile. The assault was a disaster, with the centre column, attacked from all sides by snipers taking advantage of the narrow streets and tall houses, taking heavy casualties. A second attempt was also unsuccessful. The Egyptians then blockaded Alexandria by land. The intractable nature of the conflict led the British to abandon their presence.

The same year, the limitations of British power at sea were seen when Vice-Admiral Sir John Duckworth failed to obtain the surrender of the Ottoman fleet. He sailed through the Dardanelles on 19 February 1807, repelling bombardment from the coastal forts, and destroying a squadron of Ottoman frigates, but the Ottomans refused to yield to his intimidation. When, on 3 March, Duckworth returned through the Strait he ran the gauntlet of Ottoman cannon firing stone shots of up to 363 kg (800 lb): one took away the wheel of the *Canopus*.

Further west, bitter resistance to brutal French occupation in Calabria and Spain demonstrated the determination of Mediterranean peoples to fight on even when their state structure had collapsed. The French had to commit 48,000 men to suppress the Calabrian rising which began in 1806, and even greater efforts were unsuccessful in Spain in 1808–13.

The navy also gave the British a reach throughout the Mediterranean. For example, in 1812–14, a squadron under Vice-Admiral Thomas Fremantle drove the French from much of the Dalmatian coast, playing a major role in the capture of Fiume in 1813 and Trieste in 1814. In 1814, Captain William Hoste established batteries on difficult positions, commanding Cattaro and Ragusa, leading their garrisons to surrender.

The new order: rivalry resumed

The Congress of Vienna of 1814–15 did not return Minorca (yielded under the Peace of Amiens of 1802) to the British, but, instead, left them with Malta and the Ionian Islands to add to Gibraltar, which had been captured in 1704. Thereafter, the British navy played a major role in the Mediterranean. The bombardment of Algiers by an Anglo-Dutch fleet in 1816 led to an agreement to end the taking of Christian slaves. It also reflected the capacity of the British industrial system. The British squadron alone fired 40,000 round-shot and shells.

The previous year, an American squadron had forced Algiers to pay compensation for attacks on American trade. The threat of naval bombardment led Algiers to capitulate to British demands in 1824. Thanks largely to superior British gunnery, an Anglo-French-Russian fleet under Sir Edward Codrington destroyed the Ottoman and Egyptian fleets at the battle of Navarino Bay in 1827, the last great battle of the Age of Fighting Sail, and one in which the Western fatalities were far lower than those of their opponents: 177 to about 17,000. This was crucial to the defeat of the Ottoman attempt to suppress the Greek struggle for independence, which was recognized in 1830. The British naval bombardment and capture of Acre, in which a shell caused the main magazine to explode, was a decisive blow in the expulsion of Egyptian forces from Syria in 1840. In 1882 a British squadron silenced the forts near Alexandria, a crucial preliminary to the British conquest of Egypt.

It was not, however, until the last quarter of the century that the British tried to use their naval superiority to gain fresh territories in the Mediterranean; indeed, in 1863, the Ionian Islands had been ceded to Greece, which had become independent, with British support, in 1830. The British change of policy in the late 1870s was prompted by anxiety about the other two states expanding in (or towards) the region: France and Russia. Having lost their first colonial empire with Napoleon, the French began their second when they occupied Algiers with 37,000 troops in 1830. This was intended not to serve as the basis of a widespread empire, but to win popularity for the last Bourbon king of France, Charles X. It failed in this, and Charles fell in the 1830 revolution, but his successor, Louis-Philippe, continued the policy. Oran was seized in 1831 and Bône in 1833, and in 1834 Louis-Philippe decided to seek the entire coastline; but from 1835 the French encountered strong resistance led by Abd el-Kader, and opposition from the interior drew them in.

The French faced political as well as military problems in extending their rule. Although they did benefit from divisions within Algerian society, and the support of some Algerians, colonialism by incorporation, in which existing power structures were adopted and accommodated by the imperial state, was made far more difficult by the seizure of land for French settlement. Nevertheless, French policy was supported by overwhelming force. By 1846, the French had 108,000 effectives, one third of their regular army, in Algeria. This was one soldier for every 25 to 30 Algerians, and a force that greatly outnumbered that of Abd el-Kader: his army consisted of a core of about 10,000 well-armed regulars and about 40,000 well-armed irregulars. Abd el-Kader surrendered in 1847; three years earlier, accusing the Sultan of helping him, the French had invaded Morocco and defeated the Sultan's forces at Isly.

Meanwhile, Russian pressure on the Ottoman Empire had become more acute. In the Russo–Ottoman war of 1806–12, the Russians occupied Moldavia and Wallachia, operated south of the Danube, and gained Bessarabia at the subsequent peace. In the wars of 1828–9, the Russians advanced as far as Adrianople, which they captured.

The next conflict, generally known as the Crimean War (1853–56), was different because the British and French came to the assistance of the Ottomans in order to prevent Russia from dominating the Black Sea and the Balkans. The origins of the conflict reflected the role of religion and the search for prestige. Napoleon III of France sought prestige in order both to strengthen his domestic position and to enhance France's diplomatic situation. French interests in the Near East led to support for demands by Catholic priests for access to the Holy Places. Ottoman concessions led to matching demands from Russia, the protector of the Orthodox clergy, but Russian pressure was resented by the Ottomans. Nicholas I sought to continue earlier Russian expansion at the expense of the vulnerable Ottoman Empire; in the past, other powers had not come to the help of the Ottomans. He, however, mishandled relations with these powers. The Sardinians joined in on the Allied side in 1855, to get a seat at the peace table and raise Italian issues, sending 15,500 troops to the Crimea.

Despite French suggestions of a march on Moscow, the Crimean War was to be no 1812: the Allies lacked the land resources of Napoleon, but, conversely, were far more powerful at sea. The Russian navy was capable of beating the Ottomans – in 1853 at Sinope – but not the British. Instead, the war focused on naval and amphibious action against the Russians. Naval operations in the Baltic, which threatened St Petersburg, were matched by a full-scale expedition to the Crimea in order to take the Russian naval base of Sevastopol. This seemed an appropriate response to the Russian naval victory off Sinope. The Mediterranean thus served as a conduit, not a sphere, for conflict in the Crimean War.

This war held the Russian advance for a quarter century, but the Russians demonstrated the weakness of the Ottomans in 1877–8 to a greater extent than in previous wars. Although the Ottomans fought hard, Russian forces advanced to within 15 kilometres (9 miles) of Constantinople. While the Ottomans had been able to defeat the Serbs in 1876, and were to defeat the Greeks in 1897, it was clear that, in the face of Russian power and ambitions, the Eastern Question had now become a matter of the fate of the Ottoman Empire. Suspicion of Russian designs led the British to take a protectorate over Cyprus in 1878 (thus gaining a base in the eastern Mediterranean) and to prepare to resist any Russian naval move through the Dardanelles.

Concern about both the Russians and the French led the British to move into Egypt: a naval base at Alexandria seemed essential. Furthermore, Egypt had become of greater strategic importance with the Suez Canal. This began as a Franco-Ottoman project in 1859 and was opened to shipping in 1869, but, in 1875, the British government purchased the shares of the Khedive (Viceroy for the Ottomans) Ismail and thus gained a direct concern in Egypt's stability. Further west, the French made Tunisia a protectorate in 1881: a force invaded from Algeria, while other units were landed at Bône and Bizerta. The navy subsequently shelled Sfax, which had rejected French control, and covered a successful landing.

In Egypt, meanwhile, anti-European nationalist action culminating in the Arabi Rebellion had challenged British interests. The British invaded in 1882 and routed the Egyptians at Tel el Kebir on 13 September 1882. After a night march, the British attacked the Egyptian earthworks at dawn without any preliminary bombardment. Sir Garnet Wolseley preferred to gain the advantage of surprise, and his infantry attacked using their bayonets. Gaining the initiative was worthwhile, because Wolseley retained control of his manoeuvrable force which displayed cohesion, discipline and high morale. After the victory, a rapid cavalry advance seized Cairo and a British quasi-protectorate over Egypt was established, although formal status as a protectorate was not given until 1914; until then, the fiction of Ottoman sovereignty was maintained.

However, Evelyn Baring, later 1st Earl of Cromer, who had been appointed British commissioner for the finances of Egypt in 1877, ran the Egyptian government from 1883 until 1907, as Consul General and Adviser to the Khedive. Egypt became the base for British intervention in the Sudan in support of Egyptian claims of authority. This intervention was finally successful in 1898 as a result of victory over the Mahdists at Omdurman.

There were to be further gains in European power around the shores of the Mediterranean in the early twentieth century. A successful Italian conquest led the Ottomans in 1912 to cede Cyrenaica, Tripoli and the Dodecanese, although bitter resistance continued in the interior of Libya; while Spain gained a protectorate over Morocco's Mediterranean coast, the interior passing to French control. As a result of the destruction of the Ottoman Empire in the First World War, in 1920, Palestine and Trans-Jordan became British mandated territories, and Lebanon and Syria French ones. The Treaty of Sèvres of 1920 temporarily left parts of Turkey under the control of the First World War victors.

Although important, these gains simply continued the pattern already set in the nineteenth century. The world of Islam was in retreat, and British naval power dominated the Mediterranean. In so far as Mediterranean Christian elements were able to gain advantage, it was as part of nation states, not as autonomous forces. Thus, it was a case of France, Italy and Spain pursuing advantages, not Marseille/ Provence, Genoa/Venice/Tuscany/Naples, or Barcelona/Catalonia.

This was an important shift in European politics, one dramatized when the forces of Philip V of Spain successfully besieged Barcelona in 1714 and brought to an end Catalan liberties, again in 1821, when Austrian regulars defeated untrained and poorly disciplined Neapolitan *Carbonari* at Rieti, and went on to occupy Naples, and also in 1849, when starvation and cholera led a rebellious Venice to surrender to blockading Austrians.

The number of states in the western Mediterranean declined. In 1860, an army under Victor Emmanuel II of Sardinia (the kingdom based in Turin) combined with a volunteer force under Giuseppe Garibaldi to overthrow the Neapolitan Bourbons. Garibaldi and 1,000 red-shirted volunteers had sailed from Genoa to Marsala to help a revolt in Sicily against the Bourbons. After defeating a Neapolitan force at Calatafimi, Garibaldi captured Palermo following three days of street fighting. He defeated the remaining Neapolitan forces on the island at Milazzo and, having crossed the Strait of Messina, marched north to defeat the Neapolitans at the Volturno and to capture Naples. Meanwhile, Victor Emanuel II had marched south from Bologna, winning battles at Castelfidardo and Macerone, against the small Papal army and the Neapolitans respectively. Garibaldi handed over his conquests to Victor Emmanuel, enabling the latter to create the kingdom of Italy. Gaeta continued to defy the invaders, but fell in February 1861 after a long siege. This conquest of the Kingdom of the Two Sicilies was one of the most complete victories of the period 1816–1913. The ability of Garibaldi to invade Sicily denied the Bourbons the safe haven they had enjoyed when Napoleonic forces had conquered Naples.

Churches and states

The ending of the old order was even more clearly demonstrated in 1870 when the Papal States were successfully invaded by the new Italian army. Papal control had only lasted so long because French forces had restored Papal authority in 1849 and defeated an attack by Garibaldi in 1867.

As with the Ottomans, although far more so, the now old Mediterranean order had been reliant on the support of 'modern' forces. The French troops that helped overthrow the Roman republic in 1849 and restore Papal authority had been brought by steamships (from Toulon to Civitavecchia) and rail.

The end of the Papal States signalled a major collapse in the power of traditional Catholicism. Although the Church retained the support of much of its flock, its institutions were considerably weaker, and the fabric of Counter-Reformation Catholicism had been destroyed. This was a long process in which the policies of secular nationalist governments in the second half of the nineteenth century was only the final stage. Earlier, there had been inroads at the hands first of Enlightenment governments and then as a result of the policies of the French Revolutionaries and their clients.

The suppression of the Jesuits was a decisive break with Counter-Reformation Catholicism. An international Order with a special oath of loyalty to the papacy, the Jesuits were envied within the Church, but their fall was rather a triumph of state over church. Expelled from Portugal in 1759, the Order was suppressed in France in 1764, and in Spain and Naples in 1767. Clement XIV was bullied by the Bourbon rulers, who seized the Papal enclaves of Avignon and Benevento, into abolishing the Order in 1773. This reflected the declining prestige of the papacy. The Order was then suppressed in the remaining Catholic states.

The Jesuits' educational and pastoral roles were largely taken over by other bodies, but the suppression of the Order reflected little credit on those who carried it out. Many of the Jesuits were brutally treated, and many useful institutions were destroyed or harmed. Two Hungarian ex-Jesuit poets, Ferenc Faludi and David Szabó, saw the suppression as the death of a culture that was a symptom of the decline of European society. It certainly marked the passing of the old Europe.

The Church also lost authority in other respects, as rulers sought to secure and maintain control over the religious life of their territories. The clerical role in censorship, education and marriage was ended or reduced. Concordats limited the fiscal privileges of the clergy. However, attacks on traditional religious practices could be resisted. Attempts to regulate or limit traditional practices, such as images, pilgrimages, festivals and confraternities, led to protests, non-compliance, law suits, and sometimes, as in Florence and Livorno in 1790, violence.

This regulation became more insistent in the nineteenth century, particularly as support for the Church ceased to be universal and became, instead, a political position viewed with suspicion by influential political groups in France, Italy and Spain. At the same time as international relations were changing, the traditional assumptions of politics and the culture of society were being transformed.

Trade and industry

The old order, of a mighty empire in the eastern Mediterranean and a more fragmented pattern of sovereignty further west, had gone. The whole sea had been opened up to outside interests. This can be seen clearly with one set of economic statistics. Whereas in 1660 Marseille imported only 19,000 quintaux (100 kilograms/ 220 lbs to a quintal) of coffee, of Yemeni origin from Egypt, in 1785 it imported 143,310 quintaux, of which 142,500 came from the West Indies. The Europeans had taken over the bulk of world trade in coffee. Introduced to Martinique and Guadeloupe in 1725, and to Saint-Domingue in 1730, French West Indian coffee was more popular than that produced by the Dutch in the East Indies, and it swiftly became the principal global source. In 1770, 350,000 quintaux were produced and in 1790 over 950,000. Most went to France and much was then re-exported, from Marseille principally to the Ottoman Empire, reversing the trade flow of 1660.

The Mediterranean still had goods to sell. Culture was one of the principal exports from Italy. Salt, from Cagliari in Sardinia, Alicante in Spain, Ibiza, and Trapani in Sicily, was recorded in the Sound Tolls moving into the Baltic. Salt in the 1780s was the largest Swedish import from Iberia and the Mediterranean, linking Sweden and Denmark to the island of Sardinia, whose leading export it was. By value, 78.7 per cent of Piedmont's exports in 1752 was silk.

Such exports helped to bring money into the Mediterranean, but they could not compete with the value of the transoceanic goods brought to Atlantic Europe: tea from China, cotton cloth from India, sugar, coffee and tobacco from the New World, gold from Brazil. Nor did the Mediterranean produce the industrial goods that were of increasing value from the late eighteenth century: the products of forges and steam-driven equipment that were starting to come from Britain.

As a consequence, trade was increasingly a matter of the penetration of the Mediterranean by foreign goods and by merchants seeking raw materials for exploitation. Attempts to free trade did not greatly help local economies. Livorno's prominence as a trading centre owed much to its designation as a free port in 1675. Other Italian rulers sought to emulate this achievement. Messina became a free port in 1728, and Ancona in 1732. When, in 1719, Austria wished to boost her Adriatic commerce, Trieste and Rijeka were given this status. In 1748, free internal trade in the Papal States was introduced.

Yet these measures could not transform the economy. Livorno was not to lead to a Tuscan industrial revolution. There was no particular Mediterranean 'reason' for this situation. Elsewhere in Europe, successful ports, such as La Rochelle and Cádiz, led to enclave economies rather than economic transformation. Similarly, Marseille in the second half of the eighteenth century contained cloth, sugar, glass, porcelain and soap factories. Indeed, since most of Europe did not experience industrialization and significant economic transformation until the twentieth century, it is not helpful to think in terms of failure. In addition, it is far from clear that the criteria adopted to define economic progress give due weight to the variety of economic activity in this period. Research on a number of areas not generally seen in terms of economic development, for example the Veneto at the close of the seventeenth century, or Spain in the eighteenth and nineteenth centuries, has indicated a considerable degree of resilience and adaptability that suggests that an economic geography of Europe portraying the south as backwards is unhelpful.

Allowing for this, the tide of revisionism has not yet managed to portray a Balkan industrial revolution in the late eighteenth century or a Sicilian counterpart as a backdrop for Garibaldi's invasion in 1860. Indeed, it is no accident that one of the major exports from Sicily and Naples was to be people, seeking for economic advantage in the New World. The same was true of Scotland, where there very much was an industrial revolution, but all the economic indicators suggest a major difference between the two.

It was not only industry that was different, but also agriculture. In Sicily, increases in wheat production could be achieved only by extending the area of land under cultivation, and crop sizes were maintained only by sowing on tilled fallow. The tilling was done by hoes that barely scratched the surface of the soil. In Lombardy, a naturally fertile agrarian region, in contrast, rice cultivation increased from the 1730s, partly as a result of the activity of the leasehold farmers, and partly because there was sufficient local capital to support the necessary irrigation. In the second half of the century, there were clear signs of Lombard agricultural expansion, particularly in the rise of rice, silk, cheese and butter exports. There were also significant improvements in the Veneto, where the cultivation of maize spread widely.

However, in general, the Italian position was bleaker, substantially a matter of traditional methods and extensive cultivation, rather than agricultural changes and intensive methods. The mixed farming of the Lombard plain, with animals providing manure and milk, made little progress elsewhere, and efforts to encourage the cultivation of the potato had little impact. The principal problems – harsh terrain, denuded soil, poor water supplies, inadequate communications and a lack of investment – still dominated the peninsula in 1800, and the major cause of increased production was the expansion, particularly from mid-century, of the cultivated area. Though commercial farming spread in most of Italy in the second half of the century, and common lands were enclosed, subsistence agriculture was still the norm.

So also was transhumance, the seasonal movement of livestock, often over very long distances, that had long been a crucial aspect of agricultural activity throughout Europe. Man's domination of upland pasture zones, and their link to the Mediterranean coastline, was only seasonal. The cattle left the Savoyard mountains for the valleys every year on 10 October. At about the same time, the sheep of the Mesta, the Spanish wool monopoly, set off on their march from their open summer grazing lands in central Spain to the lowlands, the largest annual migration of animals in Europe. Pasture was the principal benefit derived from mountainous zones, and it linked regions: the Apennines to the Emilian plain, the Abruzzi mountains to the plains of the Capitanata near Foggia, and so on, to create the complex patterns that made up the Mediterranean economy. Sheep were driven from Roussillon to Barcelona, and cattle from Piedmont to Genoa.

There were some transport improvements, but few before the coming of the train. The opening of the Col du Tende pass at the southern end of the Alps to wheeled traffic led, in 1780, to hopes in Piedmont that wine could be exported to England via Nice, although they were cut short by the outbreak of the French Revolutionary War in 1792. The following century, the spread of train routes had to cope with the difficult terrain of much of the Mediterranean littoral, especially with mountains running down to the coast. The poor shape of the economy also limited the appeal to investors. Thus, per square mile, there were far fewer railways in the Balkans, southern Italy or Spain than in Germany, the Low Countries or England. Nevertheless, each line that was built made a difference.

Similarly, steamships greatly affected sailing times and predictability in the Mediterranean. The impact of wind and tide diminished, although sailing vessels remained important, not least because they were less expensive to buy and operate. Steamships needed coal, and their requirements and capacity led to a focus of trade on a small number of ports with the necessary facilities, while a large number of ports became very much second level. This process was accentuated by the role of steamship-train transshipment at particular ports.

Demand from Europe's growing and more affluent population helped to drive production. In the nineteenth century, demand extended to the Balkans, affecting in particular cotton and tobacco production. At the same time, much activity remained subsistence in character or was only for the local economy. This was true of both agriculture and industry, and greatly affected the collective psychology of the population. The immediate area, not the distant state, was the source of identity, interest and loyalty. This was clearly seen in southern Italy after unification with the north, with strong resistance in Naples and Sicily to the new Italian régime, which was regarded as alien. Opposition was so pronounced that in 1866, when eighteen-year-olds were conscripted to fight Austria, those from disaffected Naples and Sicily were excepted. However, local feeling had not led to much support for the Neapolitan Bourbons. The regime was fairly weak, especially in Sicily, much of which was close to ungovernable as a result of widespread brigandage.

In Spain, support for the Carlists in the nineteenth century drew on local loyalties, especially in Navarre and upland Catalonia. During the Second Carlist War (1868–76), there was also a republican and anti-centralist rising at Cartagena in 1873–74. Earlier, the Corsican rising against Genoese rule in 1730 took the form of a struggle between the countryside and the towns, where many Genoese lived, both competing for the control of the fertile alluvial plains.

Localism had also been strong within the Ottoman Balkans, and it is possible there to draw connections between the decentralized power that characterized the eighteenth century and weak government in the nineteenth. In the eighteenth century, a new group of provincial rulers commonly known as *ayans* (notables) emerged with a local power base. They were often the only source of effective local administration. Powerful local families dominated Albania, central Greece and the Morea with the aid of private armies. Bosnia was run by the beys, a strong, Muslim, semi-independent nobility, who spoke the local language and understood local traditions, while the power of the Ottoman governor tended to be very restricted. The sale of state land to rich officials in much of the Ottoman Empire did little to increase central authority. The weakness of the central government forced it to co-opt many of the *ayans* into the provincial administrative system and, particularly in periods of difficulty, they were granted official appointments. At other times, determined leaders sought to curb *ayan* power; the energetic Grand Vizier Halil Hamid Pasa launched one such attempt in 1785, but abandoned it when war with Russia broke out in 1787.

Thus, alongside the apparently clear-cut themes of outside dominance, economic backwardness and the rise of nation states, can be set a more varied reality. All the three points just noted were correct, but, at the same time, there was also the diversity that is to be expected from such a varied and complex region and that helps to make the history of the Mediterranean so fascinating.

North European links with the Mediterranean were already intimate by 1450, when Bruges functioned as the great centre of exchange linking the German Hansa and its trading world in the Baltic and the North Sea to the Mediterranean, represented by the Medici and other Italians. Not merely goods but also artistic ideas were exchanged: artists as far south as Naples copied themes from the workshop of Jan van Eyck. To artists inhabiting the flat Netherlands, under vast cloud-filled skies, mountainous Mediterranean landscapes long remained attractive. But towards the end of the eighteenth century there were transformations in this intimate relationship. Hamilton's excavations at Pompeii had a startling impact on artistic styles throughout Europe, and the use of Pompeian themes in country-house architecture became the rage. As early as the 1820s the architect Charles Robert Cockerell excavated at Bassae, identifying the first use of the Corinthian column in Greek architecture, and enthusiastically incorporating the Corinthian theme in his own buildings. The Mediterranean was being actively imported into the greyer climes of the north.

The Grand Tour in which young gentlemen from the north indulged was the prelude to the emergence of a new phenomenon, cultural tourism in the Mediterranean. Others escaped south from harsh winters, as when Queen Victoria became a visitor to Menton. All this was facilitated by the development of railways linking the north and the south of France, and opening up access to northern Italy. Tired, covered in smuts, the English traveller reached Florence and Naples around 1900 certain of a handsome welcome by compatriots, and intent on immersion in the artistic culture of medieval and Renaissance Italy. Upper middle-class Englishmen and Englishwomen living in polite pensioni in Florence populate the pages of the novelist E. M. Forster, for at the start of the twentieth century the British settlers in Florence numbered several thousands. In addition, English businessmen flourished in areas such as Sicily, where the Whittakers had long handled the export of Marsala wines with aplomb; or in Naples, where handsome English tailor's shops appeared on the Via Toledo. Thus the British presence in the Mediterranean was far from being simply a political and naval presence. An educated reading public devoured large numbers of books that issued from British and German publishing houses devoted to the history of the Mediterranean lands, such as the works of the Swiss Jacob Burckhardt and the gentleman scholar John Addington Symonds on Renaissance Italy. German travellers reached Italy armed with their Baedeker guides, which assessed and ranked the buildings and art works of Italy and neighbouring lands, sometimes offering an excruciating degree of detail.

Not to be neglected is the way that north European institutions attempted to bring something of the Mediterranean back home with them. The Louvre, the British Museum and the Berlin Museums continued to enlarge their collections of classical and Renaissance art, often quite ruthlessly; the Elgin, or Parthenon, marbles mostly went to the British Museum, with only a small consolation prize for the Louvre. A massive classical monument was reconstructed in the Propyläen Museum in Berlin. Classical works were seen as models for artists seeking an elegant and precise style. In this spirit a galaxy of art institutes and archaeological schools serving different European nations became established in Rome and Athens. At the core of this interest in Italy and Greece lay the sense that northern Europe had inherited the classical culture of those lands, envisaged as something clear, clean, precise, rational, and communicated to generations of students throughout Europe by the intense study of classical languages.

One dominating influence was Benjamin Jowett, Master of Balliol College, Oxford, translator of Plato, himself a product of the prime classical academy in England, St Paul's School, founded in 1509 specifically to teach Latin and Greek. The classical model extended beyond scholarship; his avowed aim was to instil in the young men of Balliol that sense of civic duty that they could acquire from a close reading of the classical philosophers; hence, perhaps, the extraordinary ascendancy of Balliol men in British politics. But visiting Greece was not something that interested him; Greece was an idea, and its current reality, as a poor Balkan state, was of no interest to him, though others, from Byron onwards, romanticized the modern Greek as the heir to classical glories.

The idealization of the classical world can be seen in the work of the late nineteenth-century British artists who have been called 'The Olympian Dreamers'. The most relentless in his attention to the details of classical architecture, costume and landscape was Sir Lawrence Alma-Tadema. His canvases reflected serious research; yet his images of unclothed classical maidens combined the theme of purity with a voyeurism that only enhanced their appeal to the late Victorian and Edwardian public. But of capital importance not just in Germany but throughout Europe and North America was the art-historical research of Johann Joachim Winckelmann, which did much to classify, date and above all apply criteria of appreciation to classical sculpture. Classical sculpture portrayed ideal human bodies, rather than naturalistic ones, and it was precisely the classical past as an ideal that appealed to the nineteenth-century observer. Such attitudes penetrated into Greece as well. In 1890 the Acropolis was restored – that is to say, all later accretions were swept away, whatever their historical significance, and the buildings were reduced to bare skeletons.

This was a view of the Mediterranean that focused on Italy and Greece, the homes of classical culture. More ambiguous were attitudes to the Islamic past and present. David Roberts' sketches of a depopulated, impoverished Holy Land conjured up images of the biblical past; in America, Washington Irving's *Tales of the Alhambra* recalled the exotic past of Moorish Spain, often characterized as an age of glory and tolerance by comparison with the obscurantism and persecution of Inquisition times. But it was something other, an Oriental world, fascinating because hard to penetrate.

NINE

A globalized Mediterranean: 1900–2000

DAVID ABULAFIA

The Mediterranean is not a closed sea. The Strait of Gibraltar has given access to the Atlantic from the days when Phoenician traders sailed to Tartessos and as far as the tin mines of Cornwall. The Bosphorus has given access to the Black Sea and the Steppes. Since the mid-nineteenth century the Indian Ocean and the Mediterranean have been joined by the magnificent engineering achievement known as the Suez Canal, though even before then there were routes linking Alexandria overland to the Red Sea. The aim of this chapter is to examine ways in which the Mediterranean has, particularly in the twentieth century, been transformed as a result of its links to the outside world, as well as to explore the meeting of cultures within the Mediterranean in such cities as Alexandria. These changes that were not merely political (such as the build-up of French and British influence in the Mediterranean) but also cultural, as yearning for the classical past, long a significant feature of north European culture, found new expression, following the age of the Grand Tour, in the exploration of archaeological sites in Greece and Italy, and in the rediscovery of Renaissance art by German, British and other connoisseurs.

Turkish decline and renaissance

The twentieth century saw quite massive political transformations within the Mediterranean world. The great empires that had dominated the sea (in the case of the Turkish Empire for five centuries) experienced severe decline. Empires were lost, but also won: the Italians acquired territories, only to lose them within a few decades. And yet at the start of the twentieth century it seemed that a new order was coming into being in the region, the result in part of Anglo-French accord that the Mediterranean would henceforth function as the route between northern Europe and the Indian Ocean, in the years following the opening of the Suez Canal in 1869. This enterprise, French in conception, but jointly operated by the French and the British until 1956, marks the beginning of the process whereby the Mediterranean was 'globalized', for the strategic value of emplacements within the Mediterranean was increasingly determined by their relation to ambitious policies in the Middle and Far East. For Great Britain, already endowed since the Treaty of Utrecht with Gibraltar, and since 1814 with Malta, followed finally by Cyprus in 1878, the acquisition of a direct sea route to India via the Mediterranean was of massive commercial importance as well, feeding the textile industries of both India and Lancashire, as well as providing large quantities of long-fibred Egyptian cotton, cultivation of which expanded enormously; the Canal also enabled relatively rapid communication with the Empire, with approximate journey times of less than three hundred days to Alexandria and much the same from Suez to India.

Associated with the development of a route past Suez was the emergence of large steamships, metal-hulled, which serviced the route out East, gradually taking primacy from sailing vessels; for during much of the nineteenth century the steamship had remained a cumbersome, noisy and rather smelly innovation. But there were other opportunities being sought nearer home than India. Britain, with an eye on oil reserves, began to develop close ties with the Middle East. This again was the result of technological changes which, in the long term, transformed the economies of several Mediterranean lands and a good many statelets further east: the rise of the combustion engine fuelled demand for oil, and by the Second World War the battle for control of the oil fields in Iraq and Iran had a formative influence on the strategy conducted by the warring parties.

As important as British, French and eventually Italian ambitions in the Levant was the internal strife that tore apart the lumbering Ottoman Empire, which proved unable to cope with the vibrant nationalism of Albanians, Bulgars, Romanians, and indeed its own Turkish officer class, led by Mustafa Kemal, compounded by the strain of participation on the German side in the Great War. Already in the early nineteenth century Ottoman influence in North Africa had crumbled, most obviously in Egypt, where Muhammad Ali seized power in 1811, while the beys of Algeria and subsequently Tunisia proved unable to defend themselves from French encroachment, with Algeria falling into French hands as early as 1830. Moreover, the Greek government had scores to settle, and eyed the coast of Asia Minor, particularly around Smyrna (Izmir), an area which still contained a sizeable Greek population.

At its most ambitious level, Greek nationalism even aspired to the recovery of Constantinople, and this 'Great Idea' did not seem too unrealistic when the Turks themselves were experiencing internal revolution. But Greece attempted too much. The Turks proved quite resilient under their new leader Ataturk, as Mustafa Kemal chose to be known, and in 1922 the expulsion of the Greeks from Asia Minor (as well as bitter campaigns against the Armenians) proved that a new, secular, nationalistic Turkey could still have a significant military role in the region. The Turks were no longer 'the sick man of Europe'; indeed, all they possessed of Europe was a small corner around Istanbul, Edirne and Gallipoli. The Turks suffered the humiliation of the expulsion of the Muslim population of Crete, which had become independent on its own at a time when perhaps 40 per cent of the population was in fact Muslim, and had then undergone *Enosis*, union, with Greece.

Cyprus, with its mixed population, became a British colony in 1914. Yet this history of defeat did not prevent an attempt to modernize on the European model; for example, the Turkish government abandoned the Arabic alphabet, which had been a less than ideal vehicle for the Turkish language, and adapted the Latin alphabet to Turkish. Thus an interesting paradox emerged. Turkey was no longer a European state in any meaningful geographical sense, and yet it was attempting to become a European state by espousing a secularized, nationalist culture. Just as happened in the Balkans during the same period, the enthusiasm with which this policy was pursued presented difficulties to ethnic and religious minorities; the expulsion of the Greeks from Asia was matched by a population exchange bringing many Turks from Thrace and Thessaly into the Turkish homeland. And this in itself had notable effects on the ethnic balance within other parts of southeastern Europe. The important port city of Thessalonika or Salonika became increasingly hellenized, though until the Second World War a very high proportion of the population, maybe 40 per cent, consisted of Sephardic Jews who were ruthlessly exterminated by the Nazis (Jewish stevedores were so numerous that the port installations closed down on the Sabbath).

The Middle East moves to centre stage

Defeat in the First World War also brought to an end Ottoman influence in Palestine and Syria, and the British general Allenby entered Jerusalem in triumph in 1917. The victory over the Turks coincided with the recognition by the British government that Palestine would at some time in the future serve as a National Home for the Jewish people. Whether the 'Balfour Declaration' envisaged a fully independent Jewish state is another matter, and in any case Great Britain would work hard to make friends with Arab leaders in the region, setting up in the eastern part of former Palestine the Kingdom of Transjordan, as a link between the British sphere of influence in Iraq and British interests in Egypt and Palestine; nor were Arab rulers necessarily averse to the economic advantages that Jewish immigration might bring to the region. But the reality was that among the Jews of Europe, no less than the Slavic peoples, various movements for self-determination were coming into being. They were inspired in part by the suffering of the Jews in Eastern Europe, where the Tsarist government was at best uninterested in the pogroms launched against the Jews, and in part by the sense that the only land to which Jews had looked for centuries was indeed Palestine, the Holy Land, the Land of Israel. By the 1930s it was clear that the harsh anti-Semitic policies being adopted in central Europe, particularly in Germany, were also making necessary the provision of some place of refuge for the Jews. It will be necessary to return to the conflicts that emerged from Jewish immigration and state-building in the Levant in a moment.

At the same time as Britain was entrusted by the League of Nations with a mandate for the administration of Palestine, the French acquired similar obligations and duties in Syria. There France saw itself as the custodian of great traditions, the protector of the Christian population of the Lebanese highlands, but also as the heir to the French crusaders who had created the first 'nation franco-syrienne' in the twelfth and thirteenth centuries. An interesting cultural manifestation of the French mission in Syria was the project to restore the crusader castle at Crac des Chevaliers, perhaps the grandest castle in the entire Levant, but also a potent symbol that the French had returned. For Great Britain, however, much of the value of these possessions lay in their usefulness as stages on the route to India, rather than in what they meant for themselves, a good example of British pragmatism.

The collapse of Ottoman power had other effects in the Levant. After 1883 Egypt emerged as a British client state, with a king, of Albanian extraction, who shared with the British control of the Sudan (which simply means 'the south') down the Nile from Egypt. It thus possessed a special strategic role, not simply because of its position beside Suez, but also because the Nile gave access to British possessions in central and eastern Africa: Kenya, Uganda and also

Tanganyika, which Germany had lost following its defeat in the First World War (Zanzibar was acquired in the 1880s when Great Britain exchanged it for Heligoland). For a period of fifty years, Alexandria acted as a particular cultural magnet, as the home to Italians, Sephardic Jews, Greeks, Albanians, French, Coptic Christians, with an élite that eschewed their native tongue for French, a world brilliantly recreated in Lawrence Durrell's *Alexandria Quartet*. Nationalism had not yet become so fierce that several of these distinctive groups were unwelcome away from their place of birth.

Italy, 'the least of the great powers'

A gentle jostling for position, within the framework of the *entente cordiale* binding France and Great Britain together, gave some stability, therefore, to the eastern Mediterranean. The basic interests of the two former rivals did not clash. And both were democratic countries, whose governments, as events in the 1930s would show, were often prepared to go to great lengths to avoid war with aggressive competitors in central Europe. More complicated was the role of Italy, 'the fourth of the great powers', which began its empire-building in the wake of unification, led by parliamentary governments that lost power in 1922 to the first of the right-wing authoritarian dictatorships.

The role of Italy is also peculiar because Italy sits fairly and squarely in the middle of the Mediterranean; for although France has a Mediterranean coast, France was much more than a Mediterranean power, with extensive imperial possessions in West Africa, South America, Southeast Asia and the Pacific, to which, certainly, it added during the nineteenth and early twentieth centuries great swathes of North Africa: Algeria, Tunisia, much of Morocco (though Spain controlled the Mediterranean shores of Morocco). But Italy was a country whose industrialization lagged behind that of France, and by a very long distance behind Britain or Germany, a country whose south and centre, in particular, still saw desperate poverty, and whose national unity had been forged over a quarter of a century in the face of exceptionally strong regional identities. The urge to create an empire, enthusiastically supported by king and parliament, was unquestionably an expression of the search for a strong national purpose and identity. The more successful enterprises were those nearest home. Conveniently close to home, the open spaces of Libya invited conquest, as Liberal Italy, on the eve of the First World War, sought to exploit the patent weakness of Turkish power in the region; other schemes, as far afield as Eritrea and Ethiopia, were nurtured in the late nineteenth century, culminating in Mussolini's brutal war on Abyssinia in 1935. The Dodecanese, including Rhodes, constituted Italy's share of the former Ottoman possessions in the Aegean, and were occupied as early as 1912, a sideshow in the war that brought Italy control of once Turkish Libya.

Another theatre almost within sight of *la patria* was Albania, a largely Muslim land of warring tribes with weak government; even as it broke loose from Turkey during the First World War it was prey to Greek, Italian and Serbian ambitions, but it came to depend heavily on the Italians. Indeed, the National Bank of Albania was based in Rome and not the impoverished capital, Tirana, well before the Italians invaded in April 1939. The ill-fated King Zog of Albania (originally a tough tribal leader from the interior) was an Italian puppet for much of his short career, which saw him transformed from president in 1925 to king in 1928. The Italian invasion was long remembered by soldiers in the Fascist army as a long and bitter trial, and the failure of Italy to conquer Albania quickly and neatly raised eyebrows in Germany, for it suggested that Fascist Italy was not likely to be a strong military ally when the time for a wider war came.

Along the Albanian coast, malarial swamps made life insufferable; in the interior the Italians had to cope with bandits who had no interest in seeing the creation of the strong government Mussolini aspired to create. Tirana itself was turned into an Italianate capital, with ministries and one grand hotel in the monumental Roman style; and yet nothing could turn it into a real city, for it was very small and lacking in creature comforts. Despite the availability of chrome in Albania, there was not much profit to be extracted from Italy's European colony, and the major advantages gained from dominion there lay in control of its ports, Durrës (Durazzo) and Vlorë (Valona); Italy had in any case already acquired the island of Sazan (Saseno) opposite Valona in 1920, having failed to keep Valona for itself.

While the acquisition of influence in Albania appeared to consolidate Italy's hold over the Adriatic, in ways reminiscent of medieval Venice, it can hardly be said that the control of the Adriatic served a crucial strategic purpose, since there were no obvious rivals: Yugoslavia was no challenge, and one of the major ports along the Dalmatian coast, Zara (Zadar), was an Italian possession, made famous by its exports of Luxardo's cherry brandy. Trieste was won from the Austro-Hungarian Empire at the end of the Great War; it was in theory a valuable asset, since it gave access from the Mediterranean to the key cities of south-central Europe, and its commerce flourished after the opening of the Suez Canal. However, the disintegration of the Austro-Hungarian Empire and its incorporation in Italy deprived it of the easy access to central European markets that it had enjoyed in the late nineteenth century, and the city set into decline. However, one reflection of its contacts beyond Italy and the new Yugoslav state was that Trieste developed a thriving literary culture, which brought together the intellectual world of Vienna with that of northern Italy (expressed, for instance, in the works of Italo Svevo, while James Joyce was a celebrated Irish visitor).

Trieste was famous for its insurance companies that developed out of its shipping trade, and the Jewish community, drawn from Italy and Austria, was prominent in these activities and in the brandy business. At the other end of the Istrian coast, Fiume (Rijeka) had effectively become an Italian outpost after the victorious entry into the city by the poet and *condottiere* Gabriele d'Annunzio in 1919, leading a private army that sought to celebrate the glory of a victorious and united Italy by bringing the partly Italian-speaking population of the Istrian littoral under Italian rule. Italy later took over his conquest.

After 1922 the sense of Italian national rebirth was heavily emphasized by the Fascist régime. Mussolini celebrated the recreation of the Roman Empire under his direction (though in fact many of the key advances had been made by the Liberal governments that preceded the Fascist seizure of power); it was in large part a Mediterranean empire, situated in *Mare Nostrum*, 'our sea'. One manifestation was the adoption of Roman insignia by the Fascist movement, notably the *fasces* or rods of correction from which the Fascist movement acquired its name; but the Duce also wanted to bring the message of Mediterranean empire to his people, and carved a great triumphal road through the centre of Rome, right past the Roman Forum and the Palatine, adorned with a series of maps set in stone which showed the expansion of Rome from a small town on seven hills to the greatest extent of imperial glory under Trajan. Nor did his ambitions exclude territories ruled by the French and the British. One of the more peculiar propaganda efforts of the Fascist era was the series of historical journals that related the history of those lands that also constituted part of *Italia irredenta*, 'unredeemed Italy' because their populations had once been ruled by Italians: French Corsica, British Malta, Yugoslav Dalmatia.

Mediterranean rivalries, 1930–45

The assumption was, of course, that ruling lands like Libya involved bringing civilization to them, though conquest also brought careers, commercial opportunities and political clout to the victorious nation. The idea of spreading western civilization from the north of the Mediterranean to the south was particularly favoured by the French. Just as the Italians made Tripoli into a large modern city with boulevards and a fine cathedral, so too Algiers became a French city on the edge of Africa, but in many respects looking northwards, for cultural inspiration and economic ties. French Algeria was neatly divided between a rather wild Saharan interior, which stretched down to join other French protectorates and possessions in West Africa, and a northern edge which would, indeed, eventually be incorporated into metropolitan France; there was a sharp divide between the European settlers and the natives, though the Algerian Jews received a privilege granting them citizenship and, effectively, European status. Algiers was endowed with a university on the Parisian model, from which the local Arabs and Berbers were excluded; it was the training ground for distinguished historians of the Mediterranean, notably Fernand Braudel. Further along the coast looking westwards, Oran developed as a centre within French Algeria with a particularly large Spanish population, for Spain made only limited gains in the Mediterranean at this period, though it held on to its ancient possessions of Ceuta and Melilla, and extended its influence from Tetuán and Tangier, winning control over a strip of the sultanate of Morocco directly opposite ever-British Gibraltar.

France acquired control of Tunisia in 1883, taking advantage of the collapse of local power in the wake of the disintegration of the Ottoman Empire; here, not surprisingly, Italian business interests were strong, with Livorno Jews playing an especially vigorous role. Morocco proved particularly intractable, despite the willingness of the French to divide and rule with the Spaniards, and to maintain in position the sultan. One difficulty at the start of the twentieth century was the attempt by the Germans to establish themselves in Atlantic Morocco, whose major ports such as Mogador enjoyed an intimate commercial tie to England by way of Jewish merchants based there and in London. But the result of the race for empire around the Mediterranean was that France, Britain and Italy had acquired territory and influence, Britain largely with an eye to its wider imperial concerns beyond the Mediterranean, France with such concerns in mind but also seeking to acquire territory due south of her European core, and Italy in the first stages of an attempt at empire-building that would prove as short-lived as it was grandiose.

Other broadly based plans were revealed with the intervention of Fascist Italy in the civil war that wracked Spain during the 1930s. Franco's crusade against the Left, launched in Spanish Morocco, had major consequences along the Mediterranean coasts of Spain. The vigorous attempts of the Catalans and Basques to create an autonomous government were stifled, and the Civil War was accompanied by breathtaking brutality, still further compounded once it was over: garrotings continued, the press was kept under tight surveillance, Spanish refugees flooded into southern France and across the ocean to South America. The main avenues of the major Spanish towns were named after the heroes of the Falangist movement, Primo de Rivera, Franco and so on. And yet during the Second World War Generalissimo Francisco Franco was careful to distance himself from the Germans, who had given him decisive aid against his enemies during the Spanish conflict. His instinct not to join the Nazi axis (pleading Spanish exhaustion after the Civil War) would help preserve him in power after the war, as host to American air bases; and gradually a degree of cautious liberalization was permitted.

Still, times remained hard for the Catalans, the Galicians and the Basques, whose languages were no longer taught in schools. Catalan publishing was restricted, though the opportunity to publish apparently recondite works of medieval history in Catalan was eagerly seized: the days of Catalan mercantile and political glory could safely be celebrated since they were so long gone; yet in celebrating them national feeling could be subtly expressed, so that figures such as the historian Fernan Soldevila acquired a degree of influence rarely accorded to medieval scholars. Nor could the Francoist régime suppress every manifestation of Catalan culture and national sentiment, notably the dancing of the Sardana in front of Barcelona Cathedral on Saturday evenings.

Perhaps (to be counter-factual) Mussolini could have survived in similar fashion for a while, and could have preserved some of his Mediterranean interests, had he not come to terms with Nazi

Germany, and had he not seized the opportunity offered by the Fall of France in 1940 to acquire Nice and a small sphere of influence in southeastern France. He had enough points of disagreement with the Nazis, viewing the Nazi incorporation of Austria into the Reich with deep concern; and the issue of the German-speaking population of the Alto Adige region, ruled by Italy since the collapse of Austria-Hungary at the end of the First World War, was potentially a source of severe tension between Germany and Italy. Yet the firm rebuff he received from the League of Nations following his ruthless attack on Abyssinia convinced him that he should not side in the long term with the democratic powers; and there is no reason to doubt that he believed that the future lay with Fascism and authoritarian government in its various forms, which had spread to Spain, Greece, Romania and, further afield, Germany and Poland, and which was seen as a bulwark against the spread of the no less authoritarian Communism of Soviet Russia. Thus in 1938 Mussolini introduced anti-Semitic legislation on the German model, to the puzzlement of the vast majority of his nation, indicating that he was keen to tighten the bonds with the Third Reich.

While the First World War had affected the Mediterranean by drawing into the conflict the crumbling Ottoman Empire, a polity that had long dominated the eastern Mediterranean, the Second World War affected the Mediterranean in quite different ways. Italy, of course, failed in its attempt to make good out of a pact with Hitler, and the Italian army did not greatly distinguish itself in fighting in Greece, Yugoslavia or North Africa; on the other hand, Italian officers often earned a reputation as humane defenders of Jews and other persecuted minorities in southern France and Yugoslavia. Fearful of an allied invasion of Sardinia (perhaps a pointless exercise in any case), the Italians failed to notice that the real target of the Allied armies lay in Sicily. In any case, Italy's discredited generals deposed Mussolini and changed sides in 1943, which did not in any way mark the end of the period of horrors. Nor did the Italians succeed in gaining a toehold in Malta, which was stalwartly defended by the British against a German and Italian siege in 1940–43; it was the second Great Siege of Malta, and the fortifications built by La Vallette nearly 400 years earlier following the Turkish siege became the front line of the Allies in their own battle for control of the Mediterranean shipping lanes, with all that this implied for access to India and to the Far East, where British possessions had been overwhelmed by the Imperial Japanese Army.

Had the Germans succeeded in crushing the British and Commonwealth troops massed on the Egyptian frontier, that too would have decisively altered the course of the conflict, not just in the Mediterranean but in the entire war; Hitler dreamed of dominating the oil supplies of Persia, and the advance to Stalingrad was thus intimately linked to his attempts to acquire a power base in the Middle East. The victory at El Alamein (1942) saved British interests in the Middle East; the failure of the Germans to enter Palestine was also of great importance, for the virulently anti-Semitic Grand Mufti, leader of the Muslim community, decided to befriend Hitler in the hope that this would prevent Jewish immigration into the region, where tensions between his followers and the Jews, some refugees, some Zionist settlers, some ancient inhabitants, remained acute.

Allied victory and its aftermath

The Allied victory over the Nazis was partly achieved by the invasion of Italy via Sicily, and the slow but relentless march of Allied forces up the peninsula, to the Lombard plains where Mussolini had re-established himself (after dramatically escaping from captivity) in the little towns bordering Lake Garda, notably Saló; hence the term 'Saló Republic' to describe the puppet state, effectively controlled by Germany, which blocked access to the Austrian Alps. But the victory was not simply one for Western democracies. In Yugoslavia, where Nazi brutality embittered the Serb population of the centre and south and led to a fierce partisan resistance, the Allies decided eventually to support the Communist factions, not trusting the more conservative Chetniks to remain loyal. The result was the creation of a Communist state bordering Italy and Austria, aiming also to absorb Albania. The apparent victory for Stalin in this theatre of war turned sour; the Yugoslav Communist leader Tito, vain, pompous and wily, had no intention of becoming Stalin's plaything, and the physical distance from Russia made it practical for him to resist Stalin's blandishments and then denunciations, and to build an authoritarian régime which had some success in knitting together Slovenes, Croats, Bosnians, Serbs and Macedonians, Tito himself being of mixed blood. Taking advantage of the increasing concern in the West at Stalin's repression, and at the more tactful but still uncompromising position of the later Soviet leaders, Marshal Tito attempted to create a socialist state that would also enjoy good ties with the West.

By the mid-1950s, Yugoslavia sought to occupy a third position between the US and its NATO allies and Comintern, the Soviet bloc, by sponsoring meetings of the non-aligned states, including India, and, among other Mediterranean nations, the Arab Republic of Egypt, of which more later. Whether this really resulted in creating an effective third force in world affairs is a moot point; but it did preserve the Yugoslav régime in its delicate position between the Soviet Union and the West; and the reality is that the fierce national rivalries which were to erupt after the death of Tito in 1980 were held at bay. Tito even swallowed his pride and came to terms with Italy over the disputed frontier with Yugoslavia, conceding Trieste to Italy (after a brief period as the Free City of Trieste under Anglo-American protection), while Italy gained guarantees for the dwindling Italian population of the Istrian coastal towns, which were now securely under Tito's authority.

More precarious was the position of Greece and Albania, the former of which experienced the tragedy of a divisive civil war in the late 1940s, as Communists sought to gain power and to add

Greece to Stalin's empire; the consequence would have been the availability to Moscow of ports and naval facilities in the Mediterranean comparable to those it had long possessed in the Black Sea. In Albania, a Communist take-over occurred more easily, but the new leader, Enver Hoxha, reacted violently to Tito's policies, recognizing with some justice that Tito hoped to swallow Albania, even though it is not a South Slav nation. The conflict between David and Goliath was played out in a ringing propaganda war, in which Albania presented itself as the true representative of Marxism-Leninism, combating Tito's capitalist roaders and paper tigers. This worked well while Stalin and his immediate successor saw some use in Albania, and while Hoxha believed that the USSR was continuing to follow a strict Marxist line. Estrangement between Albania and the Soviet Union in the 1960s culminated in the building of close ties between Albania and Mao's China, which was held up as the paragon of true Socialism, while Khrushchev and Brezhnev in Moscow were denounced as 'Social Fascists', and busts of Stalin stood in every town square long after he had become decidedly unfashionable in the rest of Communist Europe. Hoxha delighted in telling his fellow-Albanians that Khrushchev had said to the Albanian leaders: 'Do not worry about grain, for all that you consume in a whole year is eaten by mice in our country', a clear sign of Soviet contempt for Hoxha's régime. With Chinese aid, a limited amount of industrialization took place, including the 'Mao Tse-Tung Textile Mills' in Berat.

Thus in place of the division of the Mediterranean between Islam and Christendom, there emerged a division between a new West and a new East; but neither Yugoslavia nor Albania was willing to perform the task Russia would have liked, by providing deep water ports in the Mediterranean. China, for its part, had no realistic hope of using Albania as a military outpost in Europe, preferring to employ the Albanian representative at the United Nations as its mouthpiece until, in 1971, the People's Republic of China finally displaced the Nationalist Republic of China (Taiwan) from the Chinese seat at the UN. By then, and after the death of Mao in 1976, China discovered it had little use for Albania, which became even more isolated.

Decolonization, which so deeply affected the British need for control of parts of the Mediterranean, had an even more direct effect on France. After a moderate amount of bloodshed, a 1956 independence movement in Morocco secured the union of French and Spanish Morocco (except Ceuta and Melilla), and the creation of a new state under the old Sherifian dynasty, free from European supervision; in Tunisia the Destour Party of Habib Bourguiba also gained independence for the territory in 1956, and Bourguiba thereafter became a voice of moderation in the Arab world. These were possessions that France had acquired in the relatively recent past; but the case of Algeria, linked to France since the 1830s, was far more complex. Algeria had become part of the soul of France, and indeed the northern coast, with the major towns, had been formally incorporated into metropolitan France. Thus the French government, and still more the army and the settlers, tended to see departure from Algeria as the amputation of one of France's limbs.

The Algerian civil war filled with ghastly brutality as terror groups (the OAS, loyal to France, the FLN, demanding separation) battled against one another between 1954 and 1962. In 1958, the French president, Charles de Gaulle, seized power with the support of those generals who bitterly opposed abandonment of Algeria; his Fifth Republic, despite a military plot to overthrow him, finally accepted that the situation was untenable and agreed to grant Algeria independence following a referendum. One result was the creation of an authoritarian socialist state under leaders such as President Boumedienne (between 1965 and 1978) who proved unable to tackle the country's many economic problems. Blaming them on the French legacy did not solve these problems. In the 1990s tensions between the old leadership and Islamic insurgents, and between Arabs and Berbers, erupted in massacres as horrible as anything experienced in late colonial times, though by 2000 the situation seemed a little calmer.

The other result of Algerian independence was a mass migration of French Algerians, Christian and Jewish, to France, especially cities such as Marseille and Toulon, which had close links with Algeria; this in turn was followed by the migration to France of hundreds of thousands of Algerian Muslims (as also Moroccans and Tunisians), greatly enlarging the North African population of France. Tensions between the old population and the immigrants grew in France, as in most north European countries, and during the 1990s far Right anti-immigration candidates, notably those linked to Jean-Marie Le Pen's *Front National*, became a powerful political force in such cities as Nice. These tensions reached their peak in 2002, when Le Pen survived the first round of the French presidential elections to become the sole challenger to the incumbent president, Jacques Chirac, a relaxed figure tainted by accusations of corruption; the Left had disintegrated in faction fighting. Though Le Pen was soundly beaten, his ability to reach so far in the presidential contest was a severe shock to French politics. This was a problem that did not go away, even when Le Pen's daughter, Marine Le Pen, took over leadership of her father's movement, retaining many of its ideals but attempting to make its message less toxic. All this only served as a reminder that the demographic balance in the Mediterranean was shifting; by 2000 a sizeable Muslim population (estimated 5 million in France) existed in every Western European country, many of whom came from the southern or eastern Mediterranean: North Africans in France, Turks and Moroccans in Germany and Holland.

It is now necessary to turn to the Arabs and their neighbours at the other end of the Mediterranean, where political relationships have proved even more delicate.

Israel and the Arabs

The failure of Soviet policy towards the two Communist states in the Mediterranean, Yugoslavia and Albania, did not prevent Russia from building up its links with the Arab states in the Middle East.

A key moment was the collapse of the old régime in Egypt in 1952 and the acquisition of power by a military committee, at the head of which emerged Colonel Gamal Abdal Nasser. He was a complex figure, willing to present himself as the champion of the Arab world, as a leader of the non-aligned movement, as a political and social reformer in his own country, as the enemy of colonialism and neo-colonialism, as the foe of the State of Israel. For the great transformation in Mediterranean politics that followed the Second World War was the creation of a Jewish state within mandated Palestine, as a homeland for the survivors of the Nazi persecution of the Jews, and for other Jews suffering from persecution elsewhere.

The immigrants from Eastern Europe, whose access to Palestine was frequently blocked by the British navy in the period 1945 to 1948, were joined by hundreds of thousands of refugees from Arab lands, where the issue of a Jewish state led to unprecedented attacks on Jews, seizure of Jewish property and the imprisonment of Jewish leaders. Thereby the existence of Jewish communities which had inhabited the Mediterranean and the Middle East for 2,000 years was effectively brought to an end: Nasser's policies targeted not merely the Jews of Egypt, but Italians, Greeks and other non-Arabs (one can hardly say 'foreigners' in the case of groups that had lived there so long, but that is how they were presented). Similar exoduses out of Syria and, further East, Iraq and Yemen, gave the new State of Israel a character rather different from that envisaged by some of its founding fathers, the majority of whom were central and east European Ashkenazim. Indeed, a central feature of early Zionism was the idea of a return to the land, and the establishment of the kibbutz movement, with its egalitarian socialist principles and innovative approaches to work and child-care, had great political and economic significance: the kibbutzim provided an early generation of dedicated soldiers and politicians, and the agricultural techniques developed by Israeli agronomists made the desert bloom.

The integration of Oriental Jews into Israeli society was at first achieved by expecting a degree of conformity with Westernized and partly secularized Jewish culture, an attitude that gave rise to some hostility among the immigrants. This was exacerbated by the fact that the prosperous, Westernized, francophone élite among North African Jews tended to migrate to France and Quebec, leaving many of the Maghribi Jews in Israel without the effective leadership that other communities, Oriental and occidental, retained. This later generated social problems that horrified the more idealistic among the founders of Israel.

The creation of Israel had been sanctioned on the formal basis of a two-state formula proposed by Britain in 1938 and confirmed by the UN in 1947: British Palestine was to be divided between a Jewish and an Arab state. The Arab refusal to countenance the existence of a Jewish state, coupled with attacks on the Jewish state by its Arab neighbours, helped create a massive refugee problem, as Palestinian Arabs fled from the fighting, or were forced out of the areas that fell under Jewish control. After 1948, many were miserably confined in an Egyptian-controlled corner of Palestine, the Gaza Strip, while others took refuge in shanty towns in the larger area acquired after 1948 by the king of Jordan, now generally called the West Bank. The Jordanian king had been quite willing to make a peace with Israel, dividing Palestine between Jews and Arabs, but the assassination of King Abdullah and the wish to maintain a united Arab front made this impossible. Arab pride had been severely dented. Many refugees found it impossible to shake off the idea of a victorious return to abandoned homes in Palestine, and this dream fuelled recruitment to the nascent Palestine Liberation Organization under Ahmad Shukairy, an organization whose charter made abundantly clear its intention of obliterating Israel and expelling virtually all Jews.

The presence of Israel greatly altered the politics of the eastern Mediterranean, and the question of Israel's right to exist has dominated the politics of the region since 1948. The little state was immediately recognized in 1948 by the USA and the USSR, though Stalin soon decided that he would gain nothing from the Israelis, whose kibbutznik socialists were nothing like his own socialists; later Soviet rulers gave enthusiastic support to the Arab neighbours of Israel. The Soviet Union had no qualms about Nasser's wish to nationalize the Suez Canal in the face of British and French opposition, and in any case the Suez war (1956), though humiliating to Egypt in the sense that Israel rapidly occupied the whole of the Sinai peninsula, was a convenient diversion from Russian pressure on Hungary, which was brutally invaded the same year while the West was looking in the direction of Suez. Britain and France could be presented as the villains while the Soviet Union itself acted villanously towards Hungary. The British Prime Minister, Sir Anthony Eden, was no great admirer of Israel, but he was convinced that Nasser was the new Hitler, and his obsession with Suez failed to recognize the new global reality: access to India was less important now that India was an independent republic, and access to the further corners of the Empire and Commonwealth was in any case rendered increasingly easy by the invention of the passenger jet (the first de Havilland Comet flew in 1952). Suez was no longer crucial to Britain; after 1967, the Canal was closed for over a dozen years without wrecking British trade.

The real difficulty was the build-up of Soviet influence in the Middle East. The Americans were increasingly cast in the role of capitalist-imperialist defenders of colonialist Israel, a presentation of Israel which was further embroidered by the free use of anti-Semitic motifs in the Soviet and Arab press, some of which seem to have been borrowed directly from Nazi propaganda. In particular, the USSR stepped in to replace the United States by funding the massive Egyptian project for building the Aswan Dam. Egypt, as the largest Arab state, championed the cause of Arab unity, delicately playing off its own national identity (which used as imagery the Pharaohs, Saladin and Nasser himself) against the theme of wider Arab unity. Trying to project himself as the leader of the Arab world, Nasser began to bait Israel in 1967, closing the Straits of Tiran in the Red Sea to Israeli shipping bound for Eilat; the result was the Six Day

War which lost him Sinai, forced him (briefly) to resign, and also lost Syria the Golan and, most importantly, lost Jordan the West Bank and East Jerusalem; this was an enormous humiliation for the Arab world, which responded by categorically refusing to negotiate with Israel, and to exploit the likelihood that Israel would have returned territory in exchange for peace. As one Israeli politician said, 'the Arabs have never lost an opportunity to lose an opportunity'. Following the accession to power of Benjamin Netanyahu, who became Prime Minister of Israel in 1996 and again in 2009, the same might certainly be said of the Israelis.

The Yom Kippur War of 1973, in which Egypt tried to recover Sinai, was effectively a stalemate, but it did lead in the longer term to peace negotiations between President Sadat of Egypt and the hardline government of Menachem Begin in Israel. Sinai was returned to Egypt by 1982, and ambassadors were exchanged; the USA gave enormous financial support to both parties in order to achieve and sustain peace, but no significant progress has been made on the status of the West Bank, where (in breach of international law) Israeli settlements have sprouted, with official approval and otherwise, and have become a serious obstacle to peace. This, combined with the stance taken by the Israeli government, means that the prospect of a viable Palestinian state emerging alongside the State of Israel diminishes by the day.

At the time of the Six Day War, attempts to create a single Arab entity were made, and Syria officially merged with Egypt from 1958 to 1961 using the open-ended title of 'The United Arab Republic'. Economic and political pressures soon drove the two countries apart, but schemes for unification abounded, mostly barely worth the paper they were written on. No one really wanted union with the maverick 'Libyan Arab People's Jamahiriya' founded in 1969 by Colonel Gaddafi, but all sorts of treaties were signed pretending that this was a serious intention. His own 'Green Revolution', based on an idiosyncratic mélange of socialism, ecology and Islam, did more to reveal the lack of unity between Arab nations than anything else. He imposed a ban on the public use of languages other than Arabic; and there were restrictions on the hedonistic life that many rich Libyans had led following the oil boom under King Idris. All this might have seemed rather comical, like something out of Evelyn Waugh's novels, had Gaddafi not also become a leading supporter of international terrorism, until around 2000 he sensed that his country's best interests lay in a more co-operative approach to Mediterranean and world politics. Perhaps, too, he was worried by developments in nearby Algeria, where Islamist and Berber political parties and armed rebels challenged the régime, with the horrifying result that perhaps 100,000 people died in massacres and fighting during the late 1990s.

Mediterranean tensions at the end of the twentieth century

It would be wrong to suppose that the conflict between Israel and the Arabs has been the only source of severe tension in the Mediterranean during the latter years of the twentieth century. The tendency to think that way has perhaps done as much to inflame the problem as have the difficulties on the ground. Also unresolved has been the question of Cyprus, after the withdrawal of the colonial power, Great Britain, in 1960, following rampant violence, and the creation of a republic in which power was initially shared between the Greek majority and the very substantial Turkish minority. Under the first president, Archbishop Makarios, a degree of stability was achieved, but Turkey remained highly suspicious of Greek intentions towards Cyprus, not least since many Greek Cypriots saw the way forward as *Enosis*, union with Greece. In 1974 Turkish fears of Greek intervention in Cyprus culminated in a Turkish invasion of northern Cyprus, and the flight or expulsion of Greeks out of the north and Turks out of the south. Cyprus was partitioned, though the 'Turkish Republic of Northern Cyprus' has only been recognized by the Turkish government and was in effect a province of Turkey.

Although this problem has excited far less passion outside its immediate neighbourhood than that of Palestine and Israel, it did have one highly beneficial effect: the Turkish invasion prompted the collapse of the authoritarian military dictatorship in Greece, the régime of the 'Colonels', and the restoration of democracy. The King, however, was seen as an ambiguous figure whose misconduct was believed to have made it possible for the colonels to seize power in the first place in 1967. Greece became a republic, and was granted special favours by Western Europe, which was keen to bring stability to the eastern Mediterranean; thus in 1981 the Hellenic republic acceded to the European Economic Community, even though it lagged some way behind the other EEC states in economic performance. Subsequently Greece was able to close the gap to some extent, at the price of initially quite heavy inflation; but Greece remained a favoured member of what is now called the European Union, gaining membership of the Eurozone against many expectations, and becoming one of the states that adopted the Euro as its currency in January 2002. The achievement should not be underestimated, even if the EU had to bend its rules to allow Greece to join the Euro, with savage consequences a few years later when Greece experienced economic meltdown and was unable to use its own currency to mitigate the effects.

Talk of further expansion of the European Union to include Turkey aroused a degree of unease in Greece. Though both became members of the North Atlantic Treaty Organization, and were technically allies, the relationship between Greeks and Turks has been founded on centuries of mutual suspicion. That said, membership of NATO and, in Greece's case, of the EU, acts as a firm brake on adventurism by either side in the Aegean Sea. Subsequent developments have compromised the uneasy relationship between Greece and Turkey. Turkey under President Erdoğan has looked away from Europe, has re-asserted its Islamic past, and has become deeply involved in the politics of the Middle East, taking sides against its old ally Israel, which has been embraced instead by Greece and

Cyprus. Meanwhile a solution to the problem of North Cyprus seems as remote as a solution to the Palestinian problem.

With the creation of independent states in Cyprus and Malta, Great Britain abandoned its role as a colonial power in the Mediterranean, although it retained important Sovereign Bases in Cyprus for military reasons. However, one minuscule colony persisted at the extreme end of the western Mediterranean: Gibraltar. Spanish attempts to secure Gibraltar reached a peak under General Franco, who imposed a Spanish blockade on the rock in 1965, even though this harmed the economy of the Spanish areas adjoining Gibraltar more than that of Gibraltar itself. Referenda in Gibraltar consistently showed that the population (a mix of Maltese, Genoese, Indians, Sephardic Jews and of course Spaniards) really wanted to stay under British rule. Meanwhile Britain realized it had less use of Gibraltar as a defensive base, and Gibraltar itself diversified into the provision of offshore financial services, which Spain linked to money laundering and the drugs traffic. In truth, Spain had its own similar problem in Ceuta and Melilla, the former acquired in 1415 (by Portugal originally) and the latter in 1497, outposts in North Africa which Spain saw no reason to hand over to Morocco. An apparently comical episode in which a microscopic outcrop of Spanish territory off the African coast, Perejíl ('Parsley Island') was occupied by Morocco in the summer of 2002, in fact revealed that Morocco was ready to exploit tensions over Gibraltar and over the drugs traffic out of Ceuta, in order to activate claims to territorial integrity not too dissimilar from those adumbrated by Spain over Gibraltar. Though so tiny, Gibraltar has soured Anglo-Spanish relations, with consequences for EU policy, such as financial policies and air traffic liberalization.

In other respects the European Union has provided help to poorer Mediterranean regions of member states, pumping funds into less developed areas of southern Italy, Greece and Spain. In southern Italy, this has not arrested a flight from the land, nor has it resulted in a significant increase in industrial output. In some areas heavy agricultural subsidies may indeed have dampened initiative. The accession of Slovenia, Croatia, Malta, Cyprus to the European Union has been matched by its extension northwards to the Baltic states. It will become more difficult for the sectional interests of individual members to be taken fully into account. This too is a sign of the globalization of the Mediterranean, of its integration (or at least the integration of its northern shores) into a trading and industrial complex whose centres of gravity are Brussels and Frankfurt rather than Athens and Rome.

One critical development within the Mediterranean has been the massively increased flow of migrants coming out of Asia and Africa, in search of a better life in Europe. Many do not wish to linger in Mediterranean countries: Germany, Sweden and the United Kingdom have been particular poles of attraction. However, the ethnic complexion of Mediterranean cities has changed significantly as African hawkers sell their wares on the streets of Naples or Barcelona, and as Kurdish, Syrian and Afghan refugees become a familiar sight in Greece. Small islands such as Lesbos and Pantelleria, an Italian possession not far from Tunisia, have been overwhelmed by migrants en route to continental Europe. The disintegration of Syria and the emigration of many hundreds of thousands of refugees through Turkey into Greece was matched by the arrival, after dangerous and miserable journeys across the Sahara, of asylum-seekers from sub-Saharan Africa. As the African population benefited from ever-better health care, population grew exponentially, and opportunities for employment became more restricted – many migrants are in fact middle-class, well-educated, in search of the opportunity to become an engineer or doctor in a European city. This flow will continue apace, and it is often hard to distinguish economic migrants from refugees from persecution. The exploitation of the migrants by people-traffickers has had tragic consequences time and again, as boats barely suitable for a journey downstream are launched off the coast of Libya or Turkey, carrying their occupants in many cases to a watery death. How to deal with this crisis is one of the great unsolved problems of the twenty-first century Mediterranean, and indeed the world.

North European visions: new images of the classical past

The image of the classical past as something clean, precise and pure has been discussed earlier in this volume. This was not easily dissipated: it was an ideal expressing Victorian values, whatever its relation to the harsher realities of the ancient world. However, at the start of the twentieth century a more radical reassessment of the classical past began to develop in the mind of Jane Harrison, a Fellow of Newnham College, Cambridge, and a pioneer in the study of the darker aspects of Greek culture: mystery religions devoted to Dionysos and other gods, a wilder, apparently less constrained side, that ill accorded with traditional perceptions of Greece and the Greeks. Another rebel voice was that of D. H. Lawrence, a little later; his joy at the uninhibited life of the Etruscans, displayed on the walls of the tombs he visited at Tarquinia, was volubly expressed in his book *Etruscan Places.* The sheer spontaneity of Etruscan art appealed to him, rather than the clinical coldness of the classical art then most admired. For him, Etruscan art spoke of a return to nature; it was earthy, sexually explicit, real rather than ideal:

> Art is still to us something which has been well-cooked – like a plate of spaghetti. An ear of wheat is not 'art'. Wait, wait till it has been turned into pure, into perfect macaroni. For me, I get more pleasure out of these Volterran ash-chests than out of – I had almost said, the Parthenon frieze. One wearies of the aesthetic quality – a quality which takes the edge off everything, and makes it seem 'boiled down'. A great deal of pure Greek beauty has this boiled-down effect. It is too much cooked in the artistic consciousness.

And on his travels through Tuscany, Sardinia and the Italian lakes he managed to record a less idealized Italy than his contemporaries based in Florence and Venice, an Italy of grinding poverty and of detachment from the classical and Renaissance past. It is also worth adding that Etruscan art and the art of prehistoric Sardinia had a noticeable influence on twentieth-century artists such as Giacometti, whose elongated figures closely recall the products of Nuraghic and Etruscan culture.

A further transformation in north European views of the Mediterranean occurred as a result of a spectacular series of discoveries at the end of the nineteenth and beginning of the twentieth century. They raised questions about the origins of Greek civilization, both appearing to confirm that the stories told by Homer had some basis in fact, and presenting to view a pre-classical world which was startlingly different from that of Winckelmann and Jowett. Before 1900, Heinrich Schliemann excavated Troy and Mycenae, making plenty of mistakes in the process, but extending further back in time understanding of the history of the Mediterranean; and after 1900 Arthur Evans' work in Crete conjured into life (thanks to imaginative reconstruction of the site at Knossos) a civilization midway between the European continent and Egypt, in some ways quite similar to that of Egypt, with frescoed palaces, golden drinking vessels and strange scripts, what was soon labelled 'the first European civilization'. (The concept is of course nonsensical, assuming as it does that Europe had some sort of identity around 1500 BC; but it seemed an attractive notion, showing that at this point high civilization was not just an attribute of Africans and Asiatics from Luxor and Ur of the Chaldees.) At a time when there was an assumption that long-limbed, fair-haired 'Dorians' had conquered and (to use language from the German politics of the 1930s) Aryanized Greece, the puzzle concerning who the Minoans of Crete and the Mycenaeans of the mainland were remained a difficult one, and it was only resolved as late as the 1950s when Michael Ventris and John Chadwick demonstrated that the language of the later tablets found at Knossos, Pylos and other sites, island and mainland, was an early form of Greek, as Homer had all along assumed; but even Ventris had expected that it would prove to be something else unrelated to the Indo-European languages, such as a relative of Etruscan.

This, then, was the age of the rediscovery of the Mediterranean; and the Mediterranean was certainly more than Italy and Greece. There were gaps that took long to fill. Interest in the Byzantine world had barely been ignited in the nineteenth century, notwithstanding the earlier account by one of England's greatest historians of the decline and fall of the Eastern Roman Empire; but Gibbon had already discouraged later generations from looking positively on Byzantium: 'the Greeks of Constantinople were animated only by the spirit of religion, and that spirit was productive only of animosity and discord'. Byzantium retained a negative reputation for political intrigue, Christian obscurantism and florid, debased Greek prose and poetry, setting Greek decline against the theme of Latin ascent in medieval Europe, or indeed Greek Orthodox Christianity against the pagan virtues propounded by Cicero and others. Archaeologists regularly discarded Byzantine finds when exploring classical sites in the Hellenic world, though by the Second World War academic popularizers – Runciman in England, Louis Bréhier and Charles Diehl in France – had begun to arouse wider interest in the civilization of the medieval Greek world. And the archaeologists stopped throwing away the finds of Byzantine pottery on Greek sites as (literally) trash.

Although Byzantium long retained its arcane flavour, a growing awareness of the history and art of the Islamic Mediterranean developed in popular and scholarly works from the late nineteenth century onwards. Especially powerful was the argument that Muslim Spain had been the shining beacon of civilization while the rest of Europe was immersed in the Dark Ages. Thus at the end of the nineteenth century Reinhard Dozy's romanticized studies of Islamic Spain, the work of a Dutchman writing in German and French (but rapidly translated into English) emphasized the alien character of Muslim Spain, while at the same time insisting on the legacy that it passed to Christian Europe.

The popularity of the works of an American, Washington Irving, also extended very widely, and his *Tales of the Alhambra* brought imagery from the *Arabian Nights* and the Ottoman harem in the Topkapı Seray in Istanbul to bear on the Spanish past. All this served as a reminder that the Mediterranean was a place of the meeting of cultures. Orientalist artists delighted in themes from the harem and bazaar. More impenetrable, certainly, was the Balkan side of the Mediterranean, southern Greece excepted. From the time of Edward Lear, intrepid British travellers had dived into remote areas of Albania, a tradition that remained alive, for in the 1920s and 1930s Edith Durham became a heroine among the Albanian tribes, at the same time documenting the persistence of the blood feud. But this was an isolated world that had effectively turned its back on the Great Sea, contained within narrow mountains, unconquered and ungovernable.

Travellers to the warm south

While archaeological and historical discoveries produced new ways of viewing the Mediterranean past, the continuities from the late nineteenth century to the middle of the twentieth century are also clear. The Mediterranean was a sea surrounded by lands full of museums, which documented the spread of classical culture, whether in its ancient or Renaissance form. Those who visited areas such as the interior of southern Italy were still travellers, and certainly not tourists: the Oxford historian of the Norman kingdom of Sicily, Evelyn Jamison, intrepidly made her way from archive to archive around 1910, often relying on horse and cart, in a world where hotels and restaurants were rare and simple; this was a feature of Sardinia as well, according to D. H. Lawrence's *Sea and Sardinia*: 'we saw the room. It was like a dungeon, absolutely empty, with an uneven earth floor, quite dry, and high bare walls, gloomy, with a handbreadth of window high up'. Only with the development of the Côte d'Azur at the end of the nineteenth century did a small part of the Mediterranean shores around Nice and Menton become a playground for the rich, though the rise to prominence of Monte Carlo took longer, dependent as it was on the ruling prince's decision to create a *Société des Bains de Mer* which was far more concerned with gambling than with bathing. This was also the era in which Italian spas began to develop at Montecatini, Abano and Rimini – still, the visitors to the last of these places were predominantly native Italians, and it was only with the poetry of Ezra Pound and the elegiac art appreciation of Adrian Stokes that this area of Italy entered the cultural consciousness of north European travellers. What would change dramatically in the second half of the twentieth century was the quantity of visitors, the aims of those visitors, and the ease with which they could reach the shores of nearly all the Mediterranean lands. In other words, tourists replaced travellers.

At first this invasion was a gentle one. It began after the Second World War, as ease of travel by air, rail and road made movement increasingly cheap and easy. Trainloads of Germans and Britons began to descend on Rimini and neighbouring towns in the 1950s, greatly stimulating the local economy; indeed, mass tourism, with new hotels and other infrastructure, became a significant route to economic recovery in Italy, Spain and Greece. Satellite towns swelled in size, so that Riccione, Milano Marittima and other centres began to compete with Rimini itself. Similar developments occurred near Pisa, where Viareggio became a major centre in the Tuscan tourist traffic, satisfying a clientèle apparently less interested in the artistic wonders of Florence and other Tuscan cities than in a seaside holiday, though day trips also became a standard part of the north European holiday in the Mediterranean, with the result that Pisa was and remains subject to a daily tide of humanity brought from the coastal towns in high summer to gawp at the Leaning Tower.

But the real transformation occurred with the arrival of the aeroplane. Cheap, safe air travel took time to arrive. In many respects England was the pioneer, because of the sheer inconvenience of having no direct rail link to the Mediterranean. Britain, too, was a major centre of the aircraft industry, building on successes in military aircraft during the Second World War to construct large, efficient, smooth airliners of the late 1950s and early 1960s such as the Vickers Viscount and the Britannia. So the British, and later the Germans and Scandinavians, took to the air. In the 1950s Thomson Holidays inaugurated regular charter air services to Majorca, which was to become the first target of intensive air tourism. Of course, it made excellent sense for one island, Great Britain, to send its holidaymakers by air right across Europe to another island, Majorca; otherwise a journey to Majorca would have been cumbersome indeed. This was what air travel was at first best placed to achieve. By the late 1960s, with the introduction of faster, smoother jet aircraft such as the BAC 1-11, the traffic was burgeoning; the airport at Palma remains, at least in summertime, one of the busiest in Europe. By the start of the twenty-first century, tourism accounted for 84 per cent of the Majorcan economy. Along the coast of Spain vast swathes of concrete, in largely unplanned developments, brought a degree of prosperity, but also showed a lack of consideration for the natural beauty of areas of the Costa Brava and the other Costas that stretch in an almost continuous line from the French frontier to the Strait of Gibraltar.

Travel became democratized as well as globalized. The idea of travelling from Britain to Spain began to appeal to a wide range of people of all backgrounds, aided by the creation of the package holiday. The tourist ceased being an adventurer who navigated his or her way across the towns and countryside of Mediterranean lands, since it was now possible to arrange flights, hotels, meals, even day trips, from the secure comfort of a sitting room in England or Holland or Germany, knowing (or believing) that representatives who spoke one's own language would be there to confront any difficulties with the natives. And in case the idea of being abroad seemed too threatening, there was comfort in numbers, this being mass tourism, and there was the willingness of the natives themselves to accommodate the eccentric needs of foreign visitors: fish and chips for the English, Guinness for the Irish, Bratwurst for the Germans. What also changed were the habits of travellers. While the numbers flooding into museums, and museum cities such as Venice, should certainly not be underestimated, it was not necessarily in search of culture that north Europeans took to Italy, Greece and Spain. As for the Americans and Japanese, that is a different story, and will have to be dealt with separately.

For directly associated with the idea of taking foreign holidays, Mediterranean holidays, was the idea that those, rich and not so rich, who took them should display the fact conspicuously, returning from Spain or Italy with a suitably deep tan. Indeed, for many the raison d'être of a Mediterranean holiday was precisely to acquire a tan; it became a badge indicating both prosperity and health. Whereas in the years around 1900 a tan had been associated with those who worked in the open fields, or with sailors, and certainly not with genteel women, by the eve of the Second World War it became a signal for being well-to-do; pallor was now associated with consumptives and office clerks. One sign of change, largely limited to Germany and Scandinavia, was the development of the *Frei-Korps-Kultur* ('FKK'), which preached the health-giving effects of the sun from the early twentieth century onwards, and set up naturist resorts. Much more influential, however, was the decision of that arbiter of taste, Coco Chanel, to make a fashion accessory of her sunburn after cruising the Mediterranean in the 1920s, so that her own example set a standard for generations of women.

However, this interest in bronzed flesh was also associated with changing moral standards. The display of the female body (or indeed the male one) became gradually more extensive, a particular breakthrough for women being the invention of the bikini in 1946, though it took a couple of decades to become widely adopted. It is interesting to note that the supposed immorality of the bikini led the Spanish authorities under Franco to forbid bikinis on Spanish beaches in the early days of the great tourist expansion along the Costa Brava and southwards; and indeed after the Second World War even Spanish men were expected to cover their torso on the beach. Naturally, the arrival of tourists in search of the sun and a suntan created perplexity among Mediterranean populations for whom the sun was something to be avoided at midday, if at all possible. But the clash of cultures became more obvious in the 1980s as it became more and more common for women to bare their breasts on the beach. Liberalization for some meant a dilemma for others, and the responses were varied; Italian mayors were still pursuing women accused of taking off too many clothes in the late 1990s. Southern France led the way in liberalization, not surprisingly since so many visitors to the south were in any case French. The clash of cultures was thus less extreme there, and the cult within France of physical beauty in a country with a large cosmetics industry perhaps made it inevitable that St-Tropez should be the pioneer. Nor is it surprising that more conservative societies such as Catholic Malta and Muslim Tunisia took a stricter line.

One country that seized the opportunity to profit from tourism with marked success was Yugoslavia, which determinedly built a reputation for cheap, well-organized hotel-based holidays, particularly favoured by Germans (one speciality being naturist resorts, which the Tito régime had somewhat strangely encouraged). In Spain, we can also see a response to other aspects of the mass tourist trade that have revealed deep contrasts between traditional societies within the Mediterranean and the northern 'invaders'. The development of facilities for foreign visitors that will meet their heady requirements – English- or German- style pubs, all-night night-clubs, gay bars, and so on – has been driven forward by commercial considerations, rather than by a ready adaptation of the values of the inhabitants of the Mediterranean shores to north European tastes. In some areas, notably Ibiza and parts of Majorca (notably Magaluf), the result has been the creation of extraordinary enclaves of northern culture (or lack of it), and decisive efforts began to be made in the 1990s to shake off Majorca's image as the destination of British or German 'lager louts'. However, the transformations that have occurred have also been the result of longer-term migrations, as Germans acquire houses in Majorca (for example), even planning to acquire a political voice on the island. And this also sets off a cultural clash, between the natives who are being urged to make more use of the local language, a dialect of Catalan, and settlers who are remote both from Spanish and from Catalan culture. We will look shortly at another series of migrations, from another direction, which have also begun to affect the social and cultural life of the Mediterranean towns.

For long the Mediterranean was almost the exclusive beneficiary of this expansion of mass summer tourism, though the Canary Islands and Portugal also claimed a share; only in the 1990s did long-haul holidays, including mass tourism in Florida, the Dominican Republic and even Cuba, become a significant phenomenon. But while some affluent people spent their main holidays further afield, the late 1990s also saw a very substantial expansion of short holidays, 'city breaks', as aeroplanes became faster and the skies became more densely packed with them. By 2000 a new development began to take off: price wars among airlines culminated in the emergence of 'no frills' airlines, led by British and Irish entrepreneurs, which offered some seats on flights from London to Italy or Spain for as little as £20. Once again, the sheer fact that the British Isles are islands acted as a spur to the development of air links to the Mediterranean, but by 2002 the British cut-price airlines were also creating networks based in Belgium, Germany and elsewhere, ferrying passengers towards the Mediterranean. These passengers included not just the price conscious but those with holiday homes in southern France (Provence becoming a cult centre after Peter Mayle published his books on his experiences living as an Englishman in a Provençal village), as well as Tuscany (which has had its praises sung by Italophile imitators of Mayle).

The anglicization of parts of the south European countryside, particularly marked in Atlantic France, around the Dordogne, but also visible in parts of Italy ('Chiantishire'), has proceeded by taking advantage of the flight from the countryside in rural areas of southern Europe, so that there are all too many farmhouses put up for sale; but there has also been a powerful element of cultural snobbery, and the idea of spending a fortnight in a villa in Tuscany has captivated the British upper middle classes, including then Prime Minister Blair. But it should also be stressed that natives of the Mediterranean have been avid travellers as well; Italian tourism, characterized by a remarkable homogeneity in the fashionable clothes, modish equipment and up-to-the minute taste of well-to-do Italians, has penetrated some of the more remote corners of the Mediterranean, whether Pantelleria (an island owned by Italy but close to Tunisia), or the Greek isles.

Mediterranean tastes

This tourism also produced significant cultural changes beyond the Mediterranean. The spread of Italian restaurants reflected patterns of emigration, at first, though what they offered was sometimes food radically adapted to a new environment. It is not clear that a main course of spaghetti and meat balls, New York-style, eaten around 1950, had much to do with *pasta al sugo* as a first course in Bologna; nor does the north European passion for eating pasta 'authentically' with a fork and spoon have much to do with native Italian usage. By 1970 the pizza, already a firm favourite in the United States, became well established in north European countries; more recondite dishes such as the Genoese pesto sauce, in 1970 rarely encountered outside Liguria and Provence, were so widely diffused in northern Europe that strange variants began to be introduced, such as red pesto made with sun-dried tomatoes, themselves elevated to a position of eminence in northern re-interpretations of Italian cooking that they have never had beyond certain areas of the deep south of Italy. Pasta became a staple food in England and Germany as well as in Italy. Similarly bright fortunes awaited Greek restaurants (in Britain, often Greek Cypriot), Israeli restaurants in Holland, Yugoslav and Turkish ones in Germany, Moroccan and Tunisian in France. Ethnic cooking compensated for the rather heavy qualities of English, Dutch or German food. But it was also exotic, all the more so when washed down with southern wines from Chianti (in the famous wicker bottle), rough Retsina from Greece or Spanish table wines.

By the late 1980s wine producers in Mediterranean countries had become sensitive to accusations that they produced 'plonk' and could not match French vineyards. (France, of course, with its own vibrant culinary traditions, was long more resistant to the ethnic invasion, but by 2000 it was easier to find pizza than *pissaladière* in the towns of Provence, and as easy to find couscous as *bouillabaisse*). Major improvements to vineyards throughout the Mediterranean followed: in southern Italy, in the Salentino, American wine producers placed little-known Apulian wines on the world map by 2000; in Israel, a country famous for its atrocious wines, Californian methods were applied to vineyards on the Golan Heights gained from Syria in 1967, with spectacular results; similar stories can be told about Greece and Spain, where excellent Catalan vineyards became widely appreciated throughout Europe and North America. What is important, however, is that these changes reflect a process of globalization: the Mediterranean is brought to consumers far away in a bottle. It is fair to say that this is the third great revolution in diet to have involved the Mediterranean world, in 500-year cycles: the first was the coming of exotic crops such as citrus fruits around 1000, under the Arabs, the second the impact of New World crops such as maize after 1500, the third the transfer outwards, beyond the Mediterranean, of Mediterranean cuisine around 2000.

More democratic in character has been the integration of the Mediterranean into longer-distance tourism. Two 'invasions' have been particularly significant: the American invasion, and the Japanese one. Americans were far from unknown in the watering holes of the Mediterranean before the Second World War (it was with an American friend that D. H. Lawrence visited the Etruscan tombs); but the inclusion of historical monuments in Italy, Greece, southern France and Egypt on the tourist circuit once again reflects ease of movement as cheap fares and elaborate communications networks made the Mediterranean easily accessible by air from the other side of the Atlantic. The result was that a high proportion of American visitors to Rome, Florence or Athens have been students. Generally, the American visitors have stimulated a tendency to 'dress down' while travelling on holiday, so that T-shirts, shorts and trainers have become the costume of both the young and the middle-aged throughout Europe. The Japanese have sought the explanation for the economic successes of Western Europe by interesting themselves in European culture and history; in addition, such contacts have accelerated the already rapid Westernization of Japan. The presence of American, Japanese and north European visitors has become a major area of economic growth; and yet it has also proved a precarious one, for economic downturn across the Atlantic or in Japan has periodically created deep troughs in the economies of Mediterranean regions heavily dependent on tourism.

Particularly serious has been the effect of political unrest on the income from tourism; unrest has severely damaged first the economy of Egypt (following the Luxor massacre of 1997), and subsequently that of Israel (as a result of the Palestinian uprising in 2001–2), while the once flourishing resorts of the very beautiful Dalmatian coast and islands took time to recover from the disintegration of Yugoslavia during the 1990s. None of this compares, though, with the crisis unleashed by the pandemic of Covid-19 in 2020, which devastated the travel industry – airlines grounded most of their planes; hotels, restaurants, museums and monuments closed their doors for months; cruise ships stood empty, anchored in their home waters. Covid-19 has unleashed an economic catastrophe within the Mediterranean from which recovery will be an enormous challenge.

We can thus say that two inventions, as far apart in technology as could be imagined, have transformed the relationship between the Mediterranean and the north of Europe in the second half of the twentieth century: the aeroplane and the bikini.

FURTHER READING

Introduction: What is the Mediterranean?

For an overview of the history of the Mediterranean from prehistory to the present day, see David Abulafia, *The Great Sea: A Human History of the Mediterranean* (London and New York, 2011).

For ways to approach maritime history and for the seas beyond that were linked to the Mediterranean, see David Abulafia, *The Boundless Sea: A Human History of the Oceans* (London and New York, 2019).

THE FUNDAMENTAL STUDIES OF THE MEDITERRANEAN IN HISTORY ARE:

Fernand Braudel, *The Mediterranean and the Mediterranean World in the Age of Philip II*, transl. S. Reynolds, 2 vols (London, 1972); the original French edition of 1949 was reissued in 1966, also in two volumes, after extensive revision (on the evolution of this work see: E. Paris, *La genèse intellectuelle de l'oeuvre de Fernand Braudel* [Athens, 1999]).

P. Horden and N. Purcell, *The Corrupting Sea: A Study of Mediterranean History* (Oxford, 2000), which is intended to be the first volume of a two-volume set.

P. Horden and N. Purcell have collected together a number of articles in a book rich in ideas about how to write maritime history, also coincidentally entitled *The Boundless Sea* (Abingdon, 2020), but subtitled *Writing Mediterranean History*.

J. Carpentier, F. Lebrun and others, *Histoire de la Méditerranée* (Paris, 1998), a collaborative work which is especially good on modern times.

C. Broodbank, *The Making of the Middle Sea: A History of the Mediterranean from the Beginning to the Emergence of the Classical World* (London, 2013) is fundamental for how we understand the Mediterranean before the rise of Classical Greece.

G. Woolf, *The Life and Death of Ancient Cities: A Natural History* (Oxford, 2020), mainly concentrates on the Greco-Roman Mediterranean, emphasizing the very large number of cities and their small size, apart from a very few giants such as Rome and Alexandria.

F. Tabak, *The Waning of the Mediterranean 1550–1870: A Geohistorical Approach* (Baltimore, MD, 2008), on climate change.

A. Husain and K. Fleming, *The Faithful Sea: The Religious Cultures of the Mediterranean, 1200–1700* (Oxford, 2007), on religion.

m. cooke, E. Göknar, G. Parker (eds), *Mediterranean Passages: Readings from Dido to Derrida* (Chapel Hill, NC, 2008), a collection of key sources in English translation.

THE JOURNALS MENTIONED IN THE TEXT ARE:

Mediterranean Historical Review, whose founder editor was Shlomo Ben-Ami, has been published in London and edited in Tel Aviv since 1986.

Mediterranean Studies has been published in Aldershot since 1998, and previously in the USA; the Senior Editor is Richard W. Clement of the University of Kansas.

The Journal of Mediterranean Studies: History, Culture and Society in the Mediterranean World has been published at the University of Malta since 1991, and is edited by Anthony Spiteri.

al-Masaq: Islam and the Medieval Mediterranean is published in London, previously in Turnhout and before that in Leeds; the editor since its inception in 1988 has been Dionisius Agius in Leeds.

1. The Physical Setting

A FRESH LOOK IS PROVIDED BY:

O. Rackham and A. T. Grove, *The Nature of Mediterranean Europe: An Ecological History* (New Haven, CT, 2001), with an extensive bibliography.

L. Jeftić, J. D. Milliman, G. Sestini (eds), *Climatic Change and the Mediterranean* (London, 1992).

F. di Castri and H. A. Mooney, *Mediterranean Type Ecosystems: Origin and Structure* (London, 1973).

HISTORICAL PERSPECTIVES, MAINLY ANCIENT:

C. Delano Smith, *Western Mediterranean Europe: A Historical Geography of Italy, Spain and Southern France Since the Neolithic Period* (London, 1979).

J. S. P. Bradford, *Ancient Landscapes* (London, 1957), a classic work.

R. Sallares, *The Ecology of the Ancient Greek World* (London, 1991).

T. W. Potter, *The Changing Landscape of South Etruria* (London, 1979).

R. Meiggs, *Trees and Timber in the Ancient Mediterranean World* (Oxford, 1982).

ON DESERTIFICATION:

P. Mairota, J. B. Thornes, N. Geeson (eds), *Atlas of Mediterranean Environments in Europe: The Desertification Context* (Chichester 1998).

C. J. Brandt and J. B. Thornes (eds), *Mediterranean Desertification and Land Use* (Chichester, 1996).

J. L. Rubio and A. Calvo (eds), *Soil Degradation and Desertification in Mediterranean Environments* (Logroño, 1996).

ON PLANT LIFE AND WOOD:

P. R. Dallman, *Plant Life in the World's Mediterranean Climates* (Berkeley, 1998).

J. Perlin, *A Forest Journey: The Role of Wood in the Development of Civilization* (New York, 1989).

VALLEYS, MOUNTAINS AND EROSION:

J. R. McNeill, *The Mountains of the Mediterranean World* (Cambridge, 1992).

C. Vita-Finzi, *The Mediterranean Valleys* (Cambridge, 1969).

A SELECTION OF LOCAL STUDIES:

A. Gilman and J. B. Thornes, *Land-use and Prehistory in South-east Spain* (London, 1985).

J. V. Thirgood, *Cyprus: A Chronicle of Its Forests, Land, and People* (Vancouver 1987).

O. Rackham and J. A. Moody, *The Making of the Cretan Landscape* (Manchester, 1996).

2. The First Trading Empires: Prehistory to *c.* 1000 BC

Since this chapter was first written, the major contribution to the understanding of the early Mediterranean has been C. Broodbank's masterly *The Making of the Middle Sea* (London, 2013).

This chapter owes much to the teaching of Professor Paulo Pereira de Castro thirty years ago at the Department of History, University of São Paulo, in Brazil, and the notes of F. Murari Pires.

ON EUROPEAN AND MEDITERRANEAN PREHISTORY:

L. Cavalli-Sforza and others, *The History and Geography of Human Genes* (Princeton, NJ, 2001).

J. G. D. Clark, *Prehistoric Europe: The Economic Basis* (London, 1952).

D. H. Trump, *The Prehistory of the Mediterranean* (London, 1981).

V. Gordon Childe, *The Bronze Age* (London, 1943).

R. Leighton, *Sicily Before History. An Archaeological Survey from the Palaeolithic to the Iron Age.* (London, 1999).

J. D. Evans, *The Prehistoric Antiquities of the Maltese Islands.* (London, 1971).

SOME IMPORTANT COLLECTIONS OF ARTICLES:

E. D. Oren (ed.), *The Sea Peoples and Their World: A Reassessment.* (University Museum Monograph 108. Philadelphia, 2000), articles by L. Vagnetti, P. Betancourt, D. O'Connor, N. A. Silberman, I. Singer, P. Machinist, etc.

J. Sasson (ed.), *Civilisations of the Ancient Near East* (New York, 1995), 3 vols, articles by H. G. Jansen, G. F. Bass, T. Dothan, M. L. West, A. B. Knapp, etc.

S. Gitin, A. Mazar, E. Stern (eds), *Mediterranean Peoples in Transition: 13th to early 10th century B.C.E.* (Israel Exploration Society, Jerusalem, 1998), articles by S. Bunimovitz, S. Sherratt, etc..

THE WESTERN MEDITERRANEAN AND THE AEGEAN:

R. R. Holloway, *Italy and the Aegean 3000–700 BC* (Louvain la Neuve and Providence, RI, 1981).

V. Karageorghis, 'Cyprus and the Western Mediterranean: some new evidence for interrelations', in J. B. Carter (ed.), *The Ages of Homer* (Austin, TX, 1995), pp. 93–97.

THE BRONZE AGE AEGEAN:

E. Cline, *Sailing the Wine-Dark Sea: International Trade and the Late Bronze Age Aegean* (Oxford, 1994).

O. Dickinson, *The Aegean Bronze Age* (Cambridge, 1994).

J. M. C. Driessen, *The Troubled Island: Minoan Crete Before and After the Santorini Eruption* (Liège, 1997).

A. M. Sestieri, 'The Mycenaean connection and its impact on the central Mediterranean societies', in *Dialoghi d'Archeologia* (terza serie, anno 6, n. 1), pp. 23–52.

TROY AND THE TROJAN WAR:

T. Bryce, The Trojan War in its Near Eastern Context.', *Journal of Ancient Civilizations*, vol. 6 (1991), pp. 2–21.

L. Foxhall and J. Davies, *The Trojan War, Its History and Context* (Bristol, 1984).

M. Wood, *In Search of the Trojan War* (London, 1996).

BRONZE AGE SEAFARING AND SEAMANSHIP:

R. E. Gardiner, *The Age of the Galley: Mediterranean Oared Vessels Since Pre-classical Times* (London, 1995).

S. Wachsmann, *Seagoing Ships and Seamanship in the Bronze Age Levant* (London, 1998).

ON THE HITTITES:

T. Bryce, *The Kingdom of the Hittites*. (Oxford, 1998).

J. G. MacQueen, *The Hittites and Their Contemporaries in Asia Minor*. London, 1996).

H. A. Hoffner, Jr (ed.), *Perspectives on Hittite Civilisation: Selected Writings of Hans Gustav Güterbock. Assyriological Studies* (Chicago, 1997).

H. A. Hoffner, Jr, 'New Directions in the study of Anatolian texts', in K. A. Yener and H. A. Hoffner, Jr (eds), *New Perspectives in Hittite Archaeology and History* (Winona Lake, IN, 2002).

K. A. Yener and H. A. Hoffner, Jr (eds), *Recent Developments in Hittite Archaeology and History. Papers in Memory of Hans G. Güterbock* (Winona Lake, IN, 2002).

ON THE AHHIYAWAN QUESTION:

Hans G. Güterbock, 'The Hittites and the Aegean world: part I. The Ahhiyawa problem reconsidered', *American Journal of Archaeology* 87 (1981), pp. 133–38.

Hans G. Güterbock, 'A new look at one Ahhiyawa text', in H.A. Hoffner, Jr (ed.), *Hittite and other Anatolian and Near Eastern Studies in Honour of Sedat Alp* (Ankara, 1992), pp. 235–43.

M. Marazzi, 'La "misteriosa" terra di Ahhijawa', in M. Marazzi (ed.), *Società Micenea* (Rome, 1994), pp. 323–36.

ON THE SEA PEOPLES:

See the book edited by Oren and R. D. Barnett, 'The Sea Peoples', *Cambridge Ancient History,* vol. 2 (Cambridge, 1975), part 2.

B. Cifola, 'The rôle of the Sea Peoples at the end of the Late Bronze Age: a reassessment of textual and archaeological evidence', *Orientis Antiqui Miscellanea*, vol. 1 (1994), pp. 1–21.

W. Dever, 'The Late Bronze Age-Early Iron I Horizon in Syria-Palestine: Egyptians, Canaanites, Sea Peoples and Proto-Israelites', in W. J. Ward (ed.), *The Crisis Years* (Dubuque, 1992), pp. 99–110.

O. Margalith, *The Sea Peoples in the Bible* (Wiesbaden, 1994).

A. Raban and R. Stieglitz, 'The Sea Peoples and their contribution to civilization', *Biblical Archaeological Review* vol. 17, part 6 (1991), pp. 34–42.

N. K. Sandars, *The Sea Peoples. Warriors of the Ancient Mediterranean.* (London, 1978).

I. Singer, 'The origin of the Sea Peoples and their settlement on the coast of Canaan', in M. L. Heltzer (ed.), *Society and Economy in the Eastern Mediterranean* (Leuven, 1998), pp. 239–50.

ON THE COLLAPSE OF THE BRONZE AGE SYSTEM:

R. Drews, *The End of the Bronze Age: Changes in Warfare and the Catastrophe ca. 1200 BC.* (Princeton, NJ, 1993).

A. Mazar, 'Some aspects of the 'Sea Peoples settlement', in M. L. Heltzer and E. Lipinsky (eds), *Society and Economy in the Eastern Mediterranean (c. 1500–1000 BC)* (Leuven, 1998), pp. 251–60.

S. Sherratt, 'Circulation of metal and the end of the Bronze Age in the Eastern Mediterranean', in C. F. Pare (ed.), *Metals Make the World Go Round* (Oxford, 2000), pp. 82–98.

C. S. Mathers (ed.), *Development and Decline in the Mediterranean Bronze Age.* (Sheffield, 1994).

ON THE PHILISTINES:

J. F. Brug, 1985, *A Literary and Archaeological Study of the Philistines* (BAR International Series 265, Oxford, 1985).

I. Singer, 'Egyptians, Canaanites and Philistines in the period of the emergence of Israel', in I. Finkelstein and N. Na'aman (eds), *From Nomadism to Monarchy* (Jerusalem, 1994), pp. 282–338.

C. S. Ehrlich, *The Philistines in Transition: A History from ca. 1000–730 B.C.E.* (Leiden, 1996).

R. A. Macalister, *The Philistines, Their History and Civilization* (Oxford, 1914).

ON THE IMPORTANCE OF CYPRUS:

See the article by N. P. Lemche in Sasson's volume (above) and

A. M. Snodgrass, 'Cyprus and the beginning of iron technology in the Eastern Mediterranean', in J. D. M. Muhly (ed.), *Early Metallurgy in Cyprus: 4000–500 BC* (Nicosia, 1982), pp. 285–324.

ON THE ROLE OF RELIGION:

L. E. Roller, *In Search of God the Mother: The Cult of the Anatolian Cybele* (Berkeley, CA, 1999).

3. The Battle for the Sea Routes: 1000–300 BC

C. Broodbank, *The Making of the Middle Sea* (London, 2013) is now fundamental.

FOR THE MYCENAEAN PERIOD:

A. F. Harding, *The Mycenaeans and Europe* (London, 1984).

M. Cultraro, *L'anello di Minosse* (Milan, 2001).

ON IONIAN MIGRATION AND THE ETHNIC STRUCTURE OF THE GREEK WORLD AT THE START OF THE IRON AGE:

F. Cassola, *La Ionia nel mondo miceneo* (Naples, 1957).

M. Sakellariou, *La migration grecque en Ionie* (Athens, 1958).

A. M. Snodgrass, *The Dark Age of Greece. An Archaeological Survey of the 11th to the 8th Centuries BC* (Edinburgh, 1971).

V. R. d'A. Desborough, *The Greek Dark Ages* (London, 1972).

C. J. Emlyn-Jones, *The Ionians and Hellenism. A Study of the Cultural Achievement of the Early Greek Inhabitants of Asia Minor* (London, 1980).

D. Musti (ed.), *Le origini dei Greci. Dori e mondo egeo* (Roma-Bari, 1985).

See also the collection *Griechenland, die Ägäis und die Levante während der 'Dark Ages'* (Vienna, 1983).

ON GREEK COLONIZATION:

T.J. Dunbabin, *The Western Greeks* (Oxford, 1948).

T.J. Dunbabin, *The Greeks and Their Eastern Neighbours* (London, 1957).

J. Bérard, *La colonisation grecque de l'Italie méridionale et de la Sicile*, 2nd ed. (Paris, 1957).

J. Boardman, *The Greeks Overseas*, 2nd ed. (London, 1973).

E. Lepore (ed.), *Contribution à l'étude de la société et de la colonisation eubéennes* (Paris-Naples, 1975).

A.J. Graham, *Colony and Mother City in Ancient Greece*, 2nd ed. (Chicago, 1983).

M. Casevitz, *Le vocabulaire de la colonisation en grec ancien* (Paris, 1985).

I. Malkin, *Religion and Colonization in Ancient Greece* (Leiden, 1987).

E. Lepore, *Colonie greche dell'Occidente antico* (Rome, 1989).

P. Rouillard, *Les Grecs et la péninsule ibérique du VIIIe au IVe siècle avant Jésus-Christ* (Paris, 1995).

ON ANCIENT SEAFARING AND TRADING ACTIVITIES:

H. Knorringa, *Emporos. Data on Trade in Greek Literature from Homer to Aristotle* (Utrecht, 1926).

J.S. Morrison and R.T. Williams, *Greek Oared Ships 900–322 B.C.* (Cambridge, 1968).

L. Casson, *Ships and Seamanship in the Ancient World*, 2nd ed. (Baltimore, 1995).

M. Gras, *La Méditerranée archaïque* (Paris 1995).

M. Giuffrida Ientile, *La pirateria tirrenica. Momenti e fortuna* (Rome, 1983).

G. Bunnens, *L'expansion phénicienne en Méditerranée* (Brussels-Rome, 1979).

H.G. Niemeyer (ed.), *Phönizier im Westen* (Mainz, 1982).

M.E. Aubet, *Tiro y las colonias fenicias de Occidente* (Barcelona, 1987).

M. Gras, P. Rouillard and J. Teixidor, *L'univers phénicien* (Paris 1989).

J. Quinn, *In Search of the Phoenicians* (Princeton, NJ, 2018).

S. Celestino and C. López Ruiz, *Tartessos and the Phoenicians in Iberia* (Oxford, 2008).

ON GREEK TRADE:

L. Breglia, 'Le antiche rotte del Mediterraneo documentate da monete e pesi', in *Rendiconti dell'Accademia di Napoli* 30 (1955), pp. 211–326.

E. Will, *Korinthiaka. Recherches sur l'histoire et la civilisation de Corinthe des origines aux guerres médiques* (Paris, 1955).

A. Mele, *Il commercio greco arcaico. Prexis ed emporie* (Cahiers du Centre J. Bérard 4, Naples, 1979).

A. W. Johnston, *Trademarks on Greek Vases* (Warminster, 1979).

M. Mello (ed.), *Il commercio greco nel Tirreno in età arcaica: Studi in memoria di M. Napoli* (Salerno, 1981).

A. Bresson and P. Rouillard (eds), *L'emporion* (Paris, 1993).

J. G. Manning, *The Open Sea* (Princeton, NJ, 2018) on the economy of the Greco-Roman Mediterranean.

ON EUBOEAN TRADE:

D. Ridgway, *L'alba della Magna Grecia* (Milan, 1984); English edition: *The First Western Greeks* (Cambridge, 1992).

M. Bats and B. d'Agostino (eds), *Euboica. L'Eubea e la presenza euboica in Calcidica e in Occidente: Atti del Convegno internazionale di Napoli, 13–16 Novembre 1996* (Naples, 1998).

ON EASTERN AND WESTERN GREEK TRADE:

Les céramiques de la Grèce de l'Est et leur diffusion en occident: Atti del Colloquio del Centre J. Bérard–Napoli 1976 (Rome, 1978).

C. Vandermersch, *Vins et amphores de Grande Grèce et Sicile (IVe–IIIe s. avant J.-C.)* (Naples, 1994).

ON ETRUSCAN TRADE:

M. Cristofani, *Gli Etruschi del mare* (Milan, 1983).

M. Cristofani (ed.), *Il commercio etrusco arcaico: Atti dell'Incontro di studio, 5–7 dicembre 1983* (Rome, 1985).

M. Gras, *Trafics tyrrhéniens archaïques* (Rome, 1985).

4. The Creation of *Mare Nostrum*: 300 BC–AD 500

P. Horden and N. Purcell, *The Corrupting Sea. A Study of Mediterranean History* (Oxford, 2000) is by far the most wide-ranging and subtle discussion of the Mediterranean in the ancient and medieval periods.

J. G. Manning, *The Open Sea* (Princeton, NJ, 2018).

C. Starr, *The Influence of Sea Power in Ancient History* (Oxford, 1989) is simpler but thoughtful.

G. Woolf, *The Life and Death of Ancient Cities: A Natural History* (Oxford, 2020).

FOR THE GREEK WORLD AFTER THE DEATH OF ALEXANDER THE GREAT SEE:

G. Shipley, *The Greek World after Alexander 393–30 BC* (London, 2000).

ON ROME'S RISE TO MEDITERRANEAN POWER SEE:

E. D. Rawson, 'The Expansion of Rome' in J. Boardman, J. Griffin and O. Murray (eds), *The Roman World* (Oxford, 1988), pp. 39–59.

FOR HELLENISTIC, AND, LATER, ROMAN WARSHIPS IN THIS PERIOD SEE:

J. S. Morrison, 'Hellenistic oared warships 399–31 BC', and B. Rankov 'Fleets of the Early Roman Empire 31 BC–AD 324', in R. Gardiner and J. Morrison (eds), *The Age of the Galley* (London, 1995), pp. 66–77 and pp. 78–85.

FOR SHIPS AND SEAMANSHIP GENERALLY:

L. Casson, *Ships and Seamanship in the Ancient World* (Princeton, 1971) is fundamental, and:

P. Janni, *Il mare degli antichi* (Bari, 1996) is stimulating, well-illustrated, and with a good bibliography.

ON UNDERWATER ARCHAEOLOGY SEE:

P. A. Gianfrotta and P. Pomey, *Archeologia Subacquea: storia, tecniche, scoperte e relitti* (Milan, 1980).

Also P. Throckmorton (ed.), *History from the Sea. Shipwrecks and Archaeology* (London, 1987).

For what may, and may not, legitimately be deduced from shipwreck evidence A. J. Parker is the expert, especially 'Sea transport and trade in the ancient Mediterranean', in E. E. Rice (ed.) *The Sea and History* (Stroud, 1996), pp. 97–109.

The best discussion of the tonnage of Roman merchant ships is
P. Pomey and A. Tchernia, 'Le tonnage maximum des navires de
commerce romains', *Archaeonautica* 2 (1978), pp. 233–51.

ON THE COMPLEXITIES OF THE ORGANIZATION OF ROMAN TRADE SEE:

K. Hopkins, 'Models, ships and staples' in P. Garnsey and C. R.
Whittaker (eds), *Trade and Famine in Classical Antiquity* (Cambridge,
1983), pp. 84–109; 'Introduction' in P. Garnsey, K. Hopkins, and
C. R. Whittaker (eds), *Trade in the Ancient Economy* (London, 1983),
pp. ix–xxv; and 'Roman trade, industry and labour' in M. Grant and
R. Kitzinger (eds), *Civilization of the Ancient Mediterranean* (New York,
1988) vol. 2, pp. 755–77.

A lively, contribution, with a different slant, is J. Paterson, 'Trade
and traders in the Roman world: scale, structure, and organisation'
in H. Parkins and C. Smith (eds), *Trade, Traders and the Ancient City*
(London, 1998), pp. 149–67.

J. Rougé, *Recherches sur l'organisation du commerce maritime en
Méditerranée sous l'empire romain* (Paris, 1966) is still a quarry of
information and ideas.

Discussion of the Murecine tablets is in L. Casson, 'The role of the
State in Rome's grain trade', *Ancient Trade and Society* (Detroit, 1984),
pp. 96–116, and of the Vienna papyrus in L. Casson, 'P. Vindob G
40822 and the shipping of goods from India', *Bulletin of the American
Society of Papyrologists*, 23, 1986, pp. 73–79.

Basic for an understanding of Rome's trade beyond the frontiers with
the East is L. Casson's introduction, translation and commentary on
The Periplus Maris Erythraei (Princeton, 1989), and his article, 'Rome's
trade with the East: the sea voyage to Africa and India', *Ancient Trade
and Society* (Detroit, 1984), pp. 182–98.

The outstanding single study of a Roman port is A. M. McCann, *The
Roman Port and Fishery of Cosa* (Princeton, 1987), which besides the
exemplary study of the harbour and its trade, has fascinating
information on fishing and the production of garum, fish sauce.

For harbours in general see the useful survey by D. Blackman,
'Ancient harbours in the Mediterranean', *International Journal of
Nautical Archaeology* 11, 1982, pp. 79ff. (with extensive bibliography).

The classic study of Ostia is R. Meiggs, *Roman Ostia* (Oxford, 1973);
for the harbour at Portus see G. E. Rickman, 'Portus in Perspective',

in A. Gallina Zevi and A. Claridge (eds), *'Roman Ostia' Revisited* (London, 1996), pp. 281–91; for the port area in the city of Rome see E. Rodríguez Almeida, *Il Monte Testaccio: ambiente, storia, materiali* (Rome, 1984). A succinct and perceptive account of the functioning of the whole port system is given by D. J. Mattingly and G. S. Aldrete 'The feeding of Imperial Rome: the mechanics of the food supply system' in J. Coulston and H. Dodge (eds), *Ancient Rome. The Archaeology of the Eternal City* (Oxford, 2000), pp. 142–65.

On the late Roman Empire in its widest context is A. Cameron, *The Mediterranean World in Late Antiquity AD 395–600* (London, 1993).

5. The Mediterranean Breaks Up: 500–1000

The suggestions for reading given here concentrate on the sea and trade across it. There is of course a vast literature on the barbarian invasions, beginning with the works of Edward Gibbon in the eighteenth century and Thomas Hodgkin in the nineteenth century, and on early Byzantium by such pioneers as Charles Diehl, Louis Bréhier and J. B. Bury (the role of French scholarship being particularly notable); for the rise of Islam the work of B. Lewis, *The Arabs in History* (London, 1950, and subsequent editions) is still unsurpassed.

ON THE RELATIONSHIP BETWEEN THE SEA AND THE MOVEMENT OF FLEETS:

J. H. Pryor, *Geography, Technology and War: Studies on the Maritime History of the Mediterranean* (Cambridge, 1988).

ON THE EFFECTS OF THE COLLAPSE OF THE WESTERN EMPIRE ON TRADE SEE:

for example, R. Hodges and D. Whitehouse, *Mohammed, Charlemagne and the Origins of Europe* (London, 1983); C. J. Wickham, 'Marx, Sherlock Holmes and late Roman commerce' (review discussion), *Journal of Roman Studies* 78, 1988, pp. 189–93; and G. E. Rickman, 'Mare Nostrum' in E. E. Rice (ed.), *The Sea and History* (Stroud, 1996), pp. 1–14. A brief guide to the debates is supplied by A. Havighurst (ed.), *The Pirenne Thesis: Analysis, Criticism and Revision* (Lexington, 1969).

ALSO ON EARLY MEDIEVAL TRADE ACROSS THE MEDITERRANEAN THERE IS A MASSIVE AND IMPORTANT REASSESSMENT:

M. McCormick, *Origins of the European Economy* (Cambridge, 2001).

FOR OTHER VIEWS SEE:

A. R. Lewis, *Naval Power and Trade in the Mediterranean, AD 500–1100* (Princeton, NJ, 1951) (though marred by inaccuracies).

J. Haywood, *Dark Age Naval Power* (London, 1991) is more recent and is helpful on the western Mediterranean.

ON AMALFI:

P. Skinner, *Medieval Amalfi and Its Diaspora, 800–1250* (Oxford, 2013).

A. Citarella, *Il commercio di Amalfi nell'alto Medioevo* (Salerno, 1977).

M. del Treppo and A. Leone, *Amalfi medioevale* (Naples, 1977).

B. Kreutz, 'The ecology of maritime success: the puzzling case of Amalfi', *Mediterranean Historical Review*, vol. 3 (1988), pp. 103–13.

ON THE GENIZAH MERCHANTS:

S. D. Goitein, *A Mediterranean Society: The Jewish Communities of the Arab World as Portrayed by the Documents of the Cairo Genizah*, vol. 1, *Economic Foundations* (Berkeley, 1967), followed by a further five volumes up to 1993.

FOR ISLAMIC SPAIN SEE ESPECIALLY:

O. R. Constable, *Trade and Traders in Muslim Spain: The Commercial Realignment of the Iberian Peninsula* (Cambridge, 1994; Spanish ed., Barcelona, 1997).

C. Picard, *La mer et les musulmans d'occident au Moyen Âge* (Paris, 1997).

X. de Planhol, *L'Islam et la mer* (Paris, 2000).

ON BYZANTIUM:

H. Ahrweiler, *Byzance et la Mer* (Paris, 1966).

6. A Christian Mediterranean: 1000–1500

Once again this reading list concentrates on commercial exchanges, while some other items are concerned with Latin colonization of the eastern Mediterranean.

GENERAL SURVEYS INCLUDE:

M. Tangheroni, *Commercio e navigazione nel Medioevo* (Rome-Bari, 1996), a survey by one of Italy's leading medieval historians.

R. S. Lopez, *The Commercial Revolution in the Middle Ages* (Englewood Cliffs, NJ, 1971).

G. Jehel, *La Méditerranée médiévale de 350 à 1450* (Paris, 1992).

R. S. Lopez and I. W. Raymond, *Medieval Trade in the Mediterranean World* (New York, 1968), which is a collection of key documents with commentaries.

USEFUL COLLECTION OF ESSAYS ARE:

B. Garí (ed.), *El Mundo mediterráneo de la Edad Media* (Barcelona, 1987), with essays by G. Pistarino, R. S. Lopez, S. D. Goitein and others.

M. Balard (ed.), *État et colonisation au Moyen Âge et à la Renaissance* (Lyon, 1989).

M. Balard and A. Ducellier (eds), *Le partage du monde: échange et colonisation dans la Méditerranée médiévale* (Paris, 2000).

G. Airaldi (ed.), *Gli Orizzonti aperti. Profili del mercante medievale* (Turin, 1997), a collection of reprinted essays by Le Goff, Lopez, Sapori, Heers, Abulafia and others.

D. Abulafia and N. Berend (eds), *Medieval Frontiers: Concepts and Practices* (Aldershot, 2002).

ON THE EUROPEAN TRADING CENTRES (FROM WEST TO EAST) SEE:

J. Guiral-Hadziïossif, *Valence, port méditerranéen au XVe siècle (1410–1525)* (Paris, 1986).

A. Furió (ed.), *València, un mercat medieval* (Valencia, 1985).

S. Bensch, *Barcelona and Its Rulers, 1096–1291* (Cambridge, 1995).

M. del Treppo, *I mercanti catalani e l'espansione della Corona d'Aragona nel XV secolo* (Naples, 1972; Catalan edition, Barcelona, 1976).

F. Fernández-Armesto, *Before Columbus: Exploration and Colonisation from the Mediterranean to the Atlantic, 1229–1492* (London, 1987), and the same author's *Barcelona: 1000 Years of a City's Past* (Oxford, 1991).

D. Abulafia, *A Mediterranean Emporium: The Catalan Kingdom of Majorca* (Cambridge, 1994).

P. Macaire, *Majorque et le commerce international (1400–1450 environ)* (Lille, 1986).

C.-E. Dufourcq, *La vie quotidienne dans les ports méditerranéens au Moyen Âge: Provence-Languedoc-Catalogne* (Paris, 1975).

E. Bach, *La cité de Gênes au XIIe siècle* (Copenhagen, 1955).

J. Heers, *Gênes au XVe siècle: civilisation méditerranéenne, grand capitalisme, et capitalisme populaire* (Paris, 1971: or the longer version of the same work, Paris, 1961).

F. C. Lane, *Venice: A Maritime Republic* (Baltimore, MD, 1973) remains the standard history of Venice, though somewhat adulatory in tone.

F. C. Lane, *Venetian Ships and Shipbuilders of the Renaissance* (Baltimore, 1934).

S. M. Stuard, *A State of Deference: Ragusa/Dubrovnik During the Medieval Centuries* (Philadelphia, 1992).

B. Krekic, *Dubrovnik in the 14th and 15th Centuries: A City Between East and West* (Norman, OK, 1967).

RELATIONS BETWEEN THESE CENTRES AND THE STATES IN THE CENTRAL AND EASTERN MEDITERRANEAN MAY BE FOLLOWED IN:

D. Abulafia, *The Two Italies: Economic Relations Between the Norman Kingdom of Sicily and the Northern Communes* (Cambridge, 1977; Italian ed., Naples, 1991).

H. Bresc, *Un monde méditerranéen: Économie et société en Sicile* 2 vols (Rome-Palermo, 1986).

F. Thiriet, *La Romanie vénitienne au Moyen Âge* (Paris, 1975), which includes Crete.

M. Balard, *La Romanie génoise, XIIIe–début du XVe siècle*, 2 vols. (Rome-Genoa, 1978), extending into the Black Sea.

G. Airaldi and B. Z. Kedar (eds), *I comuni italiani nel regno di Gerusalemme* (Genoa, 1987), articles in Italian, English and other languages, for the Latin Kingdom of Jerusalem.

P. Edbury, *The Kingdom of Cyprus and the Crusades, 1191–1374* (Cambridge, 1991).

For the Levant trade, the most recent attempt at a major synthesis is:

E. Ashtor, *Levant Trade in the Later Middle Ages* (Princeton, NJ, 1983).

ON POLITICAL RIVALRIES AND THEIR LINK TO ECONOMIC DEVELOPMENTS SEE:

D. Abulafia, *The Western Mediterranean Kingdoms, 1200–1500: The Struggle for Dominion* (London, 1997; Italian edition, Rome-Bari, 1999).

7. Resurgent Islam: 1500–1700

F. Braudel, *The Mediterranean and the Mediterranean World in the Age of Philip II*, 2 vols (London, 1973) is the obvious starting point.

F. Tabak, *The Waning of the Mediterranean 1550–1870: A Geohistorical Approach* (Baltimore MD, 2008) is a very important contribution.

ON NORTH AFRICA SEE ESPECIALLY:

A. Hess, *The Forgotten Frontier: A History of the Sixteenth-Century Ibero-African Frontier* (Chicago, 1978).

A. Devereux, *The Other Side of Empire* (Ithaca, NY, 2020), on Spanish ambitions along the coast of North Africa.

The discussion of Mediterranean warfare in the sixteenth century draws heavily on J. Guilmartin, *Gunpowder and Galleys: Changing Technology and Mediterranean Warfare at Sea in the Sixteenth Century* (Cambridge, 1974).

AN IMPORTANT STUDY OF ITALIAN TIES TO THE TURKS IS:

K. Fleet, *European and Islamic Trade in the Early Ottoman State: The Merchants of Genoa and Turkey* (Cambridge, 1999).

A LIVELY GENERAL ACCOUNT OF THE RISE OF THE OTTOMANS CAN BE FOUND IN:

S. Runciman, *The Fall of Constantinople* (Cambridge, 1965).

The Turkish scholar Haili Inalcık has written several key studies:

H. Inalcık, *The Ottoman Empire: The Classical Age 1300–1600* (London, 1973).

See also: H. Inalcık, 'The Question of the Closing of the Black Sea under the Ottomans', *Archeion Pontou* 35 (1979), pp. 74–110; and H. Inalcık, 'Bursa and the Silk Trade', in H. Inalcık with D. Quataert (eds), *An Economic and Social History of the Ottoman Empire* (Cambridge, 1994), p. 219.

C. Kafadar, *Between Two Worlds: The Construction of the Ottoman State* (Berkeley, 1995). Kafadar discusses frontier society at length.

ON RELATIONS BETWEEN THE TURKS AND NON-MUSLIM RELIGIOUS GROUPS SEE:

P. Konortas, 'From Tâ'ife to Millet: Ottoman terms for the Ottoman Greek Orthodox Community', in D. Gondicas and C. Issawi (eds),

Ottoman Greeks in the Age of Nationalism (Princeton, NJ, 1999), pp. 169–80.

C. Wardi, 'The question of the Holy Places in Ottoman times', in M. Ma'oz (ed.), *Studies in Palestine During the Ottoman Period* (Jerusalem, 1975), pp. 385–93.

C. Frazee, *Catholics and Sultans: The Church and the Ottoman Empire 1453–1923* (Cambridge, 1983).

M. Zilfi, 'The Kadızadelis: discordant revivalism in seventeenth-century Istanbul', *Journal of Near Eastern Studies* 95 (1986), pp. 251–69.

M. Greene, *A Shared World: Christians and Muslims in the Early Modern Mediterranean* (Princeton, NJ, 2000).

More generally, see X. de Planhol, *Les minorités en Islam* (Paris, 1997).

On music, W. Feldman, *Music of the Ottoman Court: Makam, Composition and the Early Ottoman Instrumental Repertoire* (Berlin, 1996).

DEVELOPMENTS IN THE WEST CAN BE FOLLOWED IN:

D. Sella, 'Crisis and Transformation in Venetian Trade', in B. Pullan (ed.), *Crisis and Change in the Venetian Economy in the Sixteenth and Seventeenth Centuries* (London, 1968), pp. 88–105.

THE LEVANT TRADE:

P. Masson, *Histoire du commerce français dans le Levant au XVII siècle* (Paris, 1896).

R. Mantran, *Istanbul dans la seconde moitié du XVIII siècle* (Institut Français d'Archéologie d'Istanbul, Paris, 1962).

M. Greene, *Catholic Pirates and Greek Merchants* (Princeton, NJ, 2013).

M. Fusaro, C. Heywood, M.-S. Omri (eds), *Trade and Cultural Exchange in the Early Modern Mediterranean* (London, 2010).

CORSAIRS:

P. Earle, *Corsairs of Malta and Barbary* (London, 1970).

G. Fisher, *Barbary Legend: War, Trade and Piracy in North Africa 1415–1830* (Oxford, 1957).

A. Tenenti, *Piracy and the Decline of Venice 1580–1615* (London, 1967).

THE RISE OF SMYRNA AND LIVORNO:

D. Goffman *Izmir and the Levantine World 1550–1650* (Seattle, 1990).

M.C. Engels, *Merchants, Interlopers and Corsairs: The 'Flemish' Community in Livorno and Genoa (1615–1635)* (Hilversum, 1997).

Balbi de Caro, S. (ed.), *Merci e monete a Livorno in età granducale* (Milan, 1997).

THE KNIGHTS OF MALTA:

R. Cavaliero, 'The decline of the Maltese Corso in the XVIIIth century', *Melita Historica* (1959), pp. 224–38.

H.J.A. Sire, *The Knights of Malta* (New Haven, CT, 1994).

SOME FURTHER STUDIES OF INTEREST:

T. Philipp, *The Syrians in Egypt 1725–1975* (Stuttgart, 1985).

B.J. Slot, *Archipelagus Turbatus: Les Cyclades entre colonization latine et occupation ottomane c. 1500–1718* (Nederlands Historisch-Archaeologisch Instituut, Istanbul, 1982).

A. Salzmann, 'An Ancien Regime revisited: "privatization" and political economy in the eighteenth-century Ottoman Empire', *Politics and Society,* 21 (1993), pp. 393–423.

ON ITALY:

E. Cochrane with J. Kirshner, *Italy 1530–1630* (London, 1988).

J.A. Marino, *Early Modern Italy, 1550–1796* (Oxford, 2002).

T.J. Dandelet, *Spanish Rome, 1500–1700* (New Haven, CT, 2001).

8. The Mediterranean as a Battleground of the European Powers: 1700–1900

GENERAL CONTEXT:

J. Black, *Europe in the Eighteenth Century,* 2nd ed. (Basingstoke, 1999).

J. Black, *European International Relations 1648–1815* (Basingstoke, 2002).

On Spain the relevant volumes in the Blackwell History of Spain are worth consulting:

J. Lynch, *Bourbon Spain 1700–1808* (Oxford, 1989).

C.J. Esdaile, *Spain in the Liberal Age: from Constitution to Civil War, 1808–1939* (Oxford, 2000).

ITALY:

J. A. Marino, *Early Modern Italy, 1550–1796* (Oxford, 2002).

D. Carpanetto and G. Ricuperati, *Italy in the Age of Reason, 1685–1789* (London, 1987).

H. Gross, *Rome in the Age of Enlightenment* (Cambridge, 1990).

TURKISH RULE:

P. F. Sugar, *Southeastern Europe under Ottoman rule, 1354–1804* (Seattle, 1983).

ON AN IMPORTANT FORM OF CULTURAL PERCEPTION AND TRANSMISSION:

J. Black, *Italy and the Grand Tour* (New Haven, CT, 2003).

THE ROLE OF GREAT BRITAIN AND NAVAL POWER-PROJECTION:

R. Holland, *Blue-Water Empires: The British in the Mediterranean Since 1800* (London, 2012).

J. Black, *Britain as a Military Power 1688–1815* (London, 1999).

9. A Globalized Mediterranean: 1900–2000

J. Carpentier, F. Lebrun and others, *Histoire de la Méditerranée* (Paris, 1998) is especially good

FOR THE ESSENTIAL WIDER PICTURE OF POLITICS IN THE LATE TWENTIETH CENTURY SEE:

D. Reynolds, *One World Divisible: A Global History Since 1945* (London, 2000).

S. Ball, *The Bitter Sea: The Struggle for Mastery of the Mediterranean, 1935–1949* (London, 2009), including excellent coverage of the Second World War.

P. Mansel, *Levant: Splendour and Catastrophe on the Mediterranean* (London, 2010), for Smyrna/Izmir, Alexandria and Beirut.

THE FRENCH PRESENCE IN ALGERIA AND ITS NEIGHBOURS HAS GENERATED A VARIETY OF DIFFERENT APPROACHES:

ON NORTH AFRICA.

P. Laffont, *Histoire de la France en Algérie* (Paris, 1980).

M. Bennoune, *The Making of Contemporary Algeria, 1830–1967: Colonial Upheavals and Post-Independence Development* (Cambridge, 1988).

J.-P. Sartre, *Colonialism and Neocolonialism* (London, 2001) is an important text (translated from his *Situations V*), whatever one thinks of Sartre's position.

So too F. Fanon, *The Wretched of the Earth* (New York, 1965, with a preface by J.-P. Sartre).

ON LIBERAL AND FASCIST ITALY:

A. Lyttleton (ed.), *Liberal and Fascist Italy* (Oxford, 2001).

R. J. B. Bosworth, *Italy, the Least of the Great Powers: Italian Foreign Policy before the First World War* (Cambridge, 1979).

R. De Felice and L. Goglia, *Mussolini: il mito* (Rome-Bari, 1983).

D. Mack Smith, *Mussolini's Roman Empire* (London, 1976).

R. J. B. Bosworth, *Mussolini* (London, 2000).

ON SPAIN:

H. Thomas, *The Spanish Civil War* (London, 1961) remains a classic.

P. Preston, *Franco: A Biography* (London, 1993).

ON TURKEY:

B. Lewis, *The Emergence of Modern Turkey* (London, 1961), by an excellent historian who falters badly, however, on the question of Armenia.

G. L. Lewis, *Modern Turkey* (London, 1974).

ON THE EMERGENCE OF ISRAEL:

N. Bethell, *The Palestine Triangle: The Struggle Between the British, the Jews and the Arabs, 1935–48* (London, 1979) is very judicious.

M. Gilbert, *Israel: A History* (London, 1998).

A. Shlaim, *The Iron Wall: Israel and the Arab world* (London, 2000).

M. Oren, *Six Days of War: June 1967 and the Making of the Modern Middle East* (Oxford, 2002).

ON TOURISM:

B. Korte, C. Harvie, R. Schneider, H. Berghoff, *The Making of Modern Tourism: The Cultural History of the British Experience, 1600–2000* (New York, 2000).

J. Boissevain (ed.), *Coping with Tourists: European Reactions to Mass Tourism* (Oxford, 1996).

K. Hudson, *Air Travel: A Social History* (Bath, 1972) desperately needs a successor to bring the story up to date.

L. Withey, *Grand Tours and Cook's Tours: A History of Leisure Travel, 1750 to 1915* (London, 1997).

P. Brendon, *Thomas Cook: 150 years of Popular Tourism* (London, 1991).

ON THE EFFECTS OF TOURISM IN SPAIN:

M. Barke, J. Towner and M. T. Newton (eds), *Tourism in Spain: Critical Issues* (Wallingford, 1996).

A. M. Bernal and others, *Tourisme et développement regional en Andalousie* (Publications de la Casa de Velázquez 5 Madrid, Paris, 1979).

FOR ITALY AND FRANCE:

Touring Club Italiano, *Novant'anni di turismo in Italia, 1894–1984* (Turin, 1994).

H. Levenstein, *Seductive Journey: American Tourists in France from Jefferson to the Jazz Age* (Chicago, 1998).

ON THE IMPORTANCE OF FASHION TRENDS:

J. Craik, *The Face of Fashion: Cultural Studies in Fashion* (London, 1994).

C. Probert, *Swimwear in Vogue since 1910* (London, 1981).

M. and A. Batterberry, *Fashion: The Mirror of History* (London, 1982; American edition: *Mirror, Mirror*, New York, 1987).

SOURCES OF ILLUSTRATIONS

1 Henry Martellus, map of the Mediterranean, 15th century. Add. MS 15760 ff 72v–73r. British Library, London.

2 Arabic zonal world map copied from that of Al Idrisi, 1154, geographer at the court of Roger II of Sicily. Bodleian Library, Oxford.

3 Luis Meléndez (1716–1780), *Still Life of Lemons*. Courtesy of P. and D. Colnaghi and Co.

4 Detail from the Ghent Altarpiece, Cathedral of S. Bavo, Ghent. Photo Scala.

5 Aubergines from the *Cerruti Tacuinum sanitatis*, 14th century, Italy.

6 Francesco del Cossa (1436–1478), *Autumn*, Nationalgalerie, Berlin.

7 Illumination from the *Alba Bible*. Courtesy of the Duke of Alba.

8 Painting from stone coffin found at Hagia Triada, National Museum, Herakleion.

9 Wallpainting from the Tomb of Shields, Tarquinia, 350–340 BC. Photo Scala.

10 Gold earring, Greek, 330–300 BC. Metropolitan Museum of Art, New York, Rogers Fund.

11 Perfume flask from Thebes, *c.* 650 BC. British Museum, London.

12 Collar of beaten gold, National Archaeological Museum, Beirut, Lebanon.

13 Mosaic showing a trading galley, Bardo Museum, Tunis. Photo Scala.

14 Personification of one of the Four Winds; detail from a Dionysiac scene, mosaic floor of a Roman villa near Mérida, Spain. Photo Georgina Bruckner.

15 The port of Classe, Ravenna. Mosaic from S. Apollinare Nuovo, Ravenna. Photo Scala.

16 Luca Signorelli (*c.* 1450–1523), wall painting at Monteoliveto, Chiusure, Italy.

17 Siege of Thessalonika, illumination from the Skylitzes Chronicle, National Library, Madrid.

18 Detail of the wooden ceiling, Capella Palatina, Palermo, mid-12th century. Photo Maurice Babey.

19 From *Cantigas de Santa Maria. Escorial Library.* Photo Institute Amatller, Barcelona.

20 'La Contarina', pilgrim's sketch. Badische Landesbibliothek, Karlsruhe.

21 Venice. Woodcut from B. von Breydenbach, *Peregratione*, Mainz, 1486.

22 Giovanni Battista Lusieri (1755–1821), *A View of the Bay of Naples.* J. Paul Getty Museum, Los Angeles, California.

23 *Martinus Rørbye, Morning in the Piazza Marina, Palermo*, 1846, Thorvaldsen Museum, Copenhagen.

24 Promenade des Anglais, *c.* 1900. Photo Private Collection.

25 Juan les Pins, 1930s. Photo Bridgeman Art Library.

26 Henri Edmond Cross (1856–1910), *The Beach of St Clair*, Musée de l'Annonciade, St Tropez. Photo Scala.

27 Poster advertising an aviation meeting in Nice. Bibliothèque des Arts Décoratifs, Paris. Photo Bridgeman Art Library.

CONTRIBUTORS

David Abulafia is Emeritus Professor of Mediterranean History at the University of Cambridge, and a Fellow of the British Academy and of Gonville and Caius College, Cambridge.

Michel Balard is Emeritus Professor of Medieval History at the University of Paris-Sorbonne, and former President of the Society for the Study of the Crusades and the Latin East (2002–9).

Jeremy Black is former Professor of History at the University of Exeter and the author of over 100 books, mainly on aspects of eighteenth-century British, European and American political, diplomatic and military history.

Molly Greene is Professor of History and Hellenic Studies at Princeton University, with particular interest in the history of the Mediterranean Basin, the Ottoman Empire and the Greek world.

John Pryor is former Associate Professor in the Centre for Medieval Studies, University of Sydney, with a particular interest in the history of trade and commerce in the Mediterranean region in the Middle Ages.

Oliver Rackham was a Fellow of Corpus Christi College, University of Cambridge. A leading botanist and ecologist, he was the co-author (with Jennifer Moody) of The Making of the Cretan Landscape.

Geoffrey Rickman was Emeritus Professor of Roman History at the University of St Andrews and Chairman of the Council of the British School at Rome. He was a Fellow of the British Academy.

Marlene Suano, University of São Paulo, specializes in trade links and cultural contacts between the major powers of the Bronze Age in the Mediterranean.

Mario Torelli was a leading expert on Italic culture and the Etruscans at the University of Perugia, and a member of the Academia Nazionale dei Lincei.

INDEX